Walt Disney
the American Dreamer

By Tom Tumbusch

Cover Painting by Matt Busch

Tomart Publications
Dayton, Ohio

To: Ward Kimball, Lou Lispi, Bill Justice, Van France, and Ralph Kent

Tomart Publications
3300 Encrete Lane
Dayton, Ohio 45439

www.tomart.com

First printing, 2008

©2008 Thomas E. Tumbusch

Published by Tomart Publications, Dayton, Ohio.

Library of Congress Control Number: 2006906349

ISBN-10: 0-914-29361-3
ISBN-13: 978-0-914-29361-3
Manufactured in the United States of America

Acknowledgements

My take on the life of Walt Disney came from a different perspective. In researching the merchandise history of Disney Characters, I came to know a good cross section of people who worked directly with Walt and became an important part of his organization. Chief among these wonderful people were Ward and Betty Kimball, Lou Lispi, Bill Justice, Van France, and Ralph Kent. There were many others as the following pages will reveal, but these individuals provided the main insights or validated facts about Walt that I read or learned from others. Without the patience and understanding of these contributors, this book would not have been possible.

The staff of the Disney Archives, Dave Smith, Robert Tieman, and the wonderful ladies who have worked there over the years, have always been helpful and responsive with their time whenever I needed a fact checked or visited to do research.

Those who helped to get this book ready for publication included Mark Ricci who provided photos, Didier Ghez who obtained permission to use interview material published in his Walt's People interview collection, and Bob Welbaum for his Disney expertise and copy editing. Andrew Bako did the EPCOT 3-D illustration based on the computer modeling work of Richard Zyrd. Others providing encouragement when asked for help include Joshua Benesh, Ron Stark, Susanne Hattersley, Gary Schaengold, Amy Stelmack, Daniel Bauer, and Matt Busch for his cover painting.

Also a thanks to the Tomart staff for doing the actual work of getting it all ready for publication including Chris Hall, Photography; Heather Bentley, who did the graphic design of the book; and especially, Amber Henry, who had to put up with the author during the creation, numerous revisions, and final proofing of the manuscript.

*"If we can dream it,
we can do it."*

– Walt Disney

Table of Contents

Photo from the Tomart Archives

Photo of Walt Disney and Mickey Mouse sent to fans requesting a photo of Walt or Mickey (circa 1934).

Introduction

Walt Disney, the man, was a leader and creative force. He was the motivation behind Walt Disney – the brand of family entertainment. His achievements were facilitated by his brother Roy O. Disney and the staff they recruited, trained, and managed. Without Roy we may not have known the name Walt Disney. Even though they conflicted many times, Walt always reworked his ideas until he had Roy's financial expertise solidly behind him. Roy, the silent Disney, was a key factor in making Walt's dreams come true.

This book is not a biography or a studio history. There are already plenty of those. What has been attempted here is to piece together how Walt Disney accomplished so much in one lifetime…how he managed to find the right people and inspired them to want the same things he did…and how he got the results he did, even though he rarely praised anyone or gave the screen credit other animated film studios did. "Walt Disney Presents" was the one phrase Walt wanted his audience to remember.

Nearly everything written about Walt agrees he had exceptional vision and conviction. Often it has been said he was empowered with a sense of what the public wanted in entertainment. This sense didn't come with birth. It was a skill he developed in a logical way. It wasn't always perfect and there were failures in his life. How he dealt with a parade of obstacles and continually got things done, however, is truly worth studying.

The Disney Studio operated on a first name basis. Everyone called him Walt and until the company became too big, he knew his employees' first names as well. He made it his business to know his key people so he could bring out their best work to the betterment of his entertainment enterprises. And they knew him. Not everyone liked his methods or even him personally. A lot of talented people left the studio because Walt's policies just weren't for them. It was Walt's way or the highway for anyone who challenged his authority or crossed him in an unfavorable way. The artists and production people who stayed became the heart of the Disney Studio. They revered Walt and the tremendous achievements accomplished by all of them working together.

Walt Disney accepted 34 Academy Awards, over three times as many as the next highest recipient with eleven. The employees who did the work on films nominated for Academy Awards were rewarded with Mickey Mouse or Donald Duck trophies within the company. These Mousecars and Ducksters were symbols of their important contributions. Some received Oscars as well and Walt always received his Awards as producer. Walt Disney didn't create animation, but lead the team of artists who transformed it into a first-class entertainment form that rivaled live-action. His studio's animated films set the standard.

Nine of his Oscars were received for True-Life Adventure nature films. Naturalists weren't always thrilled by his films, but families saw animals like never before. Today, entire cable channels are devoted to similar types of programming.

The first Disney live-action films were done in England after World War II. The economic reconstruction policies of Europe required the money be spent in the country earned, so Walt jumped on Roy's suggestion that the company produce films there. Once established in traditional filmmaking, Walt turned his attention to television.

He did a one-hour TV special in 1950 and another in 1951. Walt decided television was the tool he needed to help finance his dream of a theme park. In the process, he showed Hollywood that TV was not the enemy it was proclaimed to be at the time, rather a new source of revenue and publicity.

Disneyland has been hailed by the trade and the American public for changing the antiquated amusement park concept. The nation's first theme park pioneered entertainment enjoyed by the whole family, led the way to the development of shopping malls in America, to the growth of fast-food restaurants, demonstrated how young people could operate a complex facility, and was once lauded as the most important piece of urban planning in America.

The material in this book is based on a lifelong interest in the Disney films and the man who was credited with creating them. It is a collection of observations learned from friendships with people who worked with Walt Disney, interviews, and the public record. My findings are presented more or less chronologically, but Walt Disney was a premiere multi-tasker. His projects overlapped, often by many years. Providing a brief overview, and then presenting major areas of achievement individually, causes certain historical facts to be presented out of order.

This work didn't begin as a book project, but rather a personal need to understand more about the man and why he strove to attain such quality and success. Early biographies by Diane Disney Miller (with Pete Martin) and Bob Thomas satisfied my curiosity for many years, but later some important facts about Walt's life seemed to be missing.

It was then I began to find out there was a lot more to Walt Disney. If we are to truly learn from his life, then we need to know more about what prompted him to operate the way he did. In that regard, this book attempts to fill in some blanks to help understand what motivated Walt and drove him to demand things be done his way at every turn, despite pressure to settle for the economies of less-expensive approaches. Life's chain of events constantly presented new directions. Often it was circumstance or a setback. Even without the benefit of higher education, Walt figured out what to do.

The Disney Research Library at a Glance (bibliography) lists over a hundred books and other research sources, most offering interesting takes on the lives and accomplishments of Walt and Roy Disney and their staffs. The number of listings is a tribute in itself to this fascinating collaboration. The purpose here is not to recount what has been written elsewhere, rather to focus on how Walt Disney extended his talents through others. This work retraces only a minimal amount of Walt's early life necessary to establish the foundation for his midwestern integrity, relationship with his brother Roy, and commitment to excellence...the foundation on which they built the Disney empire.

Readers and researchers are encouraged to read through the Disney Research Library at a Glance beginning on page 145 for many other highlights about Walt and Roy Disney and the Disney Studio. In addition to typical references, a photo of the listed work and a brief review of its contents are provided to help locate sources of further interest.

It cannot be stressed enough that getting to know Walt is not possible without an understanding of Roy and how they complimented each other. The success of "Walt Disney" is really the achievement of both men, plus their talented team of artists and production experts.

Walt Disney has been dead since 1966. Most of the people who worked directly with Walt have joined him. Rarely has a group of people created so much enjoyment for so many others worldwide. Perhaps that's why the name Walt Disney remains such a fascinating subject forty years after his death.

—Tom Tumbusch
October, 2007

Chapter I – Walt and Me

*"I became fascinated with Walt Disney at an early age.
Diane Disney Miller's book was given to me shortly
after it was published in 1957. My friends looked up
to major league baseball stars. My hero was Walt Disney."*

—Tom Tumbusch

Walt Disney was my friend! He inspired me to create, to branch out on my own and make a life doing the things I loved the most. Just knowing him made me want to strive to do the best I could; to rise from a lower income background and achieve a place in life. He did it, so could I. To watch Walt Disney was to want to emulate him. You had to admire a guy who seemed to have so much fun doing his job. As I discovered more about him, I learned his life wasn't always fun. Things were just as difficult on him as they were on me. He had trouble sleeping and an old polo injury caused him major pain through most of his adult life. (Yet, whatever adversity we shared only strengthened the bond between us. Who doesn't have a shortage of money most of their lives?) Walt never got rich until the success of Disneyland. Up until then the loans were huge and the profits went back into new projects.

Ours was a curious friendship because we never met personally. He communicated to me using a variety of media. I listened, was entertained, learned…and I wanted to be more like him. When news of Walt Disney's death reached me, I felt a personal loss. That's when I knew ours was a closer friendship than I had ever imagined. Such was the magnitude of the man.

My first personal encounter with Walt Disney was via TV. He conveyed valuable life lessons as he introduced his weekly Wednesday, then Sunday evening programs. No, I never believed he could look out of the television set and see me, but my great grandmother did! She would wave to him when he began each program. We didn't have a TV in our home until she was 85 and she never understood how television worked. She just felt if

she could see him, he could see her. No one in our family could convince her
otherwise. She always made sure she looked her best before she sat before
the TV for the *Disneyland* program. Walt's persona knew no demograph-
ics. His appeal cut across all age groups. Walt's self-assured presence and his
stories just had that kind of effect on people.

When he told his audience how his team of artists put together the
first Alice cartoons in his uncle's garage or conceived how to get *Snow
White and the Seven Dwarfs* to the big screen, we marveled. When he
brought worldwide animal habitats into our living rooms, it made us wonder
at nature. When he showed us how man was going to blast into space and
land on the moon, we knew it would happen.

Walt sure could tell a story. His animated stories made me laugh and
cry and warmed my heart, but to hear him describe just about anything was
entertaining. Who didn't learn some interesting information in the process?
If you were in Walt Disney's circle of friends or employees, you also discovered he could have a temper, swear, and was a chain smoker. He was very
direct when he spoke and demanded things be done his way. If you had a
fragile ego, you probably didn't get along with Walt. Though he was a friend
and coach to his staff, coming up with work that pleased Walt was to achieve
personal elation. Walt was never one to heap praise, but to spark his imagination and see his face light up was to knock the bell off the carnival mus-
cle meter. To help him delight a child was life-fulfilling. The Disney Studio
was a bountiful sea of ideas and Walt was King Neptune.

Part of Walt's magic was to have a similar effect on legions of people
like myself. He came across as a congenial uncle. Personable, but not too
warm. He could interest you in things you might never discover on your own.
You became interested because it was obvious he was...and wanted you to
share his enthusiasm.

Later in life, I learned much more about Walt from the people who
worked directly with him. There were close to thirty in all.

Ward Kimball, a Disney Studio animator, was the first to happen my
way. It was in the *Phil Donahue Show* greenroom in 1973. Ward and his
wife Betty were on a book tour with Christopher Finch to promote *The Art
of Walt Disney*. My *Variety* press card won me admission. Ward dominated
the gathering with tales of Walt and the studio. The hour presentation then
aired before a live studio audience. Betty and I talked in the back of Dayton's
Channel 2 Studios during the program. She had worked in the Disney Ink
and Paint Department and told how Walt was disappointed with the final cels
of Snow White. The character was just too pale. Betty had suggested the
women in the Ink and Paint Department apply cheek make-up to the front
of each cel. When Walt questioned the accuracy of such an undertaking,
Betty replied, "Well, Walt, we all apply it on our faces in the same places
each day." They did a test and Walt approved the process. If you watch the
film closely, you can spot a slight movement in the rose coloring on Snow

White's cheeks. Betty also came up with a suggestion on how to make the forest fire in *Bambi* more realistic.

After the program concluded, I spent another hour with the Kimballs and was invited to their home the next time I was in California. They were always fun to visit. Ward was proud to show off his Grizzly Flats Railroad and other collections housed in several buildings in his backyard. Two full-sized locomotives and a passenger car filled his "roundhouse." A special building was constructed for his pre-1943 toy trains…American on one side of the building, European on the other. Another building was reserved for his *Firehouse Five plus Two* Dixieland band props and vehicles seen often at Disneyland and other Southern California events. He was the leader of the group and played trombone. Many visits were made to the Kimball home between the late 1970s and throughout the 1990s. Ward was always quick with stories about Walt and the studio. His best friend from his years at the studio was *Pogo* comic-strip creator, Walt Kelly. They used to play tin whistles together in the animation building's ceramic tiled mens room. Typical Ward once remarked, "It was the greatest sound in the world" as his face beamed.

Walt became even more vibrant in tales spun by guests at the Mouse Club* Conventions starting in 1979. Clarence "Ducky" Nash, the voice of Donald Duck, was the first featured dinner speaker. Adriana Caselotti, the voice of Snow White, told how she auditioned for Walt behind a screen because he didn't want to be influenced by the appearance of any of the girls seeking the role. She sang "I'm Wishing." Her voice still sounded like the day she recorded the soundtrack over forty years earlier.

Subsequent years won more Disney artists as friends. Herb Ryman and Ken Anderson were astounded that anyone cared and eagerly awaited their stories about working at the studio. Bill Justice and I became acquainted at a chance breakfast meeting. Little did either of us know then we would later spend two-and-a-half years in a close relationship to publish his autobiography in 1992.

Frank Thomas and Ollie Johnston made a couple appearances at Mouse Club and NFFC* (National Fantasy Fan Club for Disneyana Collectors) conventions, but I never got to know them personally. They used the Disney Archives as a means to receive and answer fan mail and were there one day when I was doing research. We talked casually that day. They had done several books on animation art and they were amusing to watch as they reacted to fan and employee requests.

Marc Davis was a key artist/animator on a wide variety of studio proj-

---

* The Mouse Club was started by Ed and Elaine Levin in the mid-1970s. Originally, it provided a forum for Disney collectors via a newsletter. It grew and they decided to hold a convention in Anaheim in 1979 at which retired Disney artists and personalities were guests. The NFFC started in 1984, holding conventions and other activities for members, plus annual recognition of Disney Legends and related charitable work (www.nffc.org).

ects and one of Walt's Nine Old Men (patterned after the nine Supreme Court Justices). He joined the studio in 1935 and designed many major characters like Thumper, Cinderella, Tinker Bell, Maleficent, and Cruella De Vil. Walt also counted on Marc for input on all Disney 1964-65 New York World's Fair attractions and Disneyland's initial audio-animatronics shows, including The Pirates of the Caribbean and Haunted Mansion. Marc was another trusted Walt Disney associate whom I met and knew briefly. Marc's wife Alice also worked closely with Walt as a costume designer for theme park and other attractions. However, the biggest contributors to my firsthand knowledge of Walt's life over the longest period of time were Ward Kimball, Bill Justice, and Van France.

Van Arsdale France was hired to write the first training manuals for Disneyland. He built his training programs around the slogan "Happiest Place on Earth." He structured operations for Disneyland as a show, and those employed there, as cast members. Van became the conscience of Disneyland. He recalled for me his first welcome meeting with Walt. Walt told him he wanted the park to be run by clean-cut young people instead of unkempt carny types. He instructed Van to come up with methods to train and manage these young people who would operate a new multi-million dollar theme park. Van hired Dick Nunis (who later became Vice President of all Disney theme parks worldwide), a fresh graduate out of the University of Southern California. Together they developed the Disneyland training program that won Walt's approval.

Van left the company for several years, but later returned as a cast member and remained a consultant after his official retirement. Everybody at Disneyland knew Van. We became friends when he approached me to publish his autobiography. Though it was published by another company titled *Window on Main Street*, we remained friends and enjoyed many talks about the founding of Disneyland and the Disney University program now duplicated at every other Disney theme park. Van also founded The Disneyland Alumni Club and made me an honorary member. Every five years the Alumni Club sponsors a banquet at the Disneyland Hotel for an evening of trading memories. The Disneyland 50th Anniversary Celebration topped the previous three events attended. When 93-year-old Art Linkletter spoke about his 26-year friendship with Walt Disney, the assembled gathering learned things never before published in any book.

Van France was the human Jiminy Cricket of Disneyland for another thirty-six years after Walt's death. He once gave my son and I a backstage tour of Disneyland, being careful to mention the developments made over the years. During an inspection of the new horse barn, Van related how much Walt Disney loved horses and often took a mount around the park before it opened in the morning.

Ralph Kent went to work at Disneyland in 1963 and worked closely with Walt on the Denver, Colorado Celebrity Sports Center. It was started by a group headed by Walt's friend, Art Linkletter. Walt had purchased it as a test for expanding concepts introduced at Disneyland into other markets and as a training ground for future Walt Disney World executives. Ralph inherited the association with Walt from his boss, Disneyland merchandise director Jack Olsen. Walt was always probing every aspect of what happened at Disneyland and the Sports Center. One busy day, Jack assigned Ralph to work with Walt. The two of them hit it off and Ralph was named art director for the sports complex. Ralph and Walt made regular flights to Denver in the company plane. Walt shared his ideas about current projects; Disney World, and EPCOT during their many hours together. Ralph provided an interesting insight of Walt reflecting over the years and his last two in particular.

Others with whom I interviewed about working with Walt included Lou Lispi, Character Merchandise Division art director who started with Kay Kamen in 1934 until he retired from the Disney Licensing Division in 1971; Disney Studio artists Ken Anderson, Herb Ryman, Carl Barks, Joe Grant, Xavier Atencio, and Ron Dias; Merchandise rep and artist Al Konetzni; Bo Boyd, Vice President of Park and Character Merchandise; actor Fess Parker; Disneyland entertainer Wally Boag; and several Mouseketeers, Annette Funicello, Tommy Cole, Karen Pendleton, Bobby Burgess, and Sherry Alberoni, as well as, music composer Richard Sherman. Material was also generated from presentations made at Mouse Club, NFFC, and Disneyana collector conventions from 1979 to present; plus addresses made at Disneyland Alumni Club gatherings, particularly those made by longtime Imagineering Vice President Marty Sklar and Art Linkletter.

Disney Archives founder Dave Smith and I first met in 1977 and have shared information about Walt and the company over the years.

Diane Disney Miller, Walt's oldest daughter, was one of the first to have a book published on her father's life. It was based mainly on interviews she and Pete Martin conducted with her dad. The original recorded interviews were reviewed for this book. Bob Thomas was Walt's "official" biographer and his book remains the most definitive work on the historic details of Walt's life. He later performed the same function for Roy Disney. Walt filmed several hours of interviews shortly before his death and excerpts from these are found in theme park presentations and on video. The public record is a vast maze of books, magazine and newspaper articles spanning over 60 years, videos of old TV programs, and the studio's films, theme park work, and technological advancements.

There is so much material about Walt Disney that it is difficult to distinguish the man from his work. Because Walt Disney and his staff achieved so many things it's a mammoth task just to sort and chronicle all of them. It is easy to lose the man in the almost mythological character he has become. Walt Disney has been described as a genius, complex, moody, difficult, or a benevolent dictator, all this by friends, forgetting for the moment those who regarded him differently. At home, he was a beloved husband and father. He worked long hours at his office and still more at night after dinner, but always found time for those closest to him.

I've felt a very personal bond since we first met via TV. Walt Disney became my friend even though I never shook his hand or spoke personally to him. He spoke to me through his many media and endeared himself to me. He became my friend just as he did to thousands, if not millions, of others. That was the magic of Walt Disney...the public Walt Disney everyone got to see on TV.

Getting to know Walt more privately through many people who did shake his hand and talked and worked with him has revealed a different perspective. When you first get acquainted with people who were close to Walt, you'd get answers like "He was a great man" or "There will never be another man like Walt Disney!" or "He was just wonderful!"

Walt had an intuitive sense of public image. He never knowingly allowed a photograph to be taken of him smoking or drinking so as not to influence a child toward those vices. He was in the family entertainment business and took extraordinary steps to communicate good taste. Those who worked with him adopted a protective attitude in public and most private meetings. It wasn't until you got closer to his associates, did you learn some of Walt's more human sides.

There were elements in Walt's history some considered negative and/or less important. These events were often eliminated or glossed over in other works, yet remain important windows to Walt's life. Walt viewed adversity as an opportunity rather than a setback. The animation strike of 1941, for example, was a life-altering experience for Walt and Roy Disney, but not as disastrous as some authors have concluded. Digging through all the negative information written about Walt in harshly critical books could have put our friendship to the test. However, when you examine the sources of most accusations, the reliability of such negative contentions quickly fades. Walt Disney had every right to run his organizations as he saw fit. Most authors who have written critically of Walt rely heavily on one disgruntled employee. However, his bitter reflections on his years at the Disney Studio have not succeeded in marring Walt's positive achievements.

Few men have had to endure the scrutiny cast upon the life of Walt Disney. He was self-confident beyond measure, demanding, and could dismiss anyone on the spot who challenged his authority. Hard feelings weren't made any softer when Walt succeeded and his detractors failed. The evidence clearly shows, however, despite what some consider his human failings, Walt Disney was more loved than feared...more loving than insensitive...more fun-loving than a hard-nosed business tycoon.

Photo courtesy of Mark Ricci.

Roy Oliver Disney and Walter Elias Disney at the peak of their careers following the success of Disneyland.

Chapter II – Of Mice and Brothers – An Overview

*"It's my job to do the dreaming, it's my brother Roy's job
to figure out how to pay for them."*

—*Walt Disney*

Walt's early life mirrored the harsh fate of other rural families of the era. His father was strict and unsettled. The family moved from place to place in pursuit of the American dream. Elias, his father, and Flora, his mother, had five children, Herbert, Raymond, Roy, Walter, and Ruth.

Walt was born in Chicago in 1901. The family moved to a Marceline, Missouri farm in 1906. The boys were worked hard on the family farm in "exchange for their room and board." Discipline and hard work ethics were learned early. The two oldest boys, Herbert and Raymond, protested and ran away from home. Roy was eight years older than Walt, but both were still young and their attempt to help their father save the family farm was futile. Elias purchased a newspaper delivery route and the family moved to Kansas City. The years in Marceline would remain a strong influence on both brothers the rest of their lives.

Art interested young Walt, but his father discouraged such a frivolous pastime. Elias saw no future in drawing pictures. Walt's drawing ability was never the best. He realized his limitations when he obtained an art job at the Pesmen-Rubin Commercial Art Studio in Kansas City. There Walt found himself surrounded by more gifted artists. One was Ubbe Iwwerks. When both were laid-off after the Christmas rush, Walt talked Iwwerks into going into business together. Their art service prospered with Walt handling sales, but the project fell apart after Walt took a second job with the Kansas City Film Ad Company, a producer of advertisements for motion picture theaters. Walt later convinced the company to also hire his good friend Iwwerks, an early sign of the loyalty exhibited throughout his career toward the people he felt were important to his work. The relatively crude animation process used by the company challenged Walt's inquiring mind. He found available books on the subject and began experimenting with the process on his own. As a result, he introduced drawing techniques to replace the silhouette cut-out methods the company had relied upon. On the side, Walt founded Laugh-O-gram Films and made a deal to do six animated fairy tales. He convinced Iwwerks to join him and went out on his own. The distributor went bust after paying only $100 toward the project and Walt had to declare bankruptcy.

Roy Disney went to work in a Kansas City bank and later enlisted in the Navy. He returned to banking after his discharge and was Walt's major benefactor when things got rough.

Blackhawk Films obtained a copy of *Puss 'N Boots,* one of Walt's early "fairy tale" cartoons, and released it back in the late 1960s. Heading up the reel was a sample of a Laugh-O-gram single panel cartoon Walt drew for the local Newman Theater using stop-motion animation; a process by which a dot or short dash was added to the drawing for each frame of the film. The effect at reel's end was a completed one panel political cartoon that appeared to have been drawn in just a few seconds. Live-action footage of Walt sitting down at his board and starting to draw was also included on the film. This is the earliest surviving footage of artist Walt Disney. Perhaps it was done for promotional purposes or to satisfy Walt's sense of history, but it also displays Walt's early ego. It shows a confident young man, overacting a bit, with an apparent desire to be his own boss and dictate his own fate.

The *Puss 'N Boots* cartoon is very repetitive in keeping with the animated shorts of the late teens and those done throughout the 1920s. The drafting of the boy, cat, and king was crude in this modern telling of the fairy tale. The boy sees an appealing girl and enlists a cat to help win her heart. It is a silent film with animated title cards to help the story along. Too much footage of the boy and cat walking was the dominant memory before going back to review the film once again for this book. A new look uncovered no interesting camera angles, revealing close-ups, or other advances that would later trademark Disney animated shorts. The characters simply moved in front of a camera as if they were on stage.

Walt's next idea for a cartoon series, featuring a live girl in a cartoon world, proved more productive. The first of these *Alice Comedies* was filmed in Kansas City before Laugh-O-gram Films went bust. Walt, now 21 years old, then moved to California where his brother Roy was convalescing from his bout with tuberculosis. Animation had proved to be discouraging and Walt decided he wanted to be a film director. He applied at every studio in Hollywood without success. He soon used job-hunting as an excuse to get on studio lots, where he would spend all day watching film-making in action. The movie business was definitely for him. It was then he decided to send the *Alice Comedy* print to New York film distributor Margaret Winkler, with whom he had been corresponding. Based on the sample film, she telegraphed her company was willing to contract for twelve *Alice Comedies* at $1,500 each.

Telegram in hand, Walt went to the veterans' hospital that same night and awakened his brother. The next morning Roy left the hospital and never had a recurrence of TB. Together they formed The Disney Brothers Studio in 1923.

Margaret Winkler stipulated Walt had to use the same little girl in the sample reel provided, so he convinced the girl's family to move to California from Kansas City. The family wanted more money after her first contract expired. Walt never took kindly to this type of salary increase pressure throughout his career. He found a new girl and told his distributor the circumstances. Winkler then approved a second girl. She and other girls were used in the remaining 56 films produced before the series was considered to have run its course in 1927.

Photo courtesy of Bill Justice

Disney Bros. Studio truck decorated for Roy and Edna Disneys' wedding.

When the first Alice contract was renewed for more episodes, the prospect of a steady income was all Roy Disney needed to send for his Kansas City sweetheart, Edna Francis, and they were married in 1925. Walt married his secretary, Lillian Bounds, six months later.

When the *Alice Comedies* series ended, the small studio developed a new character named *Oswald the Lucky Rabbit*. They showed the first film to Alice distributor Margaret Winkler. She had recently married Charles Mintz, who had contacts with Universal Pictures. A contract was signed in 1927 for the Disney Brothers to deliver 27 Oswald cartoons over the next twelve months. At renewal time in 1928, Mintz informed Walt that he was exercising his ownership of the character and intended to produce the films himself. Mintz had an agent hire away most of Walt's animators while he was en route to New York to work out a new contract. Walt had always trusted Margaret Winkler. Their relationship on the Alice Comedies had gone smoothly and Walt expected similar treatment from her new husband. He was eager to get Oswald cartoons into distribution and didn't feel Mintz would enforce the ownership clause included in the standard distibution contract. Mintz didn't really want to produce cartoons. His prime motivation was to get Walt to work for him.

This was Walt's biggest test to date. The money earned on the Alice and Oswald films had mostly gone to improve quality. The studio was in dire straits, but he didn't think twice about rejecting Mintz's offer. He phoned a distraught Roy, who confirmed the staff defections. Walt simply told him everything was going to be okay.

There is a great story about Walt coming up with an idea for Mortimer Mouse just as the train back to Hollywood was passing through his old hometown of Kansas City. His wife, Lilly, remarked Mickey would be a more suitable name. Perhaps the story is true, but it has become somewhat suspect over the years. More likely, Ub Iwerks (his name now legally shortened) got to work on new characters as soon as Walt arrived from New York. They decided on the Mouse after Walt reviewed other ideas. Lilly's suggestion of the name Mickey rather than Mortimer would have been just as valid then. She proudly took credit for the name change the rest of her life.

Work on *Plane Crazy* was begun without delay in the back of Roy Disney's garage as to not tip-off the animators Mintz had hired. They were still working under Walt's direction to complete the last contracted Oswald films. Ub Iwerks did the animation on the first Mickey cartoon while Walt tried, without success, to sell the film. *Gallopin' Gaucho* was also completed without a sale.

The Jazz Singer, the first "talkie" film, was released in 1927 and Walt decided sound was just the device he needed to make Mickey Mouse a success. It fell to Roy to raise the money for a recording session while Walt, Ub, and Les Clark animated *Steamboat Willie*. Walt took the print to New York for the recording session, but the conductor refused to follow cues Walt provided and botched the synchronization. Walt had to phone Roy to raise the money again. He did so by selling Walt's prized Moon roadster. This time Walt was more involved and the scoring worked out. Walt then shopped the finished product around New York. The major film company executives liked the cartoon, but wouldn't commit.

Harry Reichenbach, who managed the Colony Theater for Universal, had seen *Steamboat Willie* at a screening and took Walt aside and told him, "These guys don't know what's good until the public tells them." He wanted to rent the cartoon for two weeks for $500. Walt resisted because he thought it might hurt his chances for a national distribution deal. Reichenbach convinced Walt getting the film direct to the public would prompt press coverage and get the theatrical bosses interested.

Walt reluctantly signed a two-week deal at the Colony Theater. (The theater still exists today as The Broadway and is used primarily for live musical productions. Before the theater's most recent remodeling, there was a bronze plaque in the lobby, noting it was the first theater to play a Mickey Mouse cartoon along with the November 18, 1928 date. When the theater reopened, the plaque had disappeared. When asked, no one knew what happened to it.)

The Barn Dance was in production as a sound cartoon while Walt was in New York recording the soundtrack for *Steamboat Willie*. Once Mickey clicked with the public Walt could offer four Mickey cartoons as fast as sound was added to *Plane Crazy* and *Gallopin' Gaucho*.

The reviews and crowds signaled a success for Mickey Mouse in *Steamboat Willie* and suddenly the majors began to call in response to Walt's earlier screenings. Like Mintz, MGM and RKO wanted to hire Walt rather than work out a distribution deal. Walt, needing money badly, still refused. Pat Powers, the owner of the sound-on-film system Walt used for *Steamboat Willie* had another suggestion. The Disney Brothers Studio should stay independent and release Mickey Mouse films on a states rights basis. Powers would handle all the arrangements for 10% of the gross. The deal was struck and Mickey Mouse became a bigger sensation than anyone could have imagined once his films achieved national distribution.

Reichenbach's advice was never forgotten. Walt's film and other promotions from then on were directed to the public whenever possible. Mickey's success reinforced his conviction to retain all rights to his characters and productions.

Most histories go on to report how Walt added Silly Symphonies in 1929 and began a long string of Mickey Mouse cartoons. Few report how virtually *every* dollar earned went back into new and better productions...or how the deal with Powers would cause big problems later on.

Fortune Magazine did an interesting account of Disney Studio activities in its November 1934 issue. The huge success of *The Three Little Pigs* Silly Symphony in 1933, during the heart of the Great Depression, prompted the financial publication to become interested. The comprehensive illustrated story shows behind-the-scenes photos of studio inner workings. One page was devoted to Roy Disney's explanation of studio finances. Most profits were still being re-channeled into cartoon production eight years after the success of Mickey Mouse.

Snow White and the Seven Dwarfs is the next major milestone in the history of the Disney Studio. But what made *Snow White* possible? As the *Fortune* magazine article relates, the money wasn't coming from cartoon income.

In March 1930, Roy Disney signed a three-year agreement with the George Borgfelt Company of New York to act as the studio's agent to license

Disney character merchandise. At the time, the studio looked upon this as mainly a publicity venture and a way to respond to requests they were getting for Mickey Mouse merchandise. It soon became apparent the deal was not what the Disney Brothers wanted for their characters. The merchandise quality didn't match the increasing high standards they set for their films.

Enter Herman "Kay" Kamen, a Kansas City advertising man who happened to see a Mickey Mouse cartoon in a local theater in 1932. He was struck by the character's merchandise potential and phoned Walt Disney about his ideas. Walt asked him to stop by the studio the next time he was in California for further discussion. Kamen promptly boarded a train for LA. Impressed with Kamen's enthusiasm, as well as his ideas, Walt

Photo courtesy of Lou Lispi

Photo of Kay Kamen taken in 1945.

and Roy Disney asked him to get it all down on paper for a future meeting. Kamen was hired later in 1932 as the Disney's personal representative to Borgfelt. His company took over all licensing activities when the Borgfeldt contract expired in 1933.

Borgfeldt built character merchandise sales to approximately $300,000 in the final year of its contract. By Christmas of 1935, Kay Kamen had increased retail sales to $35 million. The studio's share of royalties from these sales provided money over and above the constantly reinvested cartoon revenue; the seed money needed to greenlight the production of *Snow White* which had been in the planning stage since the spring of 1934. Merchandise licensing profits went straight to the bottom line and have continued to play a vital role in the success of the Disney Studio and theme parks. On December 23, 1935 Walt dictated a seven-page memo to Don Graham, the man in charge of hiring and training new animators and background painters, about gearing up the staff for his first animated feature. Hollywood film executives and insiders called the idea "Disney's Folly." They quickly changed their minds following the film's premiere in December, 1937.

The public's reaction to *Snow White and the Seven Dwarfs* was tremendous and the film put the studio on the map for good. The profits were primarily used to repay the money owed to Bank of America and build the first buildings at the existing Burbank Studio. Walt could now produce feature length films. Work had already begun on *Bambi* and *Pinocchio*. Walt's goal was to release two animated features per year in addition to continued cartoon shorts. This goal was only achieved once in Walt's lifetime. *Pinocchio* was released in February, 1940 and *Fantasia* followed in November. Both were considered financial failures in their first releases. The studio had gone public in 1939 to finance the increased production and was

Photo courtesy of Lou Lispi

Walt Disney signing Kay Kamen's contract to serve as the sole licensing agent for the Disney characters. This photo was taken at the old Hyperion Studio.

now faced with a new crisis. The moviegoing public didn't share Walt's vision. He was just too far ahead of them. They wanted warmer, happy features like *Snow White and the Seven Dwarfs*.

Walt quickly devised a plan to steer the studio past this crisis, *The Reluctant Dragon* and *Dumbo* were produced in record time despite other complications to be explained later. Just when things began to look brighter production was stalled by World War II. During the war, the studio did a lot of government work. The postwar years, however, were devastating. There had been little profit in training films and government projects.

When the War ended employees started to return to work, but it would take three years to get another animated feature to theaters and the company didn't have the money. The Bank of America, the prime lender for Disney financing over the years, was already concerned about Disney's outstanding debt and could have easily forced foreclosure. It was the combined salesmanship of Roy and Walt Disney that encouraged the bank to hang with them while they devised a solution. That solution turned out to be *Cinderella* in 1950.

Television first entered the Disney scene the same year. All the new TV networks were after the company's library of films. Walt was putting the final touches on *Alice In Wonderland* and had agreed to a Coca-Cola sponsored Christmas Special *One Hour in Wonderland*. It became the highest-rated TV program of its time. This convinced Walt that TV wasn't the enemy the other movie studios were making it out to be. He decided it would be just the vehicle he needed to sell his newest concept in family entertainment.

The experts once again predicted Walt's dream of Disneyland would turn into a nightmare within a year. The first year or so was rocky, but Walt made it go. By 1961, the company had completely repaid all the Bank of America debt. Roy and Walt Disney were now wealthy men. Studio employees who didn't sell off their stock bonuses got rich with them. Walt and Roy had always shared financial good times with the other key personnel behind the Disney name.

Walt Disney never seemed to be motivated by money or the acquisition of wealth. It only interested him in what new dreams it could help him accomplish. He had a twist on the well-used phrase "You can't take it with you." His version was, "The only fun I'm going to have is while I'm alive."

The Florida Project was the last big dream of his lifetime. His interest in short films and cartoons waned with the introduction of the *Snow White and the Seven Dwarfs* animated feature. Then going into the live-action film business captured most of his attention, followed by TV and Disneyland. Now he envisioned a City of the Future; his Experimental Prototype Community of Tomorrow (EPCOT). Sadly, Walt and Roy Disney both died before this dream could be fully realized. Many of the EPCOT concepts, however, were employed in constructing the 43.5 square miles of Walt Disney World and Celebration, the adjacent real-life planned community.

Walt and Roy Disney were unique individuals who accomplished an incredible number of important achievements in their lives. Walt often said, "If we can dream it, we can do it." Legions of men and women predicted his attempts at "impossible" goals would fail. His standard response was, "It's kinda fun doing the impossible."

Roy was as creative financially as Walt was visually. They both had different ways of approaching problems. Financing Disneyland for example, required constant re-working and new solutions. Once built, Walt noticed a large artificial tree partially obscured the view at Disneyland's Tahitian Terrace restaurant show. This was no small tree. It was constructed of steel and concrete. The engineers studied how they could raise the foliage the four feet Walt wanted and reported it would cost a huge sum of money to get underneath it and raise it up. Their thinking was limited to "raising the tree!" Walt took another look and told his engineers just to cut the trunk and splice in the needed footage in the middle to raise the top of the tree. Quality was always uppermost in Walt's mind. How they both achieved their objectives frequently surprised and impressed the best of experts.

Walt and Roy were from Missouri. Whatever truth or fallacy there may be to the old adage about people from the "show me" state asking questions, it sure applied to the Disney Brothers. Walt questioned everything! When he wasn't questioning, he observed. His formal education ended after his first year in high school and a limited amount of art training at the Chicago Institute of Art. At that point in his life, he lied about his age to join the Red Cross Ambulance Corp and was sent to France at the end of World War I. When he returned home eleven months later, he chose to start making his way in the world rather than finish school. This decision never stopped his pursuit of knowledge. What he learned from the simple techniques of asking questions and his eye for detail caused many people to call him a genius. He disliked being called a genius "because it's a lazy way of saying a man enjoys his work."

Roy was a big proponent of outside research. He was the peacekeeper among family members and working with Walt. He clearly handled all studio business operations.

Some have characterized Walt as complex and difficult to know. More realistically, Walt was committed to a brand that bore the same name as his. "Walt Disney presents" was the single image he wanted the public to remember and to rely on. New employees often got the message one on one. Long-time Disney art director, Ken Anderson, recalled being summoned to Walt's office early on. "It was during my first week at the studio. Walt called me in and said he wanted to set me straight from the start. If I was there to make a name for myself, I should leave now, because he was selling the name 'Walt Disney.' Not for his own self, but for the studio. That's what we want our audience to remember. 'If you can agree with that principle, you're my man.' I thought his manner was straightforward and I appreciated it. I came to learn why he demanded such loyalty. Artists didn't always understand why he asked for things to be redone or changed. Some had strong convictions their way was right, but they just knew when Walt asked for changes or a different approach, you did it without an argument. It saved a lot of time…and lo and behold, you usually found out you could do better."

Walt and Roys' strength of character and mid-western values were the foundation of their studio. Walt's inquiring mind, and unwavering persistence, plus a knack for common-sense solutions, were the basic tools he needed to impact the entire world. The culture he instilled at the studio was militaristic. He was the general. Other strong individuals often had problems with his almost singularly directed management style. Fortunately, enough talented people shared his vision and valued his contribution to their personal growth. Working together under Walt's leadership and Roy's financial know-how, the studio prospered by achieving one innovation after another in animation and other entertainment enterprises.

Photo from the Tomart Archives

Photo of Walt Disney and his most famous characters sent by the studio to fans requesting a photo of Walt (circa 1936-37),

Chapter III – Orchestrating Animated Entertainment

"I think if there's any part I've played...the vital part is coordinating these talents, and encouraging these talents, and carrying them down a certain line. It's like pulling together a big orchestra. They're all individually very talented. I have an organization of people who are specialists. You can't match them anywhere in the world for what they do. But they all need to be pulled together, and that's my job."

—Walt Disney

Animator Ward Kimball once pointed out Walt's luck with timing. "He was the right man in the right place for sound and color cartoons, for the animated feature, and to take advantage of the new TV medium to launch Disneyland." Walt was always fascinated by new technological developments. The revolutionary sound film, *The Jazz Singer* had everyone in Hollywood scrambling to produce their own "talkies." Just locating the proper sound recording equipment was a challenge. Walt finally found Pat Powers in New York to add sound to his *Mickey Mouse* cartoon. Powers was a slick opportunist in the early days of the motion picture business and Walt would eventually regret hooking up with him. Powers, however, did provide the necessary equipment to help Walt achieve his first historic film triumph. Every Disney follower knows what happened after *Steamboat Willie* was screened at New York's Colony Theater, November 18, 1928.

Walt Disney had worked with animation since 1920. The first ten years were spent experimenting and deciding the direction he wanted to go. His *Alice Comedies* worked on the silent screen. *Oswald the Lucky Rabbit* was doing great business when the distributor decided to produce them himself. *Mickey Mouse* was successfully launched, but Walt wanted more realistic animation. Several things held him back. There are some key facts to remember to set the stage for the Disney led animation revolution.

Cartoon animation had been around for about fifteen years by the time Mickey Mouse was introduced. It was a novelty that hung around as cinema was finding its way in the entertainment world. It was an era when comedy was king and cartoon gags seemed to fit in. Artists and audiences were content with drawings that moved and made them laugh. New interest traditionally wasn't generated by improvement of animation techniques, but rather by the introduction of new characters or the adaptation of popular newspaper comic strip characters to the cartoon media.

Meanwhile, live-action film techniques and production qualities were making giant strides forward. This caused animation to start loosing favor among theater owners and managers. The innovation of the *Steamboat Willie* sound cartoon was the beginning of a period of great advancement in animation techniques and renewed interest in the cartoon as an important part of the filmgoing experience.

The animation process began to develop years earlier. Despite attempts as early as 1906, many film historians list *Gertie the Dinosaur* as the first animated film. It was actually a background for a vaudeville performance of her creator, cartoonist Winsor McCay. It was first seen in February 1914 at Chicago's Palace Theater. McCay's humorous routine featured him talking to Gertie (a lumbering Brontosaurus) to the point where she gets fed up, chases him into the wings, picks up an animated McCay in her mouth, sets him on her shoulder and carries him into the distance.

Animation in the teens and twenties had been developed by studios in New York where the motion picture business started with Thomas Edison. Scenes were traditionally assigned to an artist to animate. They would do the drawings and others would then shoot, edit, and composite them into the final film. Often the artist had to visit the theater to see how his work turned out. Pat Sullivan's Felix the Cat was the dominant character in the 1920s along with Betty Boop. Those were the bright spots. Most other character animation didn't improve much. The surviving *Puss 'N Boots* film from Walt's 1923-24 Laugh-O-gram Company was certainly no improvement. *Steamboat Willie* was a little better. *The Skeleton Dance*, began to show some style innovations, but the key to Walt's animation through this period had been Ub Iwerks.

Disney animation style from 1922 through 1931 changed little because Walt was so dependent on him. Iwerks was such a strong animator, he had as much influence as Walt on the studio's final product. Many of the same animators were involved during this period and they took their lead from Ub Iwerks. When Carl Stalling, Walt's first musical director, suggested a new series of cartoons based on music compositions, Iwerks was so taken with the idea he demanded to draw *every frame* of *The Skeleton Dance*, the first of what became known as the Silly Symphony series. Walt felt it was wasteful to have his top artist doing all the inbetweens and it started to cause problems between the two friends.

Interviews with animators who worked with Ub Iwerks all prized him as one of the leading craftsman at the time. He drew fast and came up with immediate solutions to make all kinds of objects move. Walt always gave him the toughest scenes to do. There was a certain style to Iwerk's animation, but it was mostly geared to mechanical movement. That was the way he thought and the process that allowed him to do hundreds of drawings a day. Walt and Roy Disney valued Ub Iwerks so highly they made him a partner and gave him 20% of their studio. As far back as the *Alice Comedies*, however, Walt was pushing for more life-like animation. Friz Freleng, who worked with Walt for a brief time on later *Alice Comedies* and early *Oswald the Lucky Rabbit* films, recalled an interesting experience in an interview with J.B. Kaufman in 1991. "I was handed a scene of a mother cat bathing her little kittens. So I did the scene and added one little kitten crawling out of the tub and he's hanging on the edge of the tub and then drops down. As the mother grabbed him and put him back into the tub, a couple others were trying to escape. This was just ad-libbed because all the script said was 'A mother cat bathing her kittens.' Walt called to everybody and he says, 'I want you to see this scene.' He says, 'That little kitten didn't just jump out of the water, he climbed up and hung there and dropped down like a little kid would do. Friz did it this way and made him act like a little kid. That's what I want to see in the pictures, I want the characters to be somebody. I don't want them just to be a drawing.'"

Ub Iwerks left the Disney Studio in 1930 to do things his way and sold his interest in the company back to the Disney brothers for $2,000. Iwerks then opened his own studio, backed by Walt's former distributor, Pat Powers. Powers had an ax to grind with the Disney Brothers for taking away his lucrative distribution deal on early *Mickey Mouse* cartoons. This put Walt in a spot similar to the time when most of his Oswald animators defected to Charles Mintz. Powers knew it was Iwerks who was the most productive animator and the leader of Walt's staff. All Walt seemed to do was write the stories and time each scene until the six to seven-minute one-reel cartoon was completed. The vindictive Powers felt a deal doubling Iwerks salary to get him away from Disney would surely put Walt out of business. He was the second man to misjudge Walt's role. On his own, Iwerks developed the *Flip the Frog* series and eventually some stand-alone cartoons, the most popular being *Jack Frost*. His studio would eventually fail.

Here is a good place to bring up one of Walt's most overlooked attributes: he always seemed to know what to do when things went wrong. When Charles Mintz took his star character and most of his animators, Walt and Ub Iwerks created Mickey Mouse. When Ub Iwerks was lured away, Walt was free to pursue animation the way he envisioned it to be. Time and again, Walt's skill saved the day. Wisdom Magazine quoted him summing up his own success this way: "Somehow I can't believe there are many heights that can't be scaled by a man who knows the secret of making dreams come true.

This special secret, it seems to me, can be summarized in four C's. They are Curiosity, Confidence, Courage, and Constancy, and the greatest of these is Confidence. When you believe a thing, believe it all over, implicitly and unquestioningly."

With Ub Iwerks gone from Disney, Walt recruited animators who shared his vision for more realistic animation. He wanted to elevate the process with more life in his characters. He eventually shot each drawing before they were traced onto cels for final production. He then reviewed this "pencil test" footage with his animators in what came to be known as the "sweatbox" where Walt communicated what changes he wanted made. The term "sweatbox" comes from small cubicles where moviolas were located. A moviola is a hand-operated projection machine used to view motion picture film at any speed; forwards or backwards, even frame by frame. The device was created for film editors. One of Walt's innovations was to have the animation drawings shot on negative film so the artist's black lines showed up as white against a black background. This test film was run on a moviola to check the animation. Several people in the animation unit had to squeeze around the small screen in the hot moviola space to see the animation.

Photo courtesy of Marc Ricci

Walt Disney with a group of storymen and animators in a projection room "sweatbox". Note the large ashtray in front of Walt. He never knowingly allowed photos of him smoking.

Careers were often made or broken in the sweatbox, giving rise to a second meaning to the term – artists sweating out the acceptance of their work. When both Walt and the animator were pleased, the drawings were released for final production. The process was later refined for color and feature production.

Walt's goal was always better entertainment. Many would say he developed animation into an art using the Silly Symphony series as a proving ground for new techniques. *The Three Little Pigs*, the color Mickey cartoons, *The Old Mill*, and ultimately the animated feature demonstrated amazingly fast progress toward Walt's objective. Walt may have encouraged his artists by telling them they were creating art, but he never really bought into the "new animated art form" concept. He always said he was just trying to improve the entertainment quality of his films.

Several important tools were created to help improve Walt's animation. Animators up to 1931 were content to make drawings to show movement. Walt was driven to make his characters become more like real actors and show emotions; evilness, fear, love, or jubilation at first; more subtle feelings like thinking, shyness, or disappointment, as more human character traits were developed. An in-house art school was established in 1932 to help the process along. Disney animators were retrained in drawing and acting techniques. They learned from each other, developing new ways to communicate gags and emotions in what soon became known as the Disney style of animation. Those who did a better job of developing their characters ended up with more challenging assignments.

Walt and Ub Iwerks had developed a process to breakdown the visual story. Six drawings were done per page. With the advent of the sound cartoon, a revision to the system was required. Three drawings then appeared in the left column with dialogue, sound effects, and description of the action typed in the right-hand column. Drawing the story in this fashion allowed it to be analyzed and altered before the actual animation drawings were begun. Early storymen Ted Sears and Webb Smith are largely credited with creating the storyboard that separated the drawings from the written dialogue and actions described in script. The drawings were pinned to large 4' x 8' boards. They could be rearranged during story meetings or gag sessions. Visualizing the story and final production became easier. This proved essential to later projects and has since been adapted universally by animators, TV commercial writers, attraction designers, and for other types of visual planning. The sound for *Steamboat Willie* was synchronized using a metronome to time the exact frame where each sound should start or stop. Once the final storyboard was developed, an accompanying timing sheet or chart was drawn up to help the composer, musical director, layout man, and animators convert the "script" to the first pencil-test footage. A timing chart is almost like a musician's sheet music to an animator. It tells him how fast the characters move, exactly where the action must match pre-recorded music, dialogue,

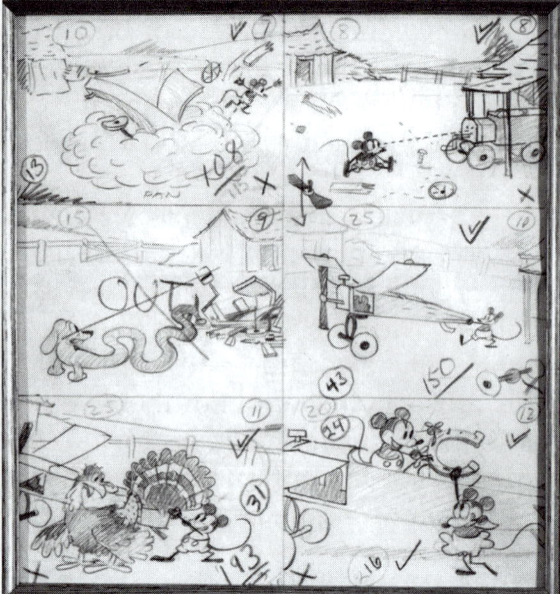

Photos Courtesy of Geppi's Entertainment Museum

Ub Iwerks storyboard for the silent *Plane Crazy*. The *Steamboat Willie* script had dialogue typed opposite the storyboard panels on a single sheet. This method was used prior to individual drawings being seperated from the script and tacked to 4'x8' panels.

sound effects, and other data about each scene before his pencil ever touches paper. This important planning step helped speed production and avoid costly reworking.

These devices helped each film improve, but the great leaps forward didn't begin to manifest themselves on film until those released beginning in 1932. Since 1926, Walt had been in the process of figuring out just how all of this progress could be achieved. To make this dream come true, he knew he needed unique individuals who were willing to learn together as a group…animators who shared his drive for more realistic animation. Then Walt made them believe animation could have a heart, describing and acting out how it could be done in minute detail. He provided the inspiration they needed to make it happen.

The hunt for the first solid animation Team Disney was ongoing. Everybody hired or interviewed was asked, "Who else do you know who's good?"

The building process actually started in 1927 with the hiring of Les Clark. He didn't join Charles Mintz along with the other deserting animators. Clark worked on Mickey Mouse projects including some animation work on *Steamboat Willie*. He later played a major role in improving cartoons and the development of Disney animated features. Norman "Fergie" Ferguson, Ben Sharpsteen, and famed gag man Roy Williams came aboard in 1929. Fred Moore, David Hand, Hamilton "Ham" Luske, and Jack Kinney joined Walt in 1930, around the time Ub Iwerks departed. So the Disney situation wasn't nearly as dire as the competition suspected. In fact, Iwerks leaving perhaps sped up the development of the Disney approach to more realistic animation. When Iwerks returned to the studio in 1940, Disney animation had passed him by and he rarely went near the animation building.

Walt and Roy moved their studio from its original Kingswell Avenue location to one on Hyperion Avenue in January 1926. Concurrently, the name was changed from The Disney Brothers Studio to the Walt Disney Studio because "that was the way Walt wanted it," Roy Disney once reported without the least hint of any envy. The branding of the "Walt Disney" name had begun. Mickey Mouse gradually developed from rascal to Mr. Nice Guy. *The Silly Symphonies* became a second cartoon product brand. Unrelated stories and characters were used throughout the series as a way to test new techniques and ideas. The company grew so fast the brothers decided to buy additional property and build the perfect environment for animation. The plan was finished in 1931, but studio growth was still skyrocketing and the plan was obsolete before the actual work was completed.

All these changes after the loss of Ub Iwerks came at a personal price. Iwerks was key to his early success. He was Walt's friend, sounding board, and confidant. Silently, Walt knew Iwerks had fallen prey to Pat Powers just as he had earlier when he was anxious to get his early *Mickey Mouse* and *Silly Symphony* cartoons into distribution and unwittingly signed an unfavorable contract with Powers. Now they were rivals. Despite the progress Walt was making with his strong new group, Iwerks was personally missed. Everyone noticed Walt was driving himself and his animators too hard.

In retrospect, the seeds of animation growth had been sown, but Walt, like a child planting his first garden, grew impatient to harvest the fruits of his labor. He slept less and became angry easier. Roy and his wife, Edna, had a son in 1930 while Walt and Lilly failed to get pregnant. This added pressure to Walt's state of mind. He drove himself into a deep depression, or what was called a nervous breakdown back then. Roy's growing concern about Walt caused him to consult with Lilly about getting Walt away for awhile. Both Walt's and Lilly's doctors felt it would help him relax and improve their chances of having a child. Walt agreed to a trip back to Missouri to fulfill a childhood dream of traveling down the Mississippi River to New Orleans...just as soon as he got *Flowers and Trees* into production. There wasn't much change after the trip to St. Louis. It seems they missed the last passenger boat to the Big Easy, so Lilly proposed they extend their trip to tour Washington, D.C. There, Walt started to improve after several days of sightseeing. The press caught word of his visit. The creator of Mickey Mouse and the *Silly Symphonies* was in town. The politicians reacted. The publicity man at their hotel had connections and asked the Disneys who they would like to meet in Washington. Walt had driven Pershing's son around France as a teenager, and the name of General John Pershing came to mind. It turned out he was unavailable and the man sheepishly asked if a meeting with President Hoover at the White House would work instead. Both Disneys were thrilled at the idea and the tide was truly turned. The trip was extended for two more months. They traveled to Florida and from Key West to Cuba, then sailed through the Panama Canal and back to California. Walt was totally rejuvenated. Lilly soon confided she thought she was pregnant. It turned out to be a false alarm, but they were later successful and Lilly gave birth to Diane Marie Disney in 1933. The Disneys adopted a second daughter, Sharon Mae Disney, shortly after she was born December 21, 1936.

While Walt was away, Roy was busy changing the company's film distributor. Columbia had loaned Disney the money to get out of their deal with Pat Powers, but the arrangement made it increasingly difficult to pass along raising production costs. Roy shopped around and found an even better deal with United Artists, an independent company founded by Mary Pickford, Douglas Fairbanks, D. W. Griffith, and Walt's longtime favorite film comic, Charlie Chaplin.

There were almost immediate improvements in *Mickey* and *Silly Symphony* shorts as the new staff learned what Walt was after. Drafting and character development showed the first signs of improvement. The *Mickey Mouse* series took a giant leap forward with *Touchdown Mickey* and *The Klondike Kid* in 1932. The stories were better and there was less repetition in the animation. The characters were more real, the action more exciting.

Art Babbit had joined Disney in 1932. He was largely responsible for creating the in-studio art training program, and turning Dippy the Goof into a major studio star, re-named Goofy. Walt hired Albert Hurter the same year, not only to do backgrounds, but also to work on story and concept art to fuel ideas among his leading animators.

Flowers and Trees was completely drawn and already in production in 1932 when Walt returned from his extended trip, but he was unhappy with the results. All those colorful flowers just didn't look right in black & white. He had been following the development of the new three-color Technicolor process and asked for a demonstration. He had heard Ub Iwerks was considering using the process and set out to convince Roy color would be worth the extra cost. When he told Technicolor he needed help to win Roy's approval, they granted a two-year exclusive deal permitting only Disney to use their new three-color system for cartoon production. Roy reluctantly agreed to the cost increase in return for Walt's promise to use color only for Silly Symphonies. Filming in color was easy compared to all the preparation required. A color pallette had to be designed, suitable paints had to be manufactured, cel techniques had to be revised, backgrounds had to be painted in color; all major adjustments the studio took in stride. *Flowers and Trees* won the Academy Award, the first awarded to a cartoon. The great period of animation experimentation and discovery took another giant leap forward.

In 1933, Walt added Eric Larson, Jack Hannah, and Wolfgang "Woolie" Reitherman, all of whom became longtime employees. They soon began to rise through the animation ranks to become directing animators

Promotional drawing released in conjunction with *Two-Gun Mickey*. This publicity still captures the type of action drawn into the new breed of Disney animated shorts.

and an inspiration to new recruits.

Black & white classics like *Mickey's Gala Premiere* and *The Mail Pilot* in 1933, and *Playful Pluto* and *Two-Gun Mickey* in 1934 were outstanding examples on how much *Mickey Mouse* and other Disney cartoons had progressed with character development, timing, and drawing techniques. Ward Kimball remembered *Playful Pluto* with particular fondness. "Norm Ferguson animated Pluto dealing with pesky fly-paper unlike anything ever done before. Pluto didn't talk, but Fergie captured him thinking as he plotted each new move to rid himself of his sticky attachment. He milked that gag for everything it was worth and more." These films remain a marvel today...and are still exciting to watch.

The next great Disney animation achievement came during the depths of the Great Depression in 1933. The stock market had crashed back in 1929, but the effects got worse for six to eight years before the U.S. economy started to improve. Unemployment had reached 25%. Against this background, *The Three Little Pigs* (1933) resonated with Walt's audience like no other Disney film since *Steamboat Willie*. People related the Big Bad Wolf to the Depression and the Three Pigs to themselves. The song "Who's Afraid of the Big Bad Wolf?" by studio composer Frank Churchill became the most popular song in the country and Disney's first big musical hit. The cartoon was billed on theater marquees and was often held over, even as the feature movie changed. People wanted to see it over and over, resulting in more than four times the normal revenue for a cartoon short. This was the first Disney film where the characters were developed as actors and merged into a full-color production with special music. The pigs were largely the work of Freddie Moore, who had a natural ability to adapt characters to cute rounded-off shapes for Disney style animation. In fact, he was the major influence of the Disney cartoon character look. Moore was the artist behind several redesigns of Mickey Mouse during the '30s. He was also the person who set the final styling for the Seven Dwarfs as they appeared in *Snow White*. He designed character into his drawings. Lines seemed to flow from his pencil, prompting most other animators to comment words to the effect "Freddie Moore never made a bad drawing." In a sense, *The Three Little Pigs* was the first ani-

Sheet music from the Tomart Archives

mated feature…just a mini-version. The film was uplifting to its audience. The story conveyed the idea the average guy did have a chance in a time when people needed to hear that message. *The Three Little Pigs* was the right film at the right time, providing a lift to a little guy on the street…and to the Disney Studio, unquestionably the smallest film factory in town.

"Never repeat" was Walt's code until the day he died. This was the way he expressed his longstanding credo in his last message to employees and shareholders in the company's annual report for the fiscal year ending October 1, 1966.

"Many people have asked, "Why don't you make another *Mary Poppins*? Well, by nature I'm a born experimenter. To this day, I don't believe in sequels. I can't follow popular cycles. I have to move on to new things; there are many new worlds to conquer.

"As a matter of fact, people have been asking us to make sequels ever since Mickey Mouse first became a star. We have bowed only on one occasion to the cry to repeat ourselves. Back in the '30s, *The Three Little Pigs* was an enormous hit. Then the cry went up – "Give us more Pigs!" I could not see how we could possibly top pigs with pigs. But we tried, and I doubt whether any one of you reading this can name the other cartoons in which the pigs appeared.

"We didn't make the same mistake with *Snow White*. When it was a huge hit, the shout went up for more dwarfs. Top dwarfs with dwarfs? Why try?

"Right now, we're not thinking about making another *Mary Poppins*. We never will. Perhaps there will be other ventures with equal critical and financial success. But we know we cannot hit a home run with the bases loaded every time we go to the plate. We also know the only way we can even get to first base is by constantly going to bat and continuing to swing.

"And so we're always looking for new ideas and new stories, hoping that somehow we'll come up with a different kind of *Mary Poppins*...or even a different kind of Disneyland."

However, United Artists, the studio's film distributor in 1933, wanted Walt to try to make The Three Pigs recurring characters like Mickey Mouse. Walt figured the story and song made *The Three Little Pigs* the success it became, but did three follow-up films – *The Big Bad Wolf* (April 14, 1934) with Little Red Riding Hood, *Three Little Wolves* (April, 18 1936), and *The Practical Pig* (February 24, 1939). None approached the success of the original, prompting Walt to coin an often used phrase, "Never follow Pigs with Pigs." He never did another animated sequel.

Milt Kahl, Frank Thomas, Ward Kimball, Ken Anderson, Vladimir "Bill" Tytla, and Grim Natwick were hired in 1934 as the studio prospered from the success of *The Three Little Pigs* and increased merchandise sales. Walt was starting to gear up for something bigger. Four men from this group were destined to become studio leaders. Milt Kahl became the silent giant at the studio. "He probably designed more characters than any other studio artist," Bill Justice once recalled. Frank Thomas helped develop or perfect many unique animation techniques. Ward Kimball was a multi-talented artist, musician, director, and studio kook. Ken Anderson became a longtime art director for cartoons, feature films, and theme park attractions. These men were all to play vital roles in the years immediately ahead.

The exclusive contract with Technicolor ended in 1934. Roy Disney agreed that color helped sell Disney cartoons, and *Mickey* shorts should also be done in color. *The Band Concert* (1935) was the first *Mickey Mouse* cartoon resulting from this decision. Every cartoon short from then on used the Technicolor process. Repetitive animation, even in large crowd scenes, had completely disappeared from Disney films by this time.

The Wise Little Hen, another story with a moral, introduced Donald Duck in 1934. Walt received so many letters from mothers asking him "not to let Mickey do this, or do that" to avoid having a negative influence on their children. Mickey was reduced to a character who played by the rules, came out the hero, and won his girl, Minnie. Disney needed another mischievous foil and Donald Duck proved to be the answer. He was created to be a loser, never a winner to be emulated.

Donald Duck wasn't named in his 1934 *Wise Little Hen* film debut. His character was still in development. The idea for the character came to Walt by chance. He was always looking for unusual voices and happened to hear an amateur talent show radio broadcast featuring Clarence Nash who was doing animal imitations and bird calls. Walt called the station immediately and employees tracked down Nash. He was hired and served as the official voice of Donald for over 50 years. He represented the studio in promotional appearances using a Donald Duck ventriloquist's dummy to the

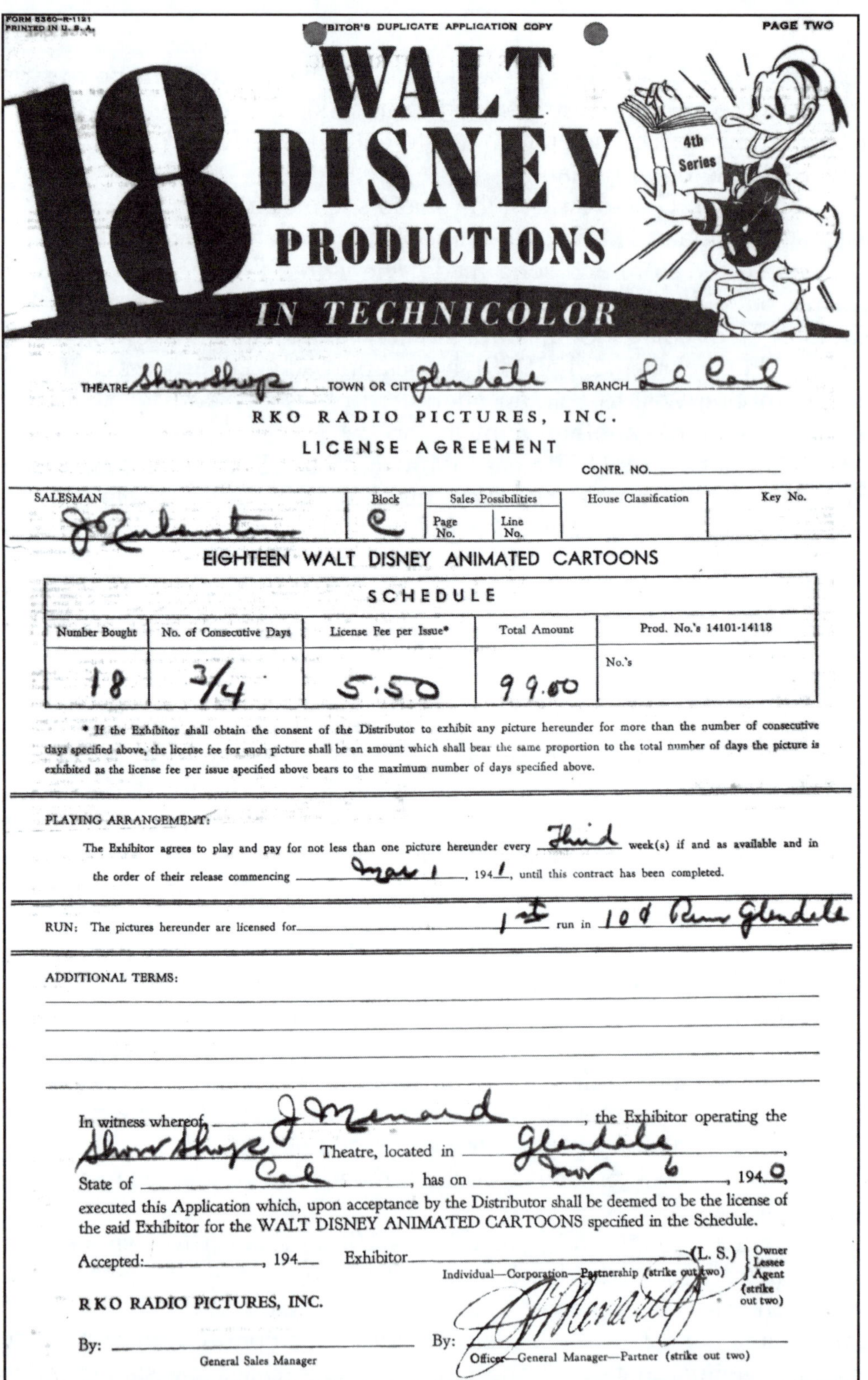

Courtesy Tomart Archives

Disney cartoons were licensed mainly in "blocks" where the exhibitor signed up to play a minimum number of shorts at a set fee per film. This 1940 contract for an eighteen-film block still prodominantly proclaimed all cartoons were in Technicolor.

delight of all who saw him perform. By 1936, Donald and Goofy appeared in *Mickey* Cartoons and Donald was soon starring in his own films.

Ollie Johnston, Marc Davis, Charles "Nick" Nicholas, John Lounsbery, and background artist Claude Coats were standout additions in the Disney Studio class of 1935. Noted illustrator Gustav Tenggren was added in 1936 for a brief time to do concept art and backgrounds for *Snow White and the Seven Dwarfs* and *Pinocchio*. Joe Grant, Bill Justice, and storyman extraordinaire Bill Peet were key additions in 1937.

Hundreds of other animators and artists worked on Disney films and many can be found on film credits for shorts and features. However, the artists mentioned in this chapter were the main shapers of the Disney brand of animation developed during the 1930s, and the principal leaders (two key exceptions to be explained later) who would guide the most notable work done by the studio over the next 25 to 30 years.

The studio had progressed in ways other than technique. Over the years, Walt developed some do's and don'ts in his approach to animation. One of his oldest was "The less dialogue, the better." He preferred sight gags to one-line or dialogue jokes. This also helped establish the Disney international market. Sight gags are funny in any language. When he felt the studio had established a good cast of cartoon characters, he was strong on keeping the total number of characters appearing in a film to 25 or less. That may sound easy, but when you start to think it wasn't unusual to use the basic eleven – Mickey, Minnie, Donald, Daisy, Goofy, Pluto, Donald's three Nephews, Chip 'n Dale – the incidental characters could add up fast. Restricting the number was to make the lead cartoon characters more valuable for licensed merchandise and more recognizable in comic strips.

Villains had to be drawn so as not to distinguish any nationality. Disney pictures were distributed throughout the entire world...by Disney in the free world and by pirates in countries not recognizing U.S. copyright or trademark protection. Walt didn't want to offend any nation or characterize them as evil. The propaganda work done during World War II was the lone exception to this rule and in this case, was carefully crafted toward the offending regimes rather than the countries themselves.

Donald was also given special consideration. He surpassed every other character in Hollywood Toontown to become the most popular cartoon character in America during the 1940s. Mickey actually came in third behind Bugs Bunny in the second slot. Walt decreed that Donald could get steaming mad in the course of his pictures, but had to be contrite or get his due before the camera irised out. Walt was all about good triumphing over evil. Donald wasn't a villain in the true sense of the word, but he could be mischievous to the point of villainy, especially with Chip 'n Dale. Even after he got his comeuppance in such tales, he always appeared to have an "I had it coming" look at the end so as not to have the audience think ill of him.

Later on, when the animated features became a factor, Walt decided that no characters from an animated feature could appear in cartoon shorts. This was to avoid overexposure to the detriment of the seven-year re-release cycle established in the '40s.

Besides convincing Walt to never repeat, *The Three Little Pigs* resulted in yet another no-no: never use ethnic humor. The Big Bad Wolf was originally disguised as a Jewish peddler when calling at one of the Pigs' homes. This raised a fuss and charges of anti-Semitism. Ethnic humor among an immigrant nation was common in the 1920s and 1930s, but the scene had to be redone for subsequent re-releases.

The Disney Studio in the '30s must have been an exciting place. Marc Davis once told the story of Walt rushing into Freddie Moore's office to reveal, "This morning while shaving I discovered that when the eye blinks, only the top lid moves." Another tiny detail was added to the growing list that went into making the human characters in *Snow White* more life-like. That's how the studio changed animation, one little detail at a time. Walt continually pushed for improved quality, sharing his observations, and getting all the other artists to do likewise. Animators learned from each other's discoveries. The whole studio hummed together to make each film better than the previous one. Work groups were established for each new title. What an animator learned from one group was passed on to the next. In addition to learning new techniques, animators were sharpening the ways they approached and drew each scene.

To better understand what the Disney animators learned, get a male friend to describe his early morning routine. His answer will be something like shave, take a shower, and eat breakfast. Ask a seasoned Disney animator like Ward Kimball the same question and the answer goes something like this, "The alarm clock rings, I squint both eyes while moving my body slightly under the covers, I open my right eye as I turn my head to look at the clock, reach out with my left hand and smack the alarm clock off, pull the covers back over me as I roll over for a few more seconds, rustle in bed a few times to shake the cobwebs from my head and joints, then I use both arms to throw back the covers from over my head, sit up in bed and stretch both arms straight in the air. Then, I reach down with my right hand and pull the covers aside, then bend my left knee, lift my leg and put my left foot on the floor. Followed by similar action with my right leg before sitting to the edge of the bed, standing up and stretching again!" This is just an abbreviated version. An animator learns to research every fiber of movement so it can be translated into 12 to 24 drawings per second depending on how fast the character being drawn moves or talks. Ward Kimball was an artist when he joined Disney, but he had never done any animation. His description of how animators think, partially recounted here, reflects what he was taught after he joined the studio. It's the same thought process that resulted from the observations of Walt and his staff as he pushed for more life-like animation.

Walt Disney didn't draw much after *Steamboat Willie,* and then only

APPLICATION FOR EMPLOYMENT

WALT DISNEY PRODUCTIONS, LTD.

NAME..........

ADDRESS.......... PHONE..........

CITY.......... STATE..........

AGE.......... SEX.......... NATIONALITY..........

MARRIED.......... DIVORCED.......... CHILDREN.......... DEPENDENTS..........

HIGH SCHOOL.......... UNIVERSITY..........

UNIVERSITY COURSE..........

ART SCHOOLS (NAME AND LENGTH OF ATTENDANCE)..........

WHAT AND HOW MUCH PRACTICAL—CARTOONING—COMMERCIAL AND FINE ARTS EXPERIENCE HAVE YOU HAD?

PRESENT EMPLOYMENT..........

HAVE YOU CONTRIBUTED TO HUMOR MAGAZINES?..........

COMIC STRIP OR GAG CONTINUITY?.......... NEWSPAPER?..........

WRITING?.......... DRAWING?.......... GAGS?..........

DO YOU COMPOSE?.......... READ?.......... OR ARRANGE MUSIC?..........

DO YOU PLAY ANY MUSICAL INSTRUMENT (INCLUDING DRUMS)..........

ACTING EXPERIENCE — VAUDEVILLE?.......... STAGE?.......... MOTION PICTURE?..........

DANCING EXPERIENCE?..........

RADIO EXPERIENCE?.......... RADIO CONTINUITY?..........

WRITING EXPERIENCE?.......... SHORT STORIES?..........

MISCELLANEOUS..........

POSTAGE IS ENCLOSED FOR THE RETURN AND INSURANCE OF SAMPLES IN THE

AMOUNT OF.......... STATE VALUATION OF SAMPLES..........

(SIGN ON REVERSE SIDE)

NAME.......... SAMPLES REC'D.......... NOTIFIED..........

INSURANCE.......... SAMPLES RETURNED.......... DECISION..........

Courtesy of the Tomart Archives

1930's Disney Studios job application shows the qualities Walt was looking for as he built his staff of artists, writers, animators, and production people.

ATTENTION: An itemized list of all drawings submitted must be furnished herewith, otherwise your portfolio cannot be released by the Mailing Department for inspection. Please identify each sample by a number or letter and refer to this identification by a corresponding number or letter on the itemized list. Your solutions to the problems should not be listed individually but should be referred to as a group.

Walt Disney Productions, Ltd.,
2719 Hyperion Avenue,
Hollywood, California.

Gentlemen:

I herewith submit on my own initiative the following material, which I am offering to you for consideration in connection with my application for a position in your organization: (Please indicate nature of material in space provided below according to above instructions.)

No.	DESCRIPTION	No.	DESCRIPTION

I appreciate the fact that your Studio has at all times many stories and situations in process of production and that it is quite possible that ideas included in my material are at this time being used by you or may be under consideration. Therefore, I realize that the menace of plagiarism claims or suits would not permit you to examine my material unless I unconditionally and fully release you from all claims, obligations and liability with reference to the same. I, therefore, hereby unconditionally and fully give and grant you such release, not only from liability for infringement but also for loss in transit, destruction by fire or otherwise, in consideration of your receiving and examining my work.

You are at liberty to retain in your files my solutions to the studio drawing problems to be used for reference in the event of future communication between us. I hereby release and assign the same to you in consideration of the premises.

NAME:...

ADDRESS:...

DATE:...

PLEASE GIVE THE NAMES AND ADDRESSES OF THREE REFERENCES:

....

....

....

Reverse side of the 1930's Disney Studios job application.

to illustrate an idea or changes he wished to make. His role was to get the best out of his artists; to provide the environment, the methods and the stimulation to help them reach a potential they didn't realize they had within themselves. He motivated by being able to act out and describe the action he wanted in great detail. He wasn't behind a desk. He worked with each unit almost on a daily basis.

Perhaps Walt Disney's greatest talent was that of a storyteller. The most important step in a Walt Disney animated production was getting the story the best it could be. Once Walt felt the story was settled and storyboarded, he turned it over to his chosen director, art directors, and lead animators. But Walt didn't merely pick artists. He selected artists/actors (often with added musical ability) and cast them in character roles. More importantly, he let them develop the characters. Then he ran their drawings through a pencil test "rehearsal" process to point out corrections and let his animators improve their work. The result was a more life-like on-screen "performance" envied by non-Disney animators who were never given the budget to review and improve their work like Disney artists could. More endearing characters were recognized by Walt's adult and child audience. "Disney characters are more lovable, they make me laugh, they make me cry, they tug at my heart strings," are all common phrases heard when people talked about the films of Walt Disney.

Frank Thomas and Ollie Johnston provided the definitive book, *Disney Animation–The Illusion of Life*, on how the Studio animators developed processes like squash and stretch, (originally pioneered by Ub Iwerks) staging, timing, secondary action, and other devices that set Disney Studio work apart from all the others. No one has reported on them better than Frank and Ollie. They lived through it. They helped create and refine the techniques. Suffice it to say the Disney staff of the very late twenties through the late 1930s developed or perfected animation techniques unique to Walt's dream of more realistic animation drawings that came alive with spirit and heart.

The Thomas/Johnston book describes the atmosphere during the mid-1930s as electric. Animators and directors worked directly with Walt, then they passed along his ideas to their assistants and inbetweeners. Several different groups worked on unrelated projects. *Mickey* cartoons had groups, *Silly Symphonies* had groups, Walt had select members of the Story Department and some concept artists doodling out how to make *Snow White* distinctively Disney. Walt simultaneously was building a small group of engineers, machinists, and other craftsmen to give him new technology to help make his films more life-like.

The United Artists contract was due for renewal in 1937. The company demanded television rights as part of a contract renewal. The Disneys hadn't considered television and were unwilling to give up rights to something they didn't know much about. It was probably a big mistake for United

Artists to be inflexible on the subject, but an important decision made by Roy and Walt. Roy Disney selected RKO to become the new distributor.

In the spring of 1934, Walt called a special evening meeting to announce *Snow White and the Seven Dwarfs* to the whole studio. Always the consummate actor, Walt played out each character as he related his version of the Grimm Brothers' fairy tale.

Preliminary work then began on *Snow White*. Most artists were so busy with their own projects that it was hard to keep up with all of Walt's dreams and experiments. Art classes continued to study human movement in preparation for the studio's first human cast of characters. Meanwhile, Walt had a small crew of specialists studying how to improve special effects animation. They filmed rain drops, clouds, bouncing balls, breaking glass, bursting bubbles, and hundreds of other actions in slow motion. They studied this film and made countless discoveries on how to faithfully duplicate these actions in frame by frame drawings. The stage was set for one of the studio's most adventuresome experiments.

The Old Mill (1937) was a landmark achievement in Walt's quest toward animation perfection. Few knew it was in the works. While most of the studio's artists were toiling on cartoons or the *Snow White* production, a small group was using special effects discoveries to set a mood and make other production elements more realistic. A new multiplane camera was developed by Walt's engineers and machine shop staff. This special camera had several levels on which cels and background elements could be placed providing greater depth to a scene. It more faithfully reproduced what the human eye saw in the real world. All the experiments came together like finding a perfect gem in a well worked mine. *The Old Mill* is simply a 24-hour period in the life of a country setting around an abandoned windmill as it experiences wildlife and the forces of nature. The little story has no words, just sound effects. The action is sublime, yet fascinating; compelling even. *The Old Mill* was the manifestation of many artistic techniques and special effects Walt had been working on for years. The results were so sensational the short film won an Academy Award all its own. No group was more blown away than animators; Disney's own and those of competitors. They knew what went into animated films. Here was a film with little character development, the mere thread of a story, the look of an Old Master, and it all moved as if photographed in live-action!

The Hyperion Studio was busting at the seams during the production of *Snow White*. The staff had grown to over 800 people. Pieces of the film were so divided up among different groups, few people knew what the final film would look like. The artists weren't prepared for the reaction to the film's premiere at Hollywood's Carthay Circle Theater on December 21, 1937.

Ward Kimball was there and often told this story, "The biggest names in Hollywood showed up; producers, directors, studio heads, and the brightest stars were there. I thought we were in for a big let down. How could all these jaded people be entertained by the longest cartoon ever made? We had some of the saddest looking costumed characters outside the theater for publicity, but everyone seemed to get into Walt's first big Hollywood opening.

"Walt introduced the film, the lights went down, and the title lit up the screen. I had worked on the film for about two years, but was seeing the completed product for the first time. Nothing seemed the same as a cartoon. There were gags, but they were more integrated into the characters. It was impressive to see what we had accomplished. At the end, these hard-

Snow White Cathay Circle Premier Program

hearted Hollywood types were crying. I couldn't believe it! They were crying at our drawings. They were moved just as Walt had envisioned they would be. It was amazing!"

Unfortunately, Ward Kimball's work on *Snow White* mostly ended up on the cutting-room floor. Two major Dwarf sequences he animated – the Dwarfs building Snow White a bed and the often-talked-about soup-slurping scene, were cut from the film. They were good scenes, but Walt told Ward, "They didn't advance the story like I wanted."

Snow White and the Seven Dwarfs was a sensation when released to the general public on February 4, 1938. The studio had a strong female character to merchandise for the first time and sales took off, led by four different doll manufacturers. Little girls had their first Disney princess. Disney's Folly turned out to be Walt's Triumph. Several of his secondary animators were lured away by other studios in an attempt to learn the Disney magic. All of the lead animators, however, remained with Walt.

Work was already under way on *Bambi*, *Pinocchio,* and a Mickey short titled *The Sorcerer's Apprentice.*

Employees shared in the success of *Snow White* via a "surprisingly large payroll bonus." Walt also invited the entire studio staff for a weekend outing at the Lake Norconian Resort, with all food and drink provided by the studio. The event became legend in studio lore. It all started with a little too much drinking around the swimming pool. Some swimsuits came off and what became known as the "Snow White orgy" got completely out of hand. Walt and Lilly Disney quietly checked out and went home. There were never any reprimands, nor was such an event ever repeated.

Walt's vindication in producing a full-length animated film prompted him to set a goal of producing two animated features per year. This goal would require a major increase in financing, so the company started a plan to go public in 1939.

Bambi was Walt's first choice to follow *Snow White*. A temporary studio was set up near Hollywood and Vine to make way for the main studio being moved from Hyperion Avenue and to facilities under construction in Burbank. The *Bambi* characters weren't the rounded cartoonish characters Disney animators were used to drawing. They had long spindly legs. Young Bambi and Faline moved totally different from more mature deer, a few of which were seen briefly in *Snow White*. There were problems adjusting to the remote location. A special art school had to be set up to study and learn to draw the woodland animals. Story and character development stalled. Work continued, but the schedule was changed to slot *Pinocchio* as the second animated feature to be released. Work on the film was started before *Snow White* was completed, but the schedule change caught the *Pinocchio* unit off guard. The sudden urgency made things more difficult.

Pinocchio was much harder to develop than *Snow White*. The book was problematic to adapt. Figaro the Cat and Cleo the Goldfish provided a few scenes of comic relief. Geppetto was a kindly old man, but that's as far as the love and warm feelings went. The lesson of *Pinocchio* was one of life's hard knocks. The story had more villains than any other Disney animated feature – five – J. Worthington Foulfellow (Honest John), Gideon, Stromboli, The Coachman, and Monstro. Still, something was missing to give the story the Disney touch. The void caused Walt to cease production until an acceptable solution could be found to add some life around the expressionless wooden marionette. Story meetings were held and drawings were made, but the missing ingredient proved elusive.

One day Ham Luske was reviewing the storyboards. One sequence had Pinocchio playing a cruel prank on Figaro the Cat. It was perfectly in character for a wooden boy without a conscience, but what if somehow he had one? This sent the storymen back to the original Collodi book. There they discovered a brief reference to a grasshopper who warned Pinocchio about his foolish ways. In the book, Pinocchio, without any regard for right or wrong, crushes the insect underfoot. Here was a conscience of sorts true to the book. The studio had previously done *Grasshopper and the Ants* and didn't want to repeat the character. Other insects were discussed. What should such a character be called? Fred Moore came up with the name Jimmy. Ham Luske came back with Jiminy...Jiminy Cricket. He would become the narrator for the story as well as Pinocchio's conscience. The story was back on track. Two songs were written for the new character by Leigh Narline and Ned Washington: "When You Wish Upon a Star" to help establish the character and "Give a Little Whistle." The entire animation unit was pleased with the story solution and work on *Pinocchio* resumed with renewed vigor, but the Cricket was to cause further delays.

Ward Kimball's major scenes for *Snow White* had been cut and he once explained, "I was ready to quit and find a studio that would think higher of me. Walt got wind of my thoughts and called me into his office. Before I could quit, he assigned the Cricket to me, most of the scenes except some that Bill Justice and Woolie Rietherman would do in conjunction with the whale. Walt had a way of building you up without ever giving you a compliment. He said he didn't like what the other fellas came up with and wanted me to give it a try. I came up with a modified insect approach. It got approved, and I was pleased as punch; but something always bothered me about the character. It took me the longest time to figure it out. He was almost completely animated as an insect. Then it hit me. One day, I went in to see Walt with some drawings and explained the problems I had with the insect look from the beginning and showed him the drawings of how I felt he should look. My Jiminy was more human and seemed to fit the story better. The animation using my original design was largely done. I didn't expect Walt to agree with me and order all the Cricket scenes to be redone, but he did. I don't think Woolie was too happy, but when Walt bought into the idea, that was it."

Ward Kimball's original Jiminy Cricket insect design.

And Woolie Rietherman wasn't happy. Walt was famous for playing up the competition between different animation units. Ward was normally assigned scenes in conjunction with Frank Thomas or Ollie Johnston, whereas Woolie Rietherman, Bill Justice, and Marc Davis would work in competing unit groups. "Rather than retrace the drawings of other characters on pages that had to have the new Cricket," Bill Justice confided, "Woolie cut the pages apart and taped fresh panels in position for the revised Cricket drawings. When the scenes were reviewed in the sweatbox, Walt reacted to all the visible tape with, "Woolie, what the hell was that?" Woolie simply responded, "It's going to be OK, Walt," and Walt knew it would. He may have been hard on his people when he felt they could do better, but Walt also respected their talent and trusted them to work out technical details the best way they saw fit.

Walt had his own problems with *Pinocchio*. Converting *The Sorcerer's Apprentice* into a feature film put a huge strain on the studio talent pool. His best artists were spread too thin. His vision for the film was not totally fulfilled. In the end, he wasn't completely satisfied with the result and that's what really counted as far as Walt was concerned.

The *Pinocchio* premiere on February 7, 1940 has never been detailed anything like all the festivities surrounding the *Snow White* opening. The film was more artistic and technically superior to *Snow White*. Extensive use of the multiplane camera, innovative layouts, photography angles, plus a subdued color pallette give it more of a Rembrandt look than Walt's first animated feature. It had all the drama Walt Disney felt he could bring to the screen. He wanted to get even further away from the long cartoon image. However, the darker story of *Pinocchio* didn't impress theater goers. The film wasn't light and happy like *Snow White*. Most critics raved, but rarely have they been in tune with the Disney audience. The film lost approximately half its investment due to the war in Europe. It was the first of several setbacks the studio would encounter in the decade.

This period prompted another major Disney innovation. Traditional film studios could only release movies once and then store them in a vault. Roy and Walt Disney reasoned a new audience of children was ready for a re-release of Disney animated features about every seven years. *Pinocchio* and every other classic animated feature eventually returned big profits to the studio from multiple theatrical releases alone.

The longest payback period for a Disney animated film was *Fantasia,* released November 13, 1940. It lost even more money than *Pinocchio* and had families wondering where Walt was going. He was way ahead of his time, as usual, but here was a case where Walt's normal impeccable timing and audience understanding was not entirely his misjudgment. *Fantasia* began as a simple short, *The Sorcerer's Apprentice*. It was conceived as a vehicle to revive the image of Mickey Mouse, who had become a mere partner to the antics of Goofy and Donald Duck. Freddie Moore, once again, drew the assignment to redesign Mickey with an even more human-like form. The featurette was to be done in a Silly Symphony style format.

Then Walt had a chance dinner meeting with Leopold Stokowski who talked Walt into conducting the music using his Philadelphia Symphony Orchestra. Discussions then evolved into other classical works. When everything was said and done, the Mickey Mouse featurette became *Fantasia*. Had Walt known the fate of *Pinocchio* before he was totally committed to *Fantasia*, the film might not have been produced. So while the timing seemed to be against Walt in 1940, the film did get done and ended up making big dollars in later releases, particularly the 1969 re-release, when the importance of the work became fully appreciated.

As conceived as a feature, it was planned to be updated every year or two, gradually building a repertoire of musical pieces that could be re-released in different feature length combinations, adding years of life to the idea. Walt figured the same could be done with concerts of more popular music. The prospect of replacing the *Silly Symphonies* with the *Fantasia* concept was just too tempting. Audiences however, still equated Disney to *Mickey Mouse* or *Snow White*, and this third animated feature was too different from their expectations. Many unique ways were attempted to market *Fantasia*. Study guides were made available through school music programs. Special promotions were offered through symphony orchestras and organizations. These extra efforts helped, but missed the mark with a large part of the traditional Disney audience.

Animating a symphonic concert was a revolutionary idea. Still, Walt wanted the music to sound more like it did in the concert hall. This led Disney sound engineer, Bill Garity, to develop Fantasound, the first stereophonic recording system ever created, and used only for *Fantasia*. The distinct tracks were multiple optical soundtracks recorded on a second reel of 35mm film synced to the regular mono sound film. It cost $10,000 – $30,000 per theater to install the system so only a limited number of audiences in major cities got to witness the Fantasound version. Had not World War II interrupted, stereophonic recordings might have been available much earlier because Walt Disney wanted his film to sound more like the concert hall.

Fantasia played best in New York City. One theater ran it for over a year on a "hard ticket" basis; reserved seats for two showings per day. Walt had to laugh at some of the highbrow symbolism some reviewers read into the film. "All I was trying to do was interpret the music," Walt confided to friends.

Meanwhile, Roy Disney was at odds with RKO over the way they released *Fantasia*. He wanted more reserved seat showings in smaller markets. RKO wanted the film length cut and put in general release sooner. When the studio refused to further cuts, RKO edited the film themselves to under 90 minutes and put it into general release.

The studio was now 4.5 million dollars in debt to the Bank of America and the value of Walt Disney Productions stock was dropping. Roy was after Walt to come up with ideas to get studio finances shored up. Employees weren't told how bad the situation was, but Walt had decided on a way to work out of the problem. Once again, he came up with a solution with his back against the wall. He would quickly manufacture a feature built around a cartoon featurette and two short films nearing completion, then wrap the package together with a filmed studio tour so often requested by the Disney audience. The featurette title *The Reluctant Dragon* was adapted as the title for the entire feature. The first short was Goofy in *How to Ride a Horse,* the first of the highly successful Goofy "How To" series developed by Jack Kinney. The second animated short was a charming story about a baby born with intelligence superior to Albert Einstein's. All the top scientists of the world came to visit *Baby Weems* to learn the answers to complex problems, until one day the infant gets a high fever and becomes a normal baby when he gets well. *The Reluctant Dragon* feature film could be produced inexpensively in a few months to get the revenue stream flowing while the second part of the puzzle was being completed.

One night Ward Kimball was on his way to his car when Walt caught him and confided how bad the studio's financial situation had become. Then he outlined the second part of his solution to get the studio back on track, *Dumbo*. Within ten minutes, Walt acted out the entire story. He must have

Photo courtesy of the Tomart Archives

1941 half-sheet poster for *The Reluctant Dragon* featuring all three animated sequences; the title featurette Goofy in *How to Ride a Horse* and the story of the genius *Baby Weems*.

received the reaction he wanted from Ward because he immediately put *Dumbo* into production. Walt told Ward this was, "The type of film his *Snow White* audience wanted." The film was completed in record time and improved the studio's financial picture just before World War II severely curtained studio activity.

Bambi, the next animated film on Walt's revised release schedule, was delayed until August 13, 1942 for the premiere and was released nationally August 21, 1942. The death of Bambi's mother in the film sparked a major controversy. Some thought it was too traumatic for children. In actuality, Bill Justice animated a much more graphic death scene. "There was the shot heard in the released version and I animated Bambi's mother as she slumped into a snow bank with some visible blood. When we ran the pencil test, Walt said, 'I don't know fellas, maybe we've gone a little too far,' and the scene was cut in favor of the stag saying, 'Your mother can't be with you anymore.'" But, even the revised version brought critism in interviews. Walt shrugged off his critics with words to the effect that death is part of life and children needed to learn it sooner or later. *Bambi*, mainly because of all the costs in its long gestation period, failed to make a profit.

Walt ran the creative side and chose all the stories to be produced.

Gradually, however, Roy found a way to impact the story choices Walt was considering. Since Roy was in charge of the film distribution organization, he used his position to become a stronger voice in the projects selected. If he questioned the saleability of a proposed film, it was unlikely to be made.

About the same time, the brothers worked out a deal with George Gallup and his Audience Research Institute (ARI). They began evaluating each phase of film development. The story concept was tested; then the storyboards, film segments, and the final production. All this research was done at the Disney Studio theater. Both cartoon shorts and animated features were improved using this method and Walt became more convinced than ever in solid research. The studio modified the ARI point system and used it not only to produce better products, but also as a means to reward directors, storymen, and key animators with cash bonuses. As a result, the Disney standard was so high that the other cartoon studios just developed characters and gag sequences to keep audiences laughing without regard for Disney realism.

Disney Studio animation continued to improve, but at a much slower rate. So much had been accomplished in films released between 1932 and 1942. World War II broke the rhythm of the great animation experience. Concurrently, events brewing outside the studio dealt a monumental change to Walt Disney and his incomparable team of artists and production people.

Perhaps Ward Kimball inadvertently summed it up best many years later while speaking at Cal Arts, the school Walt and Roy Disney established to train young people in all phases of art and the animation process. This particular morning, however, Ward's mind was on railroads and he spent the first forty minutes of his hour talking about trains. Finally, a brave student raised his hand to interrupt, "What about animation, Mr. Kimball?" "Walt Disney's dead and you missed it," came Ward's sharp reply before continuing to reminisce about trains.

Walt would remain involved with the Studio's animated films for the remainder of his life, but it would no longer be the complete focus of his time as it had been the previous 20 years. No one the author asked was quite sure when Walt designated his "Nine Old Men," a reference dating back to the days when Franklin D. Roosevelt boasted he had nominated a majority of justices to the U.S. Supreme Court. Walt supposedly joked he had his "Nine Old Men" as well. Actually the names that eventually surfaced were still much younger than any Supreme Court Justice in the early 1940s when Roosevelt made his boast. The first time a photo of them appears was in Bob Thomas' *Art of Animation* book published in 1958. Those pictured were Les Clark, Marc Davis, Ward Kimball, Milt Kahl, Woolie Reitherman, Eric Larson, John Lounsbery, Ollie Johnston, and Frank Thomas.

In his book *Walt Disney and Other Characters*, Jack Kinney states, "In the late forties he (Walt) designated a group of animators 'the nine old men'... who became Walt's Board of Advisors, and he listened to their opinions on many subjects." Kinney goes on to mention 23 other names who made significant contributions to the studio and the negative effect the choice of only nine had on the others. "But this was Walt's way, keeping everyone off balance and stirred up." In their book on the Disney Villains, Ollie Johnston and Frank Thomas reused the photo from the Bob Thomas book. The caption states, "The nine-old men in their mid-forties, some twelve years after being given their unusual title." If their memories are correct, the exact year would have been 1946.

Both recollections match the timeframe when Walt decided to go into live-action production and reduce his animation activities. It seems the most logical time for him to have named his "Nine Old Men," but such things were done without a press release back then. Whenever the actual designation took place, Walt knew he had a solid staff to which he could entrust the important keystone of the Disney Studio…animation.

Walt Disney, however, remained in control, as is probably best illustrated in a decision he made near the end of his life. Walt had assigned Bill Justice to WED Enterprises because he wasn't completely happy with the way the audio-animatronics figures moved at the New York World's Fair. Bill's first assignment was to work on The Pirates of the Caribbean attraction, but production of the robotic figures was running behind schedule and they weren't ready for him. So he returned to the studio to help Woolie Reitherman animate the first Winnie the Pooh featurette. As a result, he was in the sweatbox when the pencil test for *Winnie the Pooh and the Honey Tree* was unreeled for Walt's approval. Here is how Bill Justice remembered the moment … "Walt sat motionless when the lights came up. Then he started to drum his right thumb on the chair. Everyone remained quiet until Walt decided to speak. We were all prepared for Walt to start picking the film apart bit by bit as he had done so many times in the past.

"When he spoke he asked, 'How long is that thing, Woolie?,' 'About 33 minutes,' came Woolie Reitherman's reply. 'Cut it to about twenty minutes,' was Walt's response as he got up and left the room."

Walt felt confident Woolie would make the right cuts and the film would be better as a result. Walt's judgement proved correct and Disney's Winnie the Pooh became one of the studio's most popular characters. The first Pooh film was personally cut by Woolie Reitherman, the man who would become the head of all Disney animation after Walt's death.

Bill Justice did this drawing of Walt to characterize "The Look" on his face when he was questioning an artist or drumming his thumb trying to figure out how to fix a particular scene in a film. Bill decided to use a more cartoon style for Walt in his book *Justice for Disney*. This more realistic drawing was given to the author. Originally, it was done with Walt smoking a cigarette, but Bill changed it to him holding a pencil at a later date. If you look closely, you can still see both versions.

Chapter IV – Reversal of Fortune

"All the adversity I've had in my life, all my troubles and obstacles have strengthened me."

—Walt Disney

The unfavorable contract clause resulting in the loss of their Oswald the Lucky Rabbit franchise caused the Disney Brothers to adopt a whole new legal stance. They realized they had to get better advice on how to protect what they created. Characters were not only copyrighted, but trademarked as a result. It didn't take long for them to learn that more than their characters were at stake.

The first situation was with Pat Powers, the distributor of the earliest *Mickey Mouse* and *Silly Symphony* cartoons. The Disneys suspected him of cheating on their agreement and keeping a larger portion of the revenues. He admitted as much when confronted, but wanted an even better deal in order to fork over the money rightfully due to them. That was not the way to do business with Walt and Roy Disney. They sought legal counsel and broke the deal with Pat Powers, salvaging only five thousand dollars of at least $150,000 Roy eventually learned was owed to the studio. To add insult to injury, they had to pay Powers another $50,000 to get out of their distribution contract to regain the rights to the early *Mickey Mouse* and *Silly Symphony* cartoons they had assigned to him.

The second was a challenge to the ownership of Mickey Mouse. Rene D. Grove, founder and owner of the Performo Toy Company of Middletown, Pennsylvania, was the manufacturer of wooden toys. On August 17, 1926 he received a patent for his mouse "animal toy." The name "Micky" was established by an employee naming contest after the patent was granted. The name Micky was copyrighted by Performo, but not connected to the toy patent. This Micky Mouse toy was distributed primarily on the East Coast by the George Borgfeldt Company, the same agent that acquired exclusive licensing rights to Disney's characters in 1930. After Mickey Mouse's sensational film debut in 1928, the two characters co-existed until 1931. Since Borgfeldt was primarily an importer for foreign manufacturers, hardly any Disney Mickey Mouse merchandise reached retail before 1931. Until then, the sales of Micky merchandise zoomed in the blurred eyes of the buying public. Borgfeldt was using one license to sell another. Roy Disney protested. Civic leaders in Middletown, PA claimed there was a lawsuit at the time and provided details on their website, but no record of legal action could be found. They further claimed Walt had seen the toy in New York while getting the bad news about losing Oswald and used their successful toy on which to build a new cartoon character. In fact, Micky was more like Ignatz Mouse and the mice in Aesop Fable cartoons done years earlier. Micky had no resemblance to the Disney's Mickey. Another similar altercation occurred with the producers of the Aesop Fable Cartoon series.

Gunther R. Lessing, a hard-fisted entertainment attorney, who reportedly once represented Mexican outlaw Poncho Villa in a silent-film movie deal, was hired by Disney in 1929 to handle the Pat Powers situation and presumably these other early legal conflicts. He later joined the company to head its legal department. Lessing was so aristocratically formal, he refused to participate in the company's first name policy, prompting Walt to conceed, "The only mister we have at the studio is our lawyer, Mr. Lessing."

Lessing reportedly was a factor in getting Walt to tie every production to his own name to better prevent further ownership disputes. The studio name change had already occurred in 1926, but the concept of branding was strengthened by Lessing's advice. The lawyer also believed in not crediting animators. He felt this policy would obscure their value, helping to safeguard against animator defections.

Snow White and the Seven Dwarfs grossed over $8 million, more than any film up to that time, let alone an animated one. Walt used the proceeds and merchandise revenue to build a $3.2 million dollar studio in Burbank. *Pinocchio* and *Fantasia* both lost money in their 1940 releases, mainly due to Hitler invading Poland to start World War II. The European film market that contributed 40% of the *Snow White* gross was cut off from the company. It was a time when the country was still recovering from the Great Depression. Wages for the average worker were $20 to $25 per week. Ward Kimball once told me Walt was only making around $400 per week; Roy around $300, while directing animators were making $200 to $300. Ward, who started for a $15 weekly wage in 1934, remembered his weekly salary had increased to about $200 by the time the studio found itself in financial trouble in early 1941.

On the low end of the spectrum, Ward's wife, Betty, was making around $28 a week in the Ink and Paint Department. Some newer women were only making $18. Inbetweeners and assistants were taking home $50 to $80. When Walt was doing *Snow White*, he recruited some of the best New York animators and paid them extra to get them to move to the West Coast. Often they were making more money than the people supervising them. Most of these wages, particularly the animators, were much greater than what artists at other Hollywood cartoon studios were taking home.

In my many visits with Ward Kimball, you never quite knew what stories you might hear, but he was one of the most articulate of the animators and other Disney artists I came to know. He kept diaries during his years at Disney. On two occasions he pulled these out and read responses to my questions. He was quite sure about the money issues because one of the things the studio had to do to finance more animated features was to go public and sell stock. Key animators received stock and bonuses as one of Walt's ways of sharing his success.

The loss of the European film market revenue affected the whole industry. All live-action and animation studios were forced to cut back. Roy Disney held a meeting with all the studio personnel to announce across-the-board wage cuts.

There was some discontent at Disney because of pay inequities, but it was mainly cartoon industry workers at Warner Brothers and MGM that wanted a union. They sought to organize the Screen Cartoonists Guild, but they knew such a union could never have teeth without involving the Disney Studio.

Gunther Lessing attempted to counter this move by forming a Disney company union called the Federation of Screen Cartoonists. It was later reorganized into the Association of Screen Animators, a unit of the American Federation of Labor. His intention was to have animator Art Babbit head this company union.

Art Babbit seemed like a good choice. He had been a major player in the improvement of *Mickey Mouse* cartoons, starting with *The Klondike Kid*, the transformation of Goofy, animator on *The Three Little Pigs*, Donald's first appearance in *The Wise Little Hen*, the Wicked Queen and Dopey in *Snow White*, Geppetto in *Pinocchio*, and several sequences in Fantasia. He reportedly was making well over $200 a week as a major leader at the studio. Employees liked him, but a supporter of the Screen Cartoonists Guild managed to turn Babbit's head. Herb Sorrell, a noted West Coast union organizer, was the real man behind the scene. He guided Art Babbit through organizing Disney employees and getting them to strike.

Union organizers had been salting the growing Disney workforce since 1938. Animator Frank Toshlin admitted to taking a pay cut to accept an entry-level job at Disney in 1938 to promote unionization. In his testimony before the House Committee on Un-American Activities in 1947, Walt named another animator, David Hiberman, as a 1938 union infiltrator and possible communist.

The day pickets went up prompted an agonizing decision between friends. Art Babbit was committed. Bill Tytla went along because he felt it was the right thing to do for his friends. Like Art Babbit, he made a superior income and had a similarly impressive record at the studio, most notably doing Dwarfs in *Snow White*, Stromboli in *Pinocchio,* and Chernabog in *Fantasia*. Neither of these men could gain much from a strike. They were key because Disney viewed them as supervisors and part of management, but the union ruled they could be part of the strike because they were still part of the creative process. Using the union's logic, so was Walt!

Walt's first reaction to the strike, by all published reports, was one of hurt. These men were not only his employees, but friends. Together they had built animation into a major entertainment form. Walt knew he always provided better working conditions, better pay, and more challenging work than the rest of the animation industry. He strongly felt, as was the popular belief of the day, the union people behind the strike were all communists. While unionism was socialistic, none of the irritants in the Disney animation strike were ever proven to be communists. Walt also felt his people would come to their senses and return to work...and many did.

All the other key animators mentioned in the previous chapter crossed the picket lines and were hard at work on *Dumbo*. The majority of the assistants, inbetweeners, and other workers did also. The union claimed 55% of the work force went out on strike. A more accurate estimate would be less than a third of the studio employees, mainly the lower-paid workers, who joined the picket lines. Walt claimed many on the picket lines were not his employees. He had photographs taken and had large blow-ups of the strikers in his office. He agonized over people he had personally helped in times of need who rewarded him by striking. He could also point out people who never worked at the studio. There were supporting picketers from other cartoon studios and unions, but it was never proven the union inflated the crowd with hired bodies.

One of the biggest decisions the day the pickets went up was made by Ward Kimball. Art Babbit, Bill Tytla and Walt Kelly were close friends. They knew if they could get Ward to strike, others might follow. Ward recalled circling the Disney lot from the gate on Alameda Street to the one on Buena Vista Street. His friends were calling to him not to go in. "In my mind, I knew Walt might not survive if a strike persisted. I recalled when I was walking to the parking lot, Walt came up to me and confided the losses the studio had taken on *Pinocchio* and *Fantasia*. He acted out the story of *Dumbo*, then Walt added, 'We need to do this one fast!' Despite the strike, *Dumbo* was finished in nine months. 'It was the only Disney animated feature to cost less than a million dollars to produce," Ward reported.

Ward Kimball did go to work even though he sympathized with the striking workers, particularly his friends who were among the strike leaders. Walt Disney was also beginning to see some of the mistakes Gunther Lessing had made in dealing with Art Babbit, but still took his advice in pushing for a National Labor Relations Board election to install whatever union his employees wanted. Herb Sorrell wanted no part of an election. Too many employees continued to work and the people on strike knew they had to work for Walt after it was settled. The odds were not favorable to Sorrell's goal of organizing the other cartoon studios if a NLRB election was held. The strike dragged on for over two months. The mudslinging on both sides obscured the atmosphere and caused what was sure to be lasting damage to the studio.

Various meetings were held to attempt a settlement. Art Babbit claimed Lessing and Roy Disney tried to buy him off and used threatening tactics when the approach didn't work. Maybe Lessing overreacted in an angry moment, but Roy was too smart to make such a mistake. Years later, when Babbit recalled the events surrounding the strike, he remained a bitter man. He often said he had proof of many more serious claims beyond the evidence presented in his hearings, but none of it ever surfaced. Time has a way of making once-heated issues cool to the point they become meaningless to pursue any further. If indeed anything more serious ever existed, it was never given to authors unfavorable to Walt who would have welcomed anything supportable.

Walt remained convinced he would win a NLRB election. Roy Disney, on the other hand, was worried about all the negative public relations and a possible secondary boycott against theaters and Disney licensees nationwide. Such union activity has since been made illegal by the Taft-Hartley Act, but was still a weapon in 1941. A brief lockout occurred out of financial necessity and an adequate explanation was never communicated to studio employees. It probably helped prolong the walkout. Sources believe it was Lessing who went to Nelson Rockefeller, then a coordinator of Latin America Affairs at the U.S. State Department with the idea of getting Walt out-of-the-way so the strike could be settled. His proposal made sense. The Department was worried about Nazi sympathizers in South America and felt a visit from Walt Disney would help.

The Department approached Walt about the goodwill tour, but he turned them down, citing the strike and the fact he was "no good at shaking hands." The State Department countered with the idea he should go and learn more about his audience in the Southern Hemisphere and shoot footage for pictures he might make as a result. The Department promised to pay $70,000 in travel expenses and $50,000 each toward any films that might result. Walt countered affirmatively with the added consideration that federal mediators be sent in to legally settle the strike. It was probably his hope they would enforce the solution prescribed by law...an NLRB election. An agreement was reached for the goodwill mission. Walt, Lillian, plus seventeen artists and film-crew members then took off for the tour of South America. All reports indicate the change was good for Walt's spirit and got him back on track creatively. He found the people of South America were big Disney fans. The esteem in which they held him was never adequately reflected in box-offices grosses because the countries were very poor. Children paid only pennies to see a Disney film. The people, the animals and birds, the scenery, and the colorful festival costumes captivated Walt. The footage shot was later used in only two films after the State Department rejected Walt's proposal to do a film on each country visited.

Meanwhile, back at the studio, Lessing and Roy Disney welcomed the federal mediators. They didn't press for the NLRB election as Walt had hoped. Instead, the leading negotiators were summoned to Washington. President Franklin Roosevelt was pro-union. His staff advised Roy to settle the strike without an election. Herb Sorrell got most of what he wanted. The cartoon industry was unionized under his control.

Walt was livid upon learning the results. When he returned to the studio, Lessing was kicked upstairs with a vice-president title, but he lost Walt's respect for many years, perhaps forever. Sorrell was later discredited and his union voted out in favor of an IATSE (International Alliance of Theatrical Stage Employees) controlled union, similar to one the company had wanted.

Art Babbit was fired, but filed suit to get his job back. He went into the Marine Corps while his case worked its way through the courts. He won back pay and reinstatement in 1947, but left the studio for good in 1949. Neither he or Bill Tytla, who left the studio within two years after the settlement, ever regained the importance as animators they had enjoyed at the Disney Studio.

The biggest casualty of the strike was perhaps the studio's in-house art training program. Union rules and pay scale made continuation of the program impossible. The art training so vital to the development of the Disney Studio during the 1930's ended with the strike settlement. Over twenty years passed before a similar school could be established at Cal-Arts. Getting the school running properly proved much more difficult than establishing the first studio training classes in 1932, an enterprise spearheaded and championed by Art Babbit.

Dumbo was finished and premiered on October 23, 1941. Less then two months later, the United States was drawn into World War II when Pearl Harbor was attacked. The profits from *Dumbo* helped reduce the Bank of America debt or the studio could have easily gone under.

It is probably difficult for baby boomers and more modern generations to understand the mood of the country back then. It was a united country, infinitely stronger than the United States in the aftermath of the 9/11 terrorist attack on New York's World Trade Center.

Pearl Harbor was a surprise attack, but the war in Europe had been brewing for years before the hot war exploded. Americans were well aware of potential involvement. Overnight people pitched together to gird for the years ahead. Residents on the West Coast feared a land attack on our shores.

There was confusion in those initial days. An army anti-aircraft unit, 500 strong, moved into the Disney Studio. They cleared every available space to install equipment to repair anti-aircraft guns damaged in the Pearl Harbor attack. Some reports suggest they were also there to protect the nearby Lockheed Aircraft plant and other likely targets. Over three million rounds of ammunition were stored at the studio. Apart from this occupation came government funding for training films and other wartime projects. The Disney Studio was the only one in Hollywood taken over by the government. Walt always felt Washington was punishing him for his independent position on the strike and other matters. And he was probably right. The studio take-over delayed the release of *Bambi* and it proved to be the last fully animated feature of the decade.

Key animators and other important studio employees enlisted or were drafted into the war effort. There was little the Disneys could do, but they found ways to survive. The South American market did prove valuable in the near and longterm. The footage from Walt's South American goodwill tour was woven into *Saludos Amigos* and *The Three Caballeros* with great success in the Southern Hemisphere and fairly good reception in the United States. Production costs were low and with so many employees transferred to Uncle Sam's payroll the studio survived, but failed to reduce the debt to Bank of America. The State Department promise to pay $50,000 toward each picture was never realized.

Walt's decision to do *Victory Through Air Power,* in support of saving Allied ground troop lives, lost money and added to the studio's financial burden. The themed cartoon composite pictures – *Make Mine Music, Fun and Fancy Free*, and *Melody Time* cost less, but didn't fool the public. They were simply a parade of cartoon shorts, not a substitute for the return to animated features the public wanted from Disney.

During the war, Walt continued his experimentation with a variety of ideas. Many different artistic styles were tried for *Don Quixote, The Emperor's New Clothes, The Emperor's Nightingale, The Swan of Tuonela* (a Viking tale), *Insect Ballet*, and a number of Hans Christian Andersen stories, including the first work-up on *The Little Mermaid*. *Peter Pan* was completely storyboarded for the first-time during the war and extensive work was done on *Alice in Wonderland* and what would later become *Lady and the Tramp*. *Hiawatha* was envisioned as an animated feature, but was reduced to a featurette in more of a cartoon style than originally planned. It was released later as *Little Hiawatha*. The culmination of these efforts was an attempt to do an avant-garde animated film titled *Destino* with surrealist artist Salvador Dali in 1946. By then, the number of unproduced projects and the mediocre box-office results of the pasted together features had caused a renewed period of financial doldrums for the studio.

The war ended, but merchandise licensing continued to be confounded by postwar rationing. No metal was allocated for toy use. Automobiles, then TV sets, were the main priorities for returning GI's. Licensing revenue was dealt another serious setback with the sudden death of Kay Kamen and his wife in a 1949 airplane crash. Roy Disney then decided to take over the licensing operation rather than hire another outside company and the Disney Character Merchandise Division was formed.

When the government military work ceased after the war, Walt looked at several new approaches to build business. He tried his hand at industrial and educational films…and started to make plans to go into live-action productions. There were several false starts on industrial training films before the studio landed a lucrative deal for Kleenex brand tissues. *How to Catch a Cold* was produced for film distributors to schools, churches, hospitals, and others dealing with health concerns. Special presentations were made for the company's sales staff. Each industrial project required an extensive sales effort. Since the studio did nothing on speculation, as did many companies specializing in this type of production, the business was abandoned.

Walt hired leading educators to help him research the type of educational films the studio should make. He found there was no common ground among his experts. Each person had his own plan to revolutionize education and seemed to see no merit in other "expert" views. Walt gave up in disgust, vowing to "stick to entertainment."

Woolie Reitherman, who animated Monstro the Whale so vividly in *Pinocchio,* returned from his World War II pilot's commission to do the stirring Headless Horseman in *The Adventures of Ichabod and Mr. Toad,* the 1949 two-story epic that signaled Disney's progress toward the return to feature animation. One day, Woolie looked up from his drawing board and made a chance remark to Bill Justice, "You know, Bill, I think these cartoons of ours will be around long after we're gone."

The last three fully animated features – *Pinocchio, Fantasia,* and *Bambi* – failed to return the investment the studio had in them, but the tide was about to turn. *Lady and the Tramp, Alice in Wonderland,* and *Peter Pan* had all been in development, along with the never-produced *Through the Picture Frame,* since the late '30s to early 1940s. The financial crisis in 1947, resulted in layoffs Walt didn't want. The following year was also financially rough as the studio started to pour more assets into an animated feature. Roy had been dead set against another animated feature at this time. Walt insisted they go forward with a full-length story, while Roy was satisfied with smaller, safe profits from films which cost less to produce. This prompted a significant debate between the two brothers. Things had been rough for so long, Roy preferred a more conservative approach. Walt wanted to pick up from the point of the *Snow White* success. He prepared his reasoning well. Walt was ready with the pros and cons of each and why he thought *Pinocchio, Fantasia,* and *Bambi* failed at the box office. Disney audiences had their fill of makeshift features and expected more of the Disney brand. Calmer heads prevailed and Roy made his case for one of the feature films in which the company had already made a substantial investment. This time it was Walt who questioned the sales appeal of each. Together they decided to go forward with a new animated feature. Picking the wrong story could have easily closed the studio. Instead of choosing a project already on the books, Walt won his case to start from scratch on *Cinderella*.

Picking the story for his return to animated features was a do-or-die decision, and once again demonstrates Walt's ability to make the correct decisions in such a situation. This was no time for further experimentation. What happened on *Pinocchio* and *Fantasia* wasn't simply the loss of the European market. The American public wanted the joy, heart, and triumph over evil of *Snow White*. Walt knew he had to deliver such a product. The parallels between *Snow White* and *Cinderella* are unmistakable. Snow White is a princess in rags/Cinderella a soon-to-be princess in rags; Wicked Queen/Wicked Stepmother and Stepsisters; woodland animal allies/mice allies; Dwarfs/Fairy Godmother for light-hearted humor, warmth, and to help fortify the heroine; and a Prince in both stories to win the fair maiden so all may live happily *ever after*.

Cinderella regained the public's confidence in Disney family entertainment and the profits were used to reduce the company debt and free up its credit line for the busy decade ahead. Once again, the tide had turned. The frustrating forties were now just a bad memory.

There's no question Walt's judgment was correct. *Alice In Wonderland* failed at the box office the following year and was probably never in contention for the all-important 1950 release. *Peter Pan* did well in 1953 and *The Lady and the Tramp* did even better in 1955 with the first-ever major TV advertising support. However, Walt decided *Cinderella* seemed right for the time and history shows that he was right once again.

Sleeping Beauty went into production right after the success of *Cinderella*, but now that the Disney Studio was back on top of its game, Walt had a new diversion.

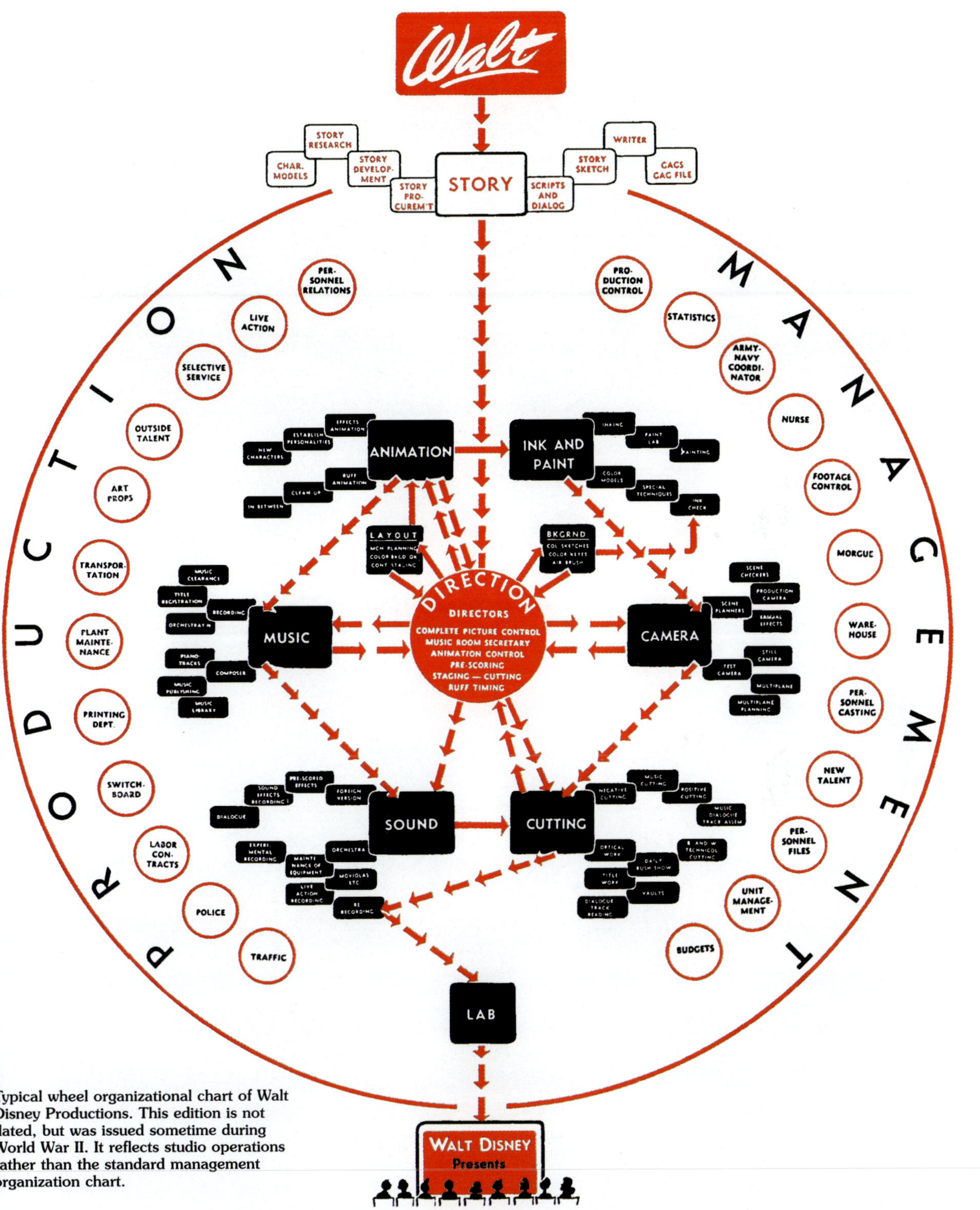

Typical wheel organizational chart of Walt Disney Productions. This edition is not dated, but was issued sometime during World War II. It reflects studio operations rather than the standard management organization chart.

Ward Kimball with his full-size Baldwin 2-6-0 Mogul backyard locomotive that he dubbed the "Emma Nevada." He purchased this 1881 steam engine as scrap from the Nevada Central Railroad in 1938 and fully restored it to running condition.

Photo by Tom Tumbusch

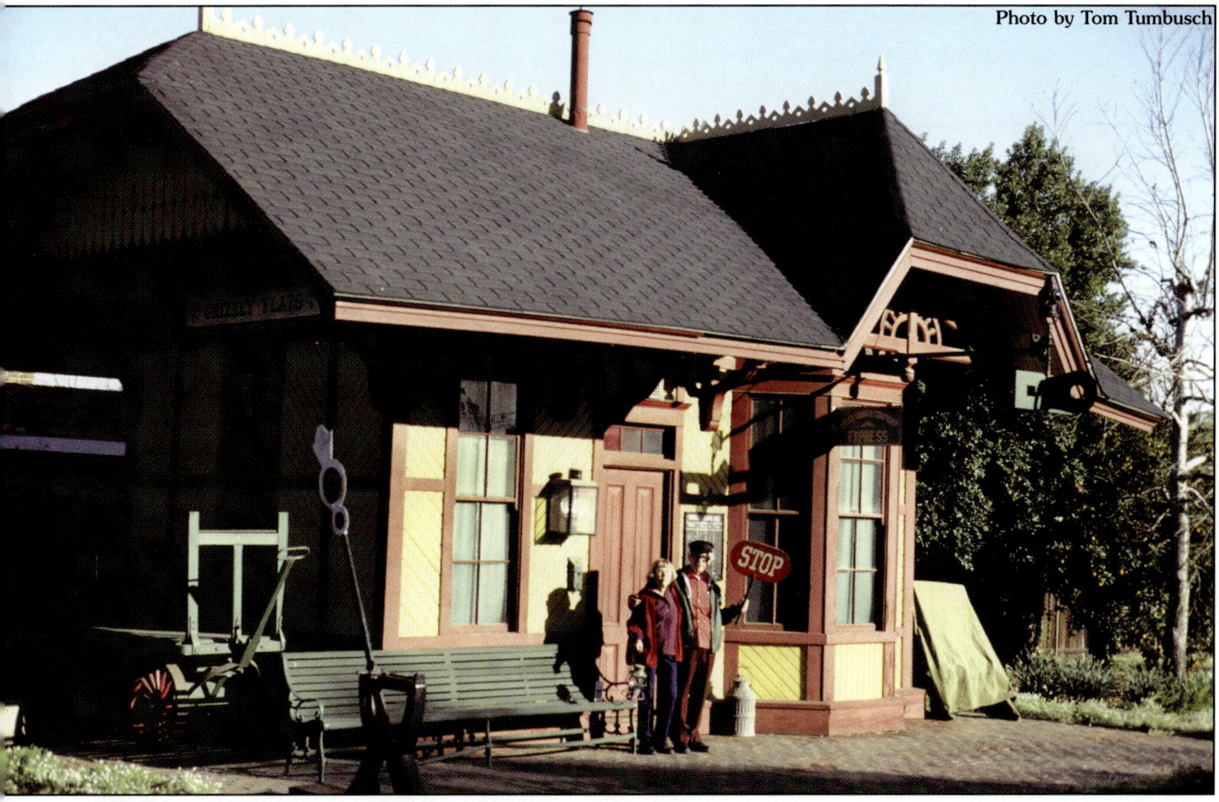

Above – Rural railroad station seen in *So Dear to My Heart* that Walt Disney sent to Ward Kimball for use with his full-size backyard trains.

Below – Roy E. Disney with the surviving Nine Old Men at the dedication of The Magic of Disney Animation attraction opening day at the Disney MGM Studio Theme Park. Left to Right - Roy E. Disney, Ward Kimball, Marc Davis, Ollie Johnston, and Frank Thomas.

Photo by Tom Tumbusch

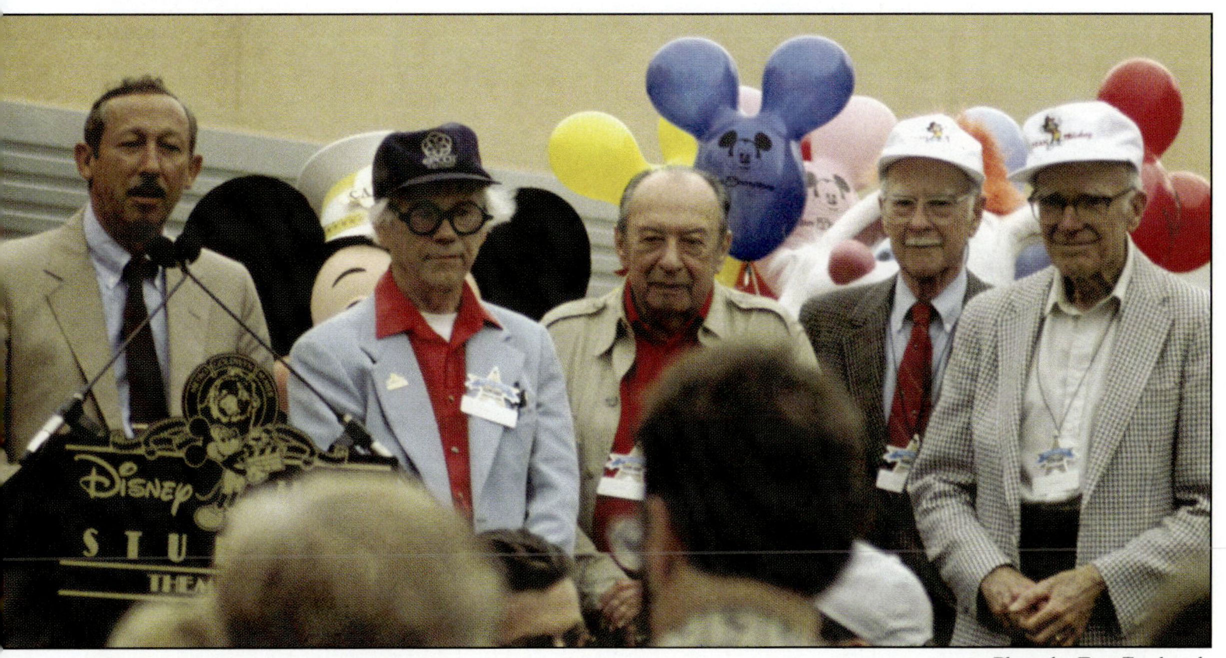

Above – Composer Richard M. Sherman, responsible for such Disney hits as "Supercalifragilisticexpialidocious", "It's a Small World", and "The Bare Neccessities".
Right – Artist and Imagineer Ralph Kent
Bottom – Animator, Director, and Imagineer Bill Justice

Right - Author Tom Tumbusch with Character Merchandise Division Art Director Lou Lispi. He was hired by Roy O. Disney and Kay Kamen in 1934 and served the company as an art director until his retirement in 1971.
Middle Left - Famed Donald Duck comic book artist and writer Carl Barks. Independent of the studio, he created Uncle Scrooge, Grandma Duck, Cousin Gladstone, and many other characters.
Middle Right - Van France, The conscience of Disneyland and creator of the Park's "Happiest Place on Earth" training programs.
Below - Ralph Kent showing a completed drawing of Cinderella to a young fan.

Photo by Ann Lispi

Photo courtesy of Tomart archives

Photo by Bob Welbaum

Photo by Amy Stelmack

The first licensed Disney merchandise item was this *Oswald the Lucky Rabbit* stencil set which sold in 1927 for ten cents.

This 1930's school tablet was the first licensed Mickey Mouse item.

1938 Knickerbocker Snow White and The Seven Dwarfs composition dolls with velvet costumes.

70

The Matador in Ferdinand the Bull is a caricature of Walt Disney...his only cartoon screen appearance.

Charlotte Clark Mickey and Minnie dolls made from 1930 until 1933. These were the first Mickey and Minnie dolls.

...aracter merchandise has played a vital role in ...ccess of the Disney organization since the early ...'s. Cartoon film production had a two-year pro... ...on cost payback. Without the dramatic increase ...rchandise revenue provided by the Kay Kamen ...ization *Snow White and the Seven Dwarfs* ...not have been produced when it was.

Danny the Little Black Lamb from *So Dear to My Heart* made by Gund in 1947.

Licensing also saved Ingersoll (now Timex) and the Lionel Train company from bankruptcy.

1935 Lionel Circus Train set sold for $1.79.

All photos are from the Tomart Archives.

World War II was devastating to the Disney Studios, yet Walt Disney supported it in every way possible. The studio produced *Victory Through Air Power* because Walt felt it would save more ground troop lives. They designed over a thousand military insignia. The studio produced training films and movie trailers to persuade citizens to purchase war bonds, and pay their income taxes early. There was also support for the USO and cartoons with "win the war" themes.

All photos are from the Tomart Archives.

Chapter V – Walt Disney Live!

"Women are the best judges of anything we turn out. Their taste is very important. They are the theater-goers, they are the ones who drag the men in. If the women like it, the heck with the men."

—*Walt Disney*

Both the Hyperion and the early Burbank Disney Studios were the most unusual in Hollywood. Neither had a huge soundstage...the cavernous buildings where whole city blocks could be duplicated for filming under controlled conditions. Previously, Disney background artists simply painted the buildings or interiors needed. The clear character cels were photographed over them. No large live-action soundstages were necessary. Smaller soundstages at Disney were used mainly for recording music and sound effects.

The conductor and orchestra in *Fantasia* were photographed in the cramped quarters of the music and sound effects building. The live-action studio tour for *The Reluctant Dragon* was shot outside around the studio buildings with very limited, often close-up views in the studio's production departments themselves.

South American locations shot on Walt's goodwill tour were used for *Saludos Amigos* and *The Three Caballeros*, and the big live-action sequences for *Song of the South* and *So Dear to My Heart* used non-studio U.S. locations.

Walt knew he had to make more features to grow and the easiest way to meet his goal was with live-action films like his competitors in Hollywood. Once the war was over, he began to prepare to enter this market. The studio's first big soundstage was planned in 1946 and was completed in 1948, but his initial live-action feature was completed elsewhere.

After World War II, the important European market began to open once again to Disney films, but reconstruction policies in key Disney countries such as England and France restricted use of the profits made in those nations. The money was frozen or blocked until a way could be devised to spend it in the countries where it was earned.

Studios and location crews were available and Walt jumped on Roy's suggestion to produce his first series of live-action films in Europe, using not only the facilities, but actors and directors as well. The films were then released in the United States to relocate the money trapped in Europe. They were also released in Europe, along with animated films completed during the war to countries involved in the conflict, earning even more money for foreign production.

Walt didn't seek out this live-action film production opportunity. The "opportunity" was thrust upon him by the foreign governments restricting how he could use his profits. His animation staff often described him as a consummate actor. He sought employment as a director when he first moved to Hollywood. Now he had a great new toy and he relished every moment of his new predicament.

His methods, however, remained much the same. He started by asking a lot of questions about live-action production in England. Just like he ferreted out the animators who would become long-term assets to his animation staff, he used similar probing research to identify the production people and actors he wanted for his films. Instead of selecting animators who could draw what he envisioned and then casting a voice to match, he had to find both in a single actor. Then he had to round up a production team that understood the detail and authenticity required in every Disney film: Walt knew what he wanted and settled for nothing less.

Live-action films were storyboarded just like animated features. Walt's chosen directors liked this approach (even though "A" list directors would have probably been offended) and it allowed Walt to get comfortable with the story, particularly the more expensive action scenes, before green-lighting a film in a distant land where it would be more difficult to monitor all the production planning.

Walt needed a sure hit to establish his reputation as a live-action producer. Once again, he turned to a classic story and gave it a Disney spin. *Treasure Island* by Robert Louis Stevenson (July 19, 1950) was Disney's first fully live-action feature. Walt chose a trusted on-site producer, Perce Pearce, who had been a supervising director since *Snow White* and an associate producer on *Song of the South*, to be his chief-of-staff in England. He served Walt in that capacity for all four live-action films done abroad with restricted funds. A full British crew was used on *Treasure Island*. Bobby Driscoll as Jim Hawkins was the only American principal in the cast. Walt spent close to $2 million on the film. The box-office returns weren't as big as he had hoped, but the U.S. critics were kind and the profits earned in this country were welcome funding for other projects.

Treasure Island was followed by *The Story of Robin Hood* (June 26, 1952). The British critics panned it, but audiences everywhere found the

Cast of *Treasure Island* filmed in England with an all British cast, except Bobby Driscoll, who played Jim Hawkins.

Disney version of the Rogue of Sherwood Forest entertaining. It did better than any of the other British productions.

The addition of live-action to the studio's product mix revitalized Walt's creativity. He loved traveling to the locations on the continent and frequently took Lilly and his daughters along for extended trips. The animation staff back at the studio that had previously commanded Walt's undivided attention began to feel a little left out. Never again would he be as involved as he once was with animation. Young inbetweener Ron Dias, later a Disney animator and art director, remembered returning from lunch one day to catch a conversation Walt was having with Eric Larson on this subject as Walt said, "I did *Snow White*. I've done my *Cinderella*, I'm doing my *Sleeping Beauty*...where do I go from here?" Obviously it was on to other things. Live-action changed Walt. More importantly, once free of daily animation supervision, his mind raced.

The Sword and the Rose (July 23, 1953) and *Rob Roy* (February 4, 1954) were the last two frozen-funds live-action films. Both made money, but neither enjoyed the degree of success the first two did and fairly well dried up the reconstruction money. The rest could be used to promote U.S. made product as monetary conditions began to change back to prewar policies.

The True-Life Adventure featurettes preceded human actor live-action pictures, but the studio for these films were the animals' natural habitats. Yet there were many camera and editing lessons learned from these "nature films" used later in studio pictures. The inspiration for the True-Life

Adventure series came out of the research that studio artists were doing on *Bambi*. A six week study program was planned before actual work was scheduled to begin on the film. Walt brought in experts on animal anatomy and set up a studio zoo of deer, rabbits, birds, racoons, and other creatures appearing in the film. "But that wasn't enough," Walt once related, "Animals don't react in captivity like they do in nature. So I hired two freelance photographers to go into the woods and shoot the reference footage needed. I got some unusual things and that got me to thinking if I could find the right people, we could get some really unusual things. That's where the idea for the nature films came from."

Walt found his husband/wife nature photography team in Alfred and Elma Milotte and outfitted them with special equipment and sent them off to Alaska to capture anything interesting on film.

True-Life Adventures started as featurette shorts running about 30 minutes. They only cost about $250,000 to produce and could earn back about twice as much. Not a big deal, but important bottom-line dollars as the company struggled to return to animated features. When *Seal Island* won an Academy Award, Walt began to consider how to expand them to feature length. There were 13 True-Life Adventures in all…seven featurettes and six full-length features. Feature versions cost about $750,000 to produce, but some returned over $6 million. The studio's distributor rejected the concept at first, so Walt had a friend run *Seal Island* at the Crown Theater in Pasadena to qualify it for the Oscar competition where it won as the Best Documentary.

Back in Burbank, Walt was planning his first major home-grown live-action film based on Jules Verne's *20,000 Leagues Under the Sea*. The budget contained money to outfit his major soundstage with a gigantic water tank for filming seascapes and a submarine attacked by a giant squid. The entire film was storyboarded in great detail. The son of Max Fleischer, a New York Animation Studio head, Richard Fleischer, was the director. Walt wanted someone who understood the animation approach to moviemaking, only with some live-action directing experience. It was Richard Fleischer's first big film. Walt picked a top-flight Hollywood cast headed by Kirk Douglas, Paul Lukas, Peter Lorre, and James Mason as Captain Nemo.

The futuristic vision of Jules Verne was embellished to make his submarine more sea monsterish. The visual effects were incredibly lifelike long before Ub Iwerks developed the blue-screen moving-matte technology for the filming of *Mary Poppins* nearly 10 years later. Over a quarter million dollars was budgeted for the filming of the giant squid attack. Walt ordered segments to be re-shot, because he could detect a single wire used to animate the sea creature. When told the audience would be caught up in the action and wouldn't see it, Walt responded, "I will still be able to see it. Re-shoot!" Quality always came first.

Fess Parker, one of Walt's most famous weekly contracted stars, who

Movie still © The Walt Disney Company

Crew of the Nautilus battle a giant squid in *20,000 Leagues Under the Sea.*

worked on five Disney live-action features, made an interesting observation. He related how Walt viewed live-action footage much the same as the pencil tests done for animation. "It always seemed to me Walt wanted to see the picture, determined what was wrong, and then fix it," Parker noted. "It was his *Modus Operandi.*"

Besides the international sensation he created as Davy Crockett on the *Disneyland* TV series, Parker also starred in theatrical features as Davy Crockett, James J. Andrews in *The Great Locomotive Chase*, John "Doc" Grayson in *Westward Ho The Wagons,* the father (Jim Coates) in *Old Yeller,* and Del Hardy in *The Light in the Forest.*

"Bill Walsh, the producer of the Davy Crockett series and the TV *Mickey Mouse Club*, became Walt's top money live-action film producer in the fifties and up into the sixties, including *Mary Poppins*," Fess Parker recalled. "They really worked well together and he holds the record for the top box-office grossing films all the way to the *Star Wars* series. We were also great friends and he was the best man at my wedding. Walt could apply pressure at times and Bill's only reaction was 'Ho boy!' He loved his work, the studio, and working for Walt. Sometimes, at lunch, Bill would remark, 'Walt arrived in his bear suit today,' but calmly went about his business."

Davy Crockett, King of the Wild Frontier proved to be a box-office winner on the heels of *20,000 Leagues Under the Sea*, but live-action feature production was uneven for several years. *The Great Locomotive Chase*

77

(June 8, 1956), *Old Yeller* (December 25, 1957), *The Shaggy Dog* (March 19, 1959), *Pollyanna* (May 19, 1960), *Swiss Family Robinson* (December 10, 1960), *The Absent-Minded Professor* (March 16, 1961), and *The Parent Trap* (June 12, 1961) proved to be modest to big box-office winners. Others were less successful. *The Son of Flubber* (January 18, 1963) proved to be a bankable hit before the *Mary Poppins* blockbuster first hit theater screens on August 29, 1964. It was Walt's last major live-action success before his death. The robin on Mary's finger as she sang "A Spoonful of Sugar" employed the same technology used in the Enchanted Tiki Room introduced at Disneyland in 1963.

Movie still © The Walt Disney Company
Left, Buddy Ebsen, and right, Fess Parker from the TV show *Davy Crockett and the River Pirates.*

In all fairness, Walt Disney was extremely limited by story content for his live-action pictures. He insisted on family-oriented stories at a time when censorship on TV presented movie studios an incentive for more adventuresome entertainment. "The majors" were starting to buy into the sexual revolution, the effect of Vietnam war protesting, and the growing drug culture of the '60s. These were areas where TV couldn't go and didn't compete. And with the Disney studio now championing family entertainment, the big live-action Hollywood studios conceded the market and moved to new ground. Disney stuck with "G" rated films, but before long the "G" rating became a kiss of death to teenage and young adults, a huge share of the movie-going public, who saw themselves as too mature to patronize such films.

The first two British films, *20,000 Leagues Under the Sea*, and later *Mary Poppins*, commanded Walt's major interest in live-action films. He couldn't devote the twenty years he gave the development of his animation operation to traditional scripted films. Nor was the challenge as great. Live-action was merely an adaptation of an established form already a staple at every other Hollywood studio. Once live-action was centered in Burbank, it was simply a matter of hiring the right people for a given project. Walt brought concepts from animation, such as the storyboard to live-action production and stayed involved with his key people just as he had done with animation. However, just as live-action production diverted his full attention away from animation, Walt moved on quickly to TV production and its reason for being…Disneyland.

Chapter VI – Smaller Screen, Brighter Future

"This television thing can be the greatest thing, because we will be going direct to the public."

—Walt Disney

Hollywood film studios were dead set against the television medium when it finally caught on around 1948. The first TV set was invented in 1927...color in 1928, but the Great Depression and World War II prevented the big eye from entering most American living rooms. The CBS and NBC TV networks were formed in the late '40s out of the radio network operations founded in the 1920s. NBC once owned two networks; the NBC Red and NBC Blue. A government antitrust unit forced the sale of the NBC Blue network in 1943. It was renamed the American Broadcasting System. Leonard Goldenson purchased the near bankrupt American Broadcasting Company radio/TV systems in 1951 for $25 million and began to seek ways to make it competitive.

Walt Disney had done a Christmas TV special for NBC in 1950. *One Hour In Wonderland* was essentially an hour-long commercial for his next animated feature, *Alice in Wonderland*. It gained the highest TV rating for any show up to that time and had all three networks knocking at the Disney Studio door. Walt took notice of their interest in his vault full of cartoons and features, but declined all offers.

Back in 1940, Walt Disney began to formulate ideas about a "Mickey Mouse Park" to be built across from the studio in Burbank. Those plans evolved over the next 15 years to what became Disneyland.

Roy Disney was against the idea. This was one time he was not going to concede to one of Walt's dreams. Roy was convinced a motion picture company had no place in the amusement park business and felt Walt Disney Production shareholders would revolt at the idea.

Ever the optimist, Walt went out on his own and formed Disneyland, Inc. and WED Enterprises to develop the concept to the point he could bring his brother around. He sold his Palm Springs home at Smoke Tree Ranch and took out personal loans against his life insurance and equity in other personal property to finance the operation. He knew this money could only last for a short time and looked to television as a major source of long-term financing for the project. In 1952 he had WED acquire the TV rights to *Zorro* with the idea the studio would film the series, sell it to one of the networks, then use the profits to build his theme park. As the cost estimates to construct the park escalated, it became clear *Zorro* would never produce the capital needed and the idea was put on hold.

Walt would simply have to convince Roy on the merits of building Disneyland. He went to Roy with his television idea. The company had parted ways with United Artists, their established film distribution company, back in 1937, because the Disneys wouldn't include TV rights in the deal. They had no idea what the future of TV might be or the significance of their decision at the time. It was such a big issue with United Artists they just felt they had to know more before signing those rights away. Walt convinced Roy there was a market for a mix of old and new Disney programming that would appeal to Disney shareholders and would get a TV network to finance the controversial theme park idea.

Roy Disney presented Walt's concept of special "made for TV" programming and theme park financing idea to the two major networks – CBS and NBC – and both networks turned the proposal down flat. Their only interest was in the proven Disney cartoons and feature films. Roy had reservations about ABC, but called Goldenson in a last-ditch effort on Walt's behalf. Goldenson's response was, "Where are you? I'll be right over!" That meeting eventually resulted in a deal where ABC gave the Disneys $5 million and loan guarantees in return for a one-third ownership in Disneyland. ABC also agreed to pay $35 million in licensing fees and a major share of production costs over seven years for a new Walt Disney TV series to be called *Disneyland*. It was to premiere the following September on Wednesday nights. The deal gave Walt the Disneyland financing he needed at the time.

Tinker Bell and her pixie dust provided the visual magic for the open-

Shopping bag courtesy of the Tomart Archives

Detail from the first Disneyland shopping bag showing how television program logos were used in conjunction with the theme park.

ing of each show. The Disneyland park logo was used to banner each program, followed by special graphics for the different lands as the soundtrack proclaimed these memorable words... "Walt Disney's Disneyland" (Music: When You Wish Upon a Star). "Each week as you enter this timeless land, one of these many worlds will open to you. Fantasyland – the happiest kingdom of all. Tomorrowland – the promise of things to come. Adventureland – the wonderworld of nature's own realm. Frontierland – tales tall and true from the legendary past." Walt Disney then introduced each episode of this hit anthology series and closed every show with a preview of the next week's adventure. The show was an overwhelming success and began to turn the ABC network into a major moneymaker.

The ratings for the Disneyland show, particularly its Davy Crockett episodes, had ABC requesting other programming ideas from the studio. Lou Lispi, art director for the New York merchandise division, recalled the day after the first Davy Crockett episode aired. "There were no plans to merchandise any particular Disneyland TV episode, only a Davy Crockett coonskin hat, but the Thursday morning after the first Davy Crockett segment aired, the telephone started to ring off the hook. We heard from existing licensees and companies we never heard of before. They all wanted a license for Davy Crockett merchandise. By the end of the day, over 200 companies had called," Lou remembered. "By Friday night, a packet with a licensing agreement, photos of Fess Parker in his Davy Crockett costume, and some art pieces with logos and other copy points were in the mail 'special delivery.' Millions of dollars in Davy Crockett merchandise were sold in the next few months. It must have been important revenue for the company because it was the only time I ever got a bonus check, and I worked for the company from 1934 to 1971. Roy O. Disney gave me the check personally."

Fess Parker has vivid recollections on how his involvement as Davy Crockett came about and his career with Disney. "I had been in the film industry for about three years. My goal was to get established by the time I was 30 or find something else to do. I turned 30 in 1954 and not much had happened career-wise. Some time back, a Warner Brother casting agent had called about a small part in a science fiction movie about giant ants called *Them!* starring James Arness. I usually didn't do day work, but took the part.

"Walt Disney screened the film, perhaps to consider Jim Arness for the role of Davy Crockett. I don't know what he saw in me, but I got a call to see producer Bill Walsh and writer Tom Blackburn at the Disney Studio. We met a couple of times and talked about the part. It seemed like it wasn't a bad idea and they said to me, 'The next time you come out you will probably meet Walt.' For some reason I grabbed my guitar on my way to the meeting. We sat down and Walt said, 'Tell me about yourself, where you're from, and what you've done.'

"Well that took about two minutes. Then Walt noticed my guitar and asked me to play something. I played "Lonely," a song that I had written. It was about a cowboy late in the afternoon, just as the sun was going down, the dogs barking and the kids are still playing. Folks are about to light their coal-oil lamps. In the shadows, in the depot house is a cowboy and he could hear way out across the prairie the sounds of a train whistle which I approximated with my voice musically – the sound of the lonesome whistle.

"Two weeks later, August 1, 1954, I signed a personal contract with Walt Disney. I worked for him, not the studio, and my paycheck came from him. The first thing I was told to do was to report to the soundstage. There I recorded, I guess for the very first time it was ever done, the "Ballad of Davy Crockett." The recording session yielded a promotional record. The song took off in Boston while I was out with Buddy Ebsen and all of the people making the first film. In the meantime, Archie Bleyer heard the buzz about the "Ballad of Davy Crockett" out in Boston. He wanted to lease the master and Walt Disney said, 'No. We can't lease it, we are going to start our own record company.' You may or may not know that Davy Crockett was the beginning of (the Disney) recording and music publishing business.

"So I went off and we made the films. I had a little struggle with Norman Foster, the director, who hadn't chosen me for the part. He thought he was going to make *Zorro* and he was down in Mexico looking for locations. When he came back Walt told him, 'This is Fess Parker, he is going to play Davy Crockett.' So he was a little bit unimpressed by me. Then we went off about as far away from the studio we could get to Cherokee, North Carolina. There was a motel, a phone booth and I think a gas station. The next little place was up the road 15 or 20 miles. It had an old hotel called the Jarrod House. It wasn't much of a motel, but it had been visited by George Washington in his travels. We finished up the movie working in the Percy Warner park. The second film, *Davy Crockett Goes to Washington,* was filmed in and around Nashville. We used the State Capital building and the exterior of Andrew Jackson's home, The Hermitage. There was a banker in Nashville who owned a replica of the Hermitage. He allowed us to shoot inside. We came home and we did The Alamo movie and I went down swinging. We finished filming all three of the planned one-hour episodes in late November or early December (1954).

"Next they sent me down to Texas to do something for the Heart Fund. When I got back, the studio packed me off to Washington, D.C. where I appeared for the entire trip in my buckskin costume. It was a little awkward sitting next to the Speaker of the House, Sam Rayburn, and all the congressmen from Texas and Tennessee and having introductions to Senators Estes Kefauuer and Lyndon Johnson. I remember Sam Rayburn wouldn't speak to me for the longest time before he turned to an admiral sitting on the other side of him and asked 'Who is this boy?' The admiral said, 'Well, he's an actor who portrayed Davy Crockett for the Walt Disney movie company.' Then he talked to me and we became pretty good friends. In fact, we traveled together from Washington to Texas one time. There were two additional Davy Crockett TV shows for the 1955 season and I traveled to 42 cities and 13 foreign countries.

"Then came four non-Davy Crockett feature films. During this mix, my relationship with Walt changed. Two things prompted what happened. One day Liz Whitney stopped by where we were shooting and asked to meet me. She had friends with her and we chatted for a while. It just seemed like another PR introduction at the time. Later we were driving to the Georgia location where we were to shoot *The Great Locomotive Chase*. Jeffery Hunter was up in the front seat with the driver and I was in the back with Walt. Jeff Hunter suddenly turned to say he just had one of the greatest experiences of his career doing *The Searchers* with John Wayne and director John Ford. Walt looked at me and remarked, 'They wanted you for that.' Well that kinda ruined my afternoon. I was never consulted and nothing was ever said. I later learned Liz Whitney and her friends had been sizing me up for the part. If I was to ever get out of my buckskins, that was my chance.

"When I heard Marilyn Monroe was to film *Bus Stop,* I asked Walt if I could try out for the part. I gave him a copy of the play I got. He returned it with an inter-office memo stating he didn't think this was the type of material I should be doing.

"Those two incidents prompted me to get a new agent. I hired Ray Stark. He went to Walt and told him that he wasn't paying me enough. Walt said to renegotiate my original seven-year contract with the studio. We did and I got a higher salary, but things changed. I was reduced to second billing in later films and it seemed that Walt lost interest in me. When I was presented with a very minor part for *Tonka*, I felt it would be dishonest of me to take second billing. It was only a voice under the title and five pages of dialogue before I was killed. My contract was voided because I refused to do the picture. My feeling was some of the studio managers didn't like the new deal and wanted me out. So I left and went to Paramount."

The *Mickey Mouse Club* was the first additional concept to be purchased by ABC. It was childrens programming, featuring a group of talented youngsters called Mouseketeers. The show was filmed in one of the growing number of live-action studios on the Burbank lot. The only two adults on the program were Jimmie Dodd, a perfect role model for kids (who also composed many of the show's musical numbers); and the big Mooseketeer, Roy Williams, Walt's favorite gag man since the 1930s cartoon days at the studio.

Several of the original, now adult, Mouseketeers continue to make regular reunion appearances around the country. Tommy Cole, Doreen Tracy, Karen Pendleton, Sherry Alberoni, Bobby Burgess (also known for his many years as a featured dancer on the Lawrence Welk TV show), and I have had several conversations about the 1955 Mickey Mouse Club. Annette Funicello and I also had a brief discussion about those days at a Disneyana convention. Her memories of her three years on the *Mickey Mouse Club* set

Photo by Tom Tumbusch

Original 1955 Mouseketeers during a reunion show in Chicago. Left to right are Bobby Burgess, Doreen Tracy, Tommy Cole, Sherry Alberoni, Karen Pendleton, and Sharon Baird.

have also been documented in her autobiography, "*A Dream is a Wish Your Heart Makes – My Story.*"

Walt Disney made regular visits to the set, where the cast members called him Uncle Walt. Mouseketeers reported he always had questions about what they liked best or problems they might be having with their school teacher or on the set. They all loved him as a father figure. Sherry Alberoni, a second-year replacement, had been doing TV commercials since she was three or four years old. "I really didn't think much about the magnitude of what we were doing. An hour-long TV show, five days a week with original songs, sets, and stories was more of a major production than what I could understand at the time. It was just work for me, but the kids in my neighborhood seemed to think it was a big deal. But fame is fleeting. Not long ago, I asked my daughter if she was interested in my old *Mickey Mouse Club* souvenirs, and she told me just to sell them on eBay. We were kids and we had a great time doing the show. In addition to the promotional reunions we have become lifelong friends and get together a couple times a year for our own pleasure," Alberoni recounted. The *MMC* led to featured roles on two long-running TV sitcoms she co-starred in over the next 15 years.

Annette Funicello, the most famous Mouseketeer and star of many Disney film projects, described trying out for the *Mickey Mouse Club* early in 1955. She had to go to three auditions and was the last of the first 24 children, ages 9 to 14, to be selected.

Walt had made it clear to the show's producer, Bill Walsh, that he wanted each hour-long production to be centered around the kids. And they were not to be professional kids with a stage-door mother giving directions from the wings. Walsh sent his staff to local talent contests, school shows, and dance recitals to find the kind of kids Walt had specified. Just like the early animators after Ub Iwerks left the studio, Walt sought to mold his child actors into the Disney brand of bright, wholesome, and talented entertainers. He wanted to project the image of ordinary kids doing things any talented kid could do given the chance. And kids in the TV audience identified with what they viewed each afternoon.

Sharon Baird, Lonnie Burr, Sherry Alberoni, and Bobby Burgess had previously worked professionally, but fit the image Walt wanted. Most other Mouseketeers received their first professional show business contracts after the initial two-week trial period.

Even though the *Mickey Mouse Club* didn't premiere until Monday, October 3, 1955, segments began filming as early as May. The first TV *Mickey Mouse Club* was in production for three years and aired on ABC-TV for four. It ran as an hour show the first two seasons, but was reduced to 30-minute episodes the last two years due to ABC complaints about high production costs. Once again Walt chose to cut the length of the program rather than reduce content quality.

Bill Justice recalled the show's animated opening. "Walt asked me to direct the show's animated opening sequence. Because studio commitments had expanded so rapidly, ways had to be found to increase productivity. X (Xavier Atencio) thought of using colored cards for backgrounds. This was a big savings – no trees or buildings to paint! A radical idea at the time, no one was sure how it would look. The results were very effective. Mickey and his friends appeared to be suspended in space. The background was the only area we tried to save money. Remember the ending where Donald Duck hits the gong? Eleven different endings were animated to keep our viewers off balance. Kids never knew what Donald was going to do. The Muppets TV program used the same trick years later. We also animated the entire opening in color. Not many people have seen it this way because the broadcast was in black & white since there were so few color TV sets at the time. This opening sequence became one of the most used pieces of film in studio history."

In the show's first Nielson rating period, *Mickey Mouse Club* ranked second only to the Brooklyn Dodgers/New York Yankees World Series games. In the next rating book and for the remainder of the four years the show aired, the show ranked as the number-one daytime show for children, replacing the longtime NBC leader, *Howdy Doody*.

The Davy Crockett phenomenon changed television programming for the next ten years. The adult westerns hit in the fall of 1955 with *Death Valley Days*, *The Life and Legend of Wyatt Earp*, *Cheyenne*, and *Gunsmoke*. *Broken Arrow*, *Wells Fargo*, *Sugarfoot* and *The Adventures of Jim Bowie* followed as minor hits before *Have Gun, Will Travel*, *Wagon Train*, *Wanted–Dead or Alive*, *The Rifleman*, *Bat Masterson*, *Maverick*, and *Bonanza* filled most of the remaining prime-time program slots. By the time the genre produced the Sci-Fi Western, *The Wild, Wild West* in the mid-sixties, all facets of the horse opera had run its course.

ABC, having aired all the Davy Crockett episodes several times, pushed Walt for more western material.

The *Zorro* TV project was revived for the 1957 season, as a method to develop revenue to finance the expansion of Disneyland. This time the studio was forecasting not only the ABC licensing fees the show would generate, but also the type of merchandise revenue they enjoyed from Davy Crockett. ABC bought the idea, but once again turned down Walt's budget request to film in color. Walt, convinced programs would have value when color television made traditional black & white programs obsolete, had endured the cost of color for the Disneyland series out of the studio's funds, but declined to do so for the *Mickey Mouse Club* or *Zorro* episodes.

Casting for the *Zorro* role attracted many top TV names who had vivid recollections of what the role of Davy Crockett did for Fess Parker. David Janssen (The Fugitive), Jack Kelly (Maverick's brother) and Hugh O' Brian (Wyatt Earp) all auditioned. In the end, Guy Williams, who had all but given up Hollywood after a series of minor movie roles, won the right to play the title character and his alter ego, Don Diego de la Vega.

The Disney Studio lot is only 41 acres. The Zorro set was the first permanent outdoor set to be built there. The rear sides of the animation and other buildings became facades of the 19th Century Los Angeles structures. The town square was constructed just inside the Alameda Street entrance. It was almost like shooting a major TV series in a good size backyard. Other locations were used for the wide-open spaces, but most scenes from the old Los Angeles Pueblo were shot in very cramped quarters. The sets remained largely in place until they were severely damaged by the Northridge earthquake in 1994.

Once again, Walt ignored the conventional wisdom of the day. TV production costs were a joke compared to similar costs for a movie production. Walt put more than triple the average TV budget into each *Zorro* episode and it paid off. Nearly 40% of all TV viewers preferred *Zorro* in the 1957-58 season. It reached a slightly better rating the second season. ABC-TV, seeing what great properties Disney was delivering asked the Studio for even more program ideas. Walt presented *The Shaggy Dog* at the network annual spring meeting at the studio. ABC's new VP of programming was so turned off by the concept, he excused himself to leave for another meeting before Walt had finished. Walt was furious. ABC had begged for more new program ideas and Walt felt it was rude not to hear out his presentation. He was so angered he ordered *The Shaggy Dog* to be made into a feature film, which proved to be one of Disney's top moneymaking live-action films at the time. Its two spin-offs, which easily could have been part of the TV series...*The Absent - Minded Professor* and *Son of Flubber*...did even better business at the box office.

It was the beginning of trouble with ABC. Seeing the value in the growing syndication market, the network now claimed they owned the shows based on their payment of production costs. Disney sued and won all ownership rights. While the legal battle raged, Disney withheld what would have been another high-rated third *Zorro* season from ABC. Walt continued to pay Guy Williams to keep him under contract with the idea of reinstating the *Zorro* series. Some new color episodes were used on the *Disneyland* series to help keep the character before viewers. Once the suit was settled, however, Walt figured it was time to move on to something else, mainly the budget for color productions promised by NBC.

The show was renamed *Walt Disney's Wonderful World of Color* when the anthology series switched networks in 1961. It retained that title until 1969, when it was renamed *The Wonderful World of Disney*.

Tinker Bell was the signature character for the Disneyland TV show, but she did not talk, so Jiminy Cricket was the animated spokesman in many *Disneyland* episodes since the show's inception in 1954. He was replaced by a new character designed especially for the new *Walt Disney's Wonderful World of Color* program on NBC. His name was Ludwig Von Drake, voiced by Paul Frees, the ghost-host voice in Disneyland's Haunted Mansion. NBC's parent company, RCA, also used Ludwig in a number of special promotions.

The ABC *Disneyland* TV Program became the sixth highest-rated prime-time series in its first year on the air, where it remained a Wednesday night staple until the show was moved to Sunday night for the 1960-61 season. It remained on Sunday night on various networks for most of its continuous 29-year run, the longest in TV-programming history. The last two years on CBS, the series aired in the 8:00 p.m. Saturday time slot.

The show started to suffer a viewership decline following the death of Walt Disney. His introductions to the show gave it a quality it never regained. He was not replaced by another host until Michael Eisner tried it briefly starting in 1986. In subsequent years, the Disneyland type anthology program also aired under the title of *Walt Disney Presents* and *The Magical World of Disney*.

The Mouse Factory was a syndicated cartoon series produced by Ward Kimball in 1972. Forty-three shows were done using a guest star and a classic Disney cartoon in each themed episode. At the time all the classic shows except *Disneyland* had left the air. Hanna-Barbera and the Warner Brothers cartoon line-ups dominated the networks' kid's block. The impact of the Disney cartoon characters was largely lost to the '60s-generation kids. Despite major market-rating successes, "they canceled my show," Kimball reported. "They said the financial return wasn't up to expectations.

Management felt the Disney characters got enough exposure at the theme parks, but that was a lot of crap. Even if *The Mouse Factory* broke even, it would have been worth it to get kids who weren't lucky enough to visit one of our parks to love our characters. Those cartoons are timeless. It was a big mistake, but I guess that's why they never put me on the board," Kimball concluded.

E. Cardon "Card" Walker started in the Disney mail room in 1938. He worked his way up through the company in sales and advertising, serving a brief stint in the story department and was named to the Board of Directors as one of Walt's heirs apparent in 1960. Shortly after Walt's death, he was named Chief Operating Officer of the company before becoming President in 1971 and Chairman of the Board in 1980. Card Walker's biggest company vision was the formation of the Disney Channel, a joint venture with Westinghouse Broadcasting, for the emerging cable industry. The costs of this now valuable operation were larger than expected and one of the reasons the studio became ripe for take-over attempts in the 1980s.

The concept of going into competition with the on-air networks was just as revolutionary as Walt's decision to enter television in 1954 or to build Disneyland. It was a page from "Walt Disney Operations 101," but lacked Roy Disney's touch as much as Walt's. Card Walker's belief in The Disney Channel has been vindicated, but with much of the credit going to others.

In an ironic touch, the ABC Network that helped make Disneyland and subsequent theme parks possible sold back its 35% interest in the original park in 1960 for $7,500,000. The cash the parks generated over the years was largely responsible for Disney's ability to purchase all ABC holdings in 1995 for $19 billion.

Conceived as a means to finance Walt's theme park, television production has become a vital part of studio activity. Programs have included a wide variety of comedy, drama, documentary, made-for-TV and cable movies, animated series, and specials. Its revenue can rival the income from feature films. The biggest profit dollars, however, still come from the theme parks made possible by the first TV deal with ABC-TV.

TV helped raise the littlest Hollywood movie lot to become one of the largest entertainment giants in the industry. There is somewhat of a question if Walt would have ever wanted things to turn out as they have. Whatever the motivation, the expansion into media delivery from content producer was possible because of the foundation Walt and Roy Disney built. The Disney name brand is still a key to the studio's success long after their deaths and long after the once household names of other Hollywood giants of the '30s and '40s have all but been forgotten.

Chapter VII – Walt's Biggest Dream

"It was the second time I met Walt. We had just screened the picture (Cinderella, in the fall of 1949) and we were in a reception area. I sat down with him at the bar. We were both drinking orange juice and got to talking. He suddenly became very excited as ideas exploded. His words became chopped off as he described Disneyland and how it would be divided into Adventureland, Frontierland, Fantasyland, and Tomorrowland. He remarked how he had been thinking about it for years. I had only met Walt Disney once before–way back in 1935 or '36 when I was at the studio with Kay Kamen–but here he was telling me all about Disneyland with a gleam in his eye I will never forget."

—Lou Lispi, Art Director
Character Merchandise Division

The next time Lou Lispi saw Walt was shortly before the park opened. It was at an event for key Disney executives to brief them on the park and discuss the promotional buildup. When he found himself standing beside Walt, he remarked, "How very successful you must feel." Walt replied, "If you'd call being eight million dollars in debt a success, then I am a great success."

The Disneyland dream had been on Walt's mind for 15 years before it was realized. Sunday was his day with his daughters and it was boring sitting on a bench watching his girls have all the fun. He wanted a place where the whole family could enjoy themselves together.

Art Linkletter recalled the visit Walt, Lilly, and his wife Lois made to Tivoli Gardens in Copenhagen, Denmark, "It (Tivoli Gardens) was small, but an extremely well-kept park with little twinkling lights. Walt was making notes and I asked what he was doing." Linkletter remembered Walt saying, "Someday, I'm going to do something like this in America. Something bigger using the Disney characters." That dream would eventually become Disneyland.

Once *Cinderella* re-established the studio as the undisputed leader in animated film production, Walt began dreaming more about his new family entertainment idea. The biggest problem was convincing Roy. Every time Walt described his ideas, Roy envisioned an amusement park and all the negative aspects of a lowlife carny operation. He didn't buy it and was convinced the stockholders wouldn't either. It was Walt hardest sell. Everybody to whom Roy confided the plans thought it was a bad idea. When Roy's chief contact at the Bank of America agreed, Roy dug in, not to be swayed. Unflappable, Walt personally had Disneyland, Inc. incorporated in 1951.

Alice in Wonderland was disappointing at the box office and lost about $1 million domestically, but came close to breaking even with international sales. When *Peter Pan* did much better in 1953 and WED Enterprises planning began to take shape, Roy okayed $10,000 of corporate funds as a token to Walt for "preliminary drawings." Over time, Walt's commitment and the TV-network plan began to soften Roy. Walt, sensing a breakthrough, began to share more of his ideas and Roy gradually came around to a park estimated to cost $7 million. It wasn't something the Bank of America was willing to support alone. Some of the big New York banks would be needed to share the risk. Had it not been for the Disney reputation for pulling off *Snow White* and somehow coming up with the right answers during the difficult 1940s, the Disneys probably wouldn't have been given the chance. A meeting was set up for Roy to pitch the idea in New York and a financial prospectus was prepared. This was usually the key element for such meetings, but Walt knew how difficult it was to bring Roy around. He reasoned it would be just as difficult for the bankers to visualize his theme park as anything other than a sleazy amusement park.

Walt remembered an artist who was with him on his South American goodwill tour back in 1941. He recalled how fast Herb Ryman could capture a village, the mountains, or a marketplace with his watercolors. Ryman was called for an immediate meeting.

Ryman recalled that historic meeting one breakfast we had at the Old Emerald Hotel near Disneyland, "Walt began describing this fantastic place where whole families could go to have fun. It would have a castle, the Wild West with Indians, an Amazon River cruise with animals, a Fantasyland full of Disney characters, and a place for the future. It was so exciting, I asked to see a picture of the place. That's when Walt told me I was going to draw it."

The two worked the entire weekend coming up with the first concept drawing of Disneyland. Small photostats of this drawing were included in each prospectus binder and Roy was off to New York. In his meeting, he talked about how he was cold to the idea at first, but then launched into why he now thought the time was right to lead the way to a new form of wholesome family entertainment. The post-war baby boom had created a family market unlike any that had ever existed. The state of California was experiencing rapid growth. Travel had become easier by automobile and by plane.

Television had come of age and provided an ideal medium to promote this new concept.

Details were provided to show this wasn't just another amusement park. It was to be a land full of adventures to be enjoyed by the whole family. The sales estimates prepared by Disney's outside research company were convincing. The bankers agreed to back the idea and Disneyland was on its way to becoming a reality.

If Walt had ever been given a nickname, it would have been "budget buster." His unwavering commitment to quality must have kept Roy up nights. The basic elements depicted in Herb Ryman's drawing – the single entrance, the center hub, the four lands all surrounded by the Disneyland Railroad and a 15-foot-high berm to separate the park from the outside world – were retained. As the orange groves of Anaheim gave way to the Main Street USA gateway, rivers, a castle, and a rocket launch pad, some attractions had to be postponed. Still the cost kept increasing.

Television had figured in Walt's plan since before he had WED purchase the rights to *Zorro*. Roy was off to New York again to contact the networks and ended up with the deal at ABC. This helped with the second tier of Disneyland financing, especially when a faithful Disney licensee, the Western Printing and Lithographing Company of Racine, Wisconsin financed an additional 13% of the construction costs. Still, it was not going to be enough. The park was taking shape, but the project completion budg-

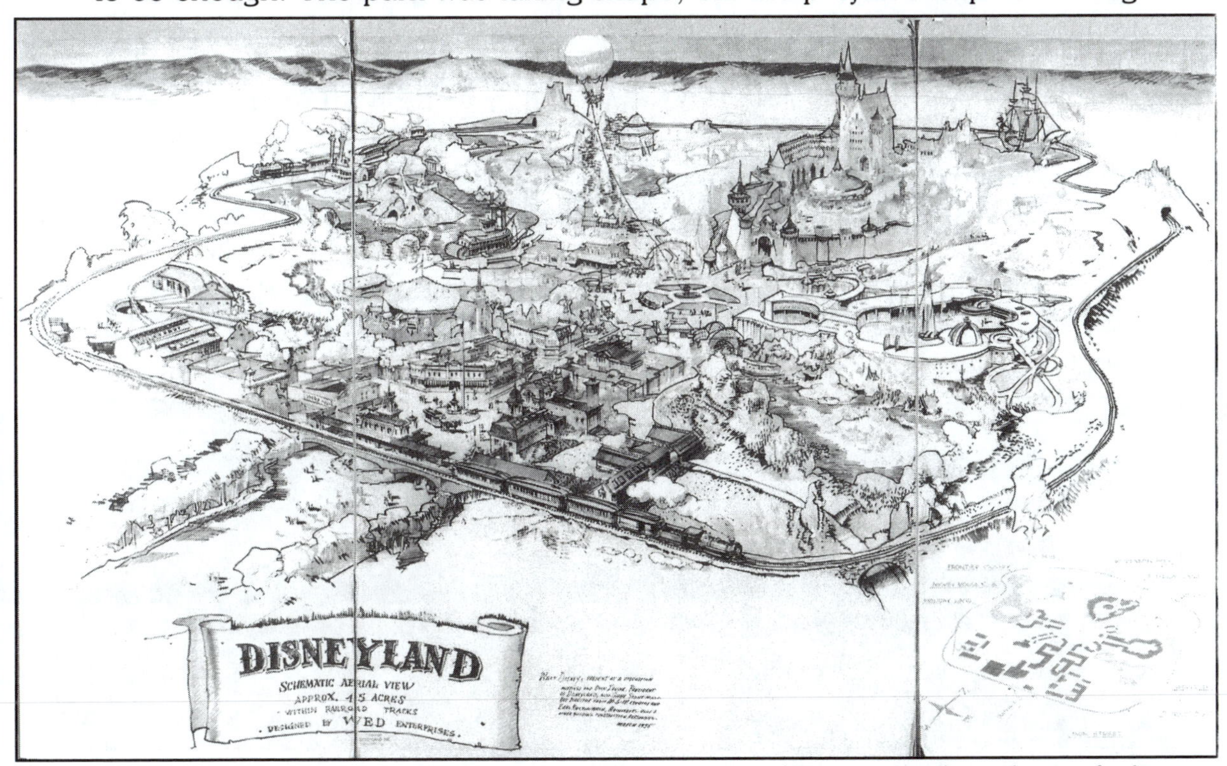

Photostat courtesy of Westmoor Consulting, sales agent for the owner

Herb Ryman's concept drawing made from Walt Disney's verbal description of his Disneyland dream.

et had now risen to $17 million: a full $10 million more than the original estimates. Every time it seemed the project was all wrapped up, Walt's changes and unforeseen expenditures kept driving the costs higher.

Normally, only governments could incur those kinds of cost overruns. The bankers wouldn't lend another penny. The major commitment by ABC and Western Publishing covered most of the cost beyond the base $7 million pledged by the banks and the initial investment the studio provided, but things were still a bit short.

Roy came up with a solution. The shops along Main Street and a few in the lands would be leased for five years with two years payable in advance – the first and the fifth. The banks understood solid leases and could then finance the middle three years. That proved to be enough to get the park open on schedule July 17, 1955. There weren't the trees and plants Walt wanted and there were problems getting everything to work reliably, but Disneyland opened on time and offered music, laughs, and adventures never before found anywhere else.

The single entrance that critics thought would never work proved to be an asset rather than a problem (except during the opening-day telecast). The bands, horse-drawn streetcars, fire wagon, and surreys created a whole different atmosphere from the established amusement parks. Those who wished to pause visited the shops, the penny arcade, or the cinema where original *Mickey Mouse* cartoons were shown. The sight of the castle, or "the weenie" as Walt liked to call it, drew the crowd away from the single entrance and channeled them into the four lands. Those focusing on Sleeping Beauty's Castle could see King Arthur Carousel through the archway. Once in Fantasyland, they found Peter Pan's Flight, Snow White's Adventure, Mr. Toad's Wild Ride, and the Mad Tea Party. These attractions were more like ones found in an amusement park, but had been given a whole new Disney twist to the point the resemblance was overlooked.

Adventureland offered the Jungle Cruise. Rain-Forest jungles were re-created with a sense of adventure not found along the real Amazon. In addition, there were some shops, but little else in Adventureland on opening day.

Panoramic Postcard of Sleeping Beauty's Castle (circa 1957). Notice the sparce vegetation found at Disneyland the first several years.

Frontierland fared much better. The Mark Twain paddle-wheeler was a moving focal point as it wound around the Rivers of America. There were Stagecoach rides on some of the most ornate hand-carved wooden stagecoaches ever built. Walt assumed if you built things so elegant, vandals would not deface them and his theory proved correct. There was a mule-pack ride and The Golden Horseshoe Revue live stage show.

Canal Boats of the World, soon to be converted to Storybook Land, provided a transition from Fantasyland to Tomorrowland. Autopia had cars children as young as four or five could drive, and Space Station X-1, was where you could catch the next rocket leaving for the moon.

When you flash back to Disneyland 1955 versus all the incredible adventures existing there today, it seems primitive, but compared to old-style amusement parks it was revolutionary. In a sense, the original Disneyland concept really wasn't completed until Tomorrowland was expanded in 1959, when the Matterhorn, Submarine voyage, and Monorail were added. True to Walt Disney's dedication message, Disneyland has never stopped growing.

The bricks, mortar, finely machined wood, and unique adventures were only part of the Disneyland story. Guests were greeted by young, enthusiastic hosts and hostesess in festive costumes themed for each land or attraction. They were cast members on stage, presenting a rehearsed show of guest kindness, enjoyment, and satisfaction.

Van France put the training package together for Walt. He was hired by C.V. Wood in 1954 when the property was still an orange grove. C.V. Wood is a little-known name in Disney history, yet he played a major role in the creation of Disneyland. Wood, with a background in the aviation industry, was a Texan who came out of the Stanford Research team that located the Anaheim site. Walt hired him to oversee the development of Disneyland. He worked out of the studio and was the man largely responsible for getting the park opened in only eleven months. Retired Navy Admiral Joe Fowler was the "Can do" man directing the on-site construction management. Fowler had been Production Officer supervising ship construction for the U.S. Navy Yard at Mare Island, California and former Commander of the San Francisco Naval Ship Yard in the 1940s. Walt and Roy coaxed him out of retirement to do a temporary consulting job…and it lasted twenty years. He supervised an army of subcontractors with an optimistic attitude, usually punctuated with the words "can do!" He was nicknamed the "miracle man" for getting the park open on schedule. Wood coordinated all the design, scheduling, off-site fabrication, and park operation functions. He hired a team, including other Texans from his background, to help. Once the park was opened, C.V. Wood was named Vice President of Operations.

Wood had worked with Van France previously in setting up training programs and invited him to the studio to meet Walt. It was a match. Van won the job to establish the training program and to get the first cast members up to speed by opening day. He spent hours with Walt to determine how he wanted his park to be run, then successfully turned Walt's ideas into the basic principles by which Disney theme parks are still run today. "It's easy when you have a boss like Walt who can tell you exactly what he wants," recalled Van France. Van details his long relationship with C.V. Wood in his book *Window on Main Street*. What is not in the book is why Wood suddenly left the company several months after Disneyland was completed. "One day Walt was going past Wood's office while he was on the phone," Van related, "and Walt overheard Wood say, 'I'm the guy who built Disneyland.' Whatever truth there was in that statement, Walt didn't appreciate it. He already felt Wood was getting out of hand, but overhearing his conversation was the last straw. Wood was gone the next morning."

Wood's history with Disneyland helped him land positions with perhaps a dozen other theme parks as the amusement park business scrambled to match Disney's success. He was instrumental in building the first Six Flags park in his native Texas. In time, however, Wood's other new and revived theme parks all failed, Once again, proving it's the mind in which the dream originated that truly mattered.

C.V. Wood's contributions to Disneyland will never be fully known, but the best one on record is the hiring of Van France. He in turn was responsible for bringing aboard and training Dick Nunis, who eventually would head all Disney theme parks worldwide. Working together, they

Replica of the first American vessel to sail 'round the world . . . three-masted and fully rigged . . . the first sailing ship of its kind built in more than 100 years . . . a thrilling voyage of exploration on the Rivers of America in Frontierland!

An exciting new attraction in "the happiest kingdom of them all" . . . travel "down the Rabbit Hole" to see Alice's thrilling dreams come to life . . . through the Oversize Chamber and the Upside Down Room . . . visit the Mad Hatter and his wild Tea Party . . . the March Hare, Cheshire Cat and White Rabbit . . . experience the astounding adventures from this famous story!

One of the wonders of the world re-created for your enjoyment . . . see the Grand Canyon at beautiful sunrise and sunset . . . during a spectacular thunder and lightning storm . . . view mountain lions, deer, wild turkeys and birds . . . and an Indian cliff dweller village . . . all inside the world's largest Diorama!

MAIN STREET — FRONTIERLAND — FANTASYLAND — TOMORROWLAND

Three elegant trains take you on a scenic tour around Disneyland . . climaxed by the majestic 306-feet long Grand Canyon Diorama . . board the new Excursion train . . the deluxe Passenger train . . or the fast Freight . . all on the Santa Fe & Disneyland Railroad!

Important! For your convenience you may purchase either Big 10 or Jumbo 15 Ticket Books, minus admission, at Ticket Booths in all the Lands, the Penny Arcade on Main Street, and Souvenir Stands.

REMEMBER! Disneyland Ticket Books offer BIGGEST SAVINGS AND MOST CONVENIENCE!

© Copyright 1958 Walt Disney Productions

Jumbo 15 — Child $2.75 — Junior $3.05 — Adult $3.35

Big 10 — Child $1.75 — Junior $2.05 — Adult $2.35

(THESE TICKET BOOKS DO NOT INCLUDE MAIN GATE ADMISSION!)

Advertising flyer distributed by ticket sellers promoting the rapid expansion of additional attractions from 1956 through the opening of the New Tomorrowland in 1959.

realized Walt's dream for how the park would be run by "fresh young people rather than carny types."

Disneyland's product would be happiness for the entire family – "The Happiest Place on Earth." Everyone from area supervisors down to the street cleaners got Van's happiness training. They were all performers – cast members – on stage in the largest show on earth – Disneyland – where they were paid to smile and make their guests happy.

Van France was perfect for the job. He was a person anyone could like. He was confident, funny, and shared Walt's way of getting people to go along with his program. A big part of Van France's success was his playful sense of humor and love of life. When he was approaching his 80th year, his personal Christmas card showed him parasailing. He loved Disneyland and practiced what he preached. Whenever he encountered litter or a carelessly placed cup, he would escort the offending object to the nearest trash container. Small bits of trash were simply stuffed unceremoniously into his pocket. Cast members had to notice his example.

Van France met all ages at their own level, one where they were not only motivated, but inspired to put on the best show they possibly could. Van knew everybody who worked at Disneyland and many leads at the other parks around the world. He had trained them or their bosses personally. A writer by trade, Van also possessed communication skills that elevated people to levels they never would have dreamed possible. Van France was simply a Pied Piper of excellence. He loved good conversation and Scotch. Like Walt, he asked a lot of questions and used the answers to improve his work. The operational policies he and Dick Nunis established at Disneyland have been adapted to different languages and cultures for Disney's international theme parks. The concept of cast members as part of a show has continued to set working at Disney apart from any other job a college-age student can find…and it can be an important asset to any resume.

C.V. Wood lured Van away from Disneyland for several years to develop training programs at non-Disney theme parks. "But I never had the wonderful things Walt provided at Disneyland. Walt wanted things done right, the other parks were poor attempts to copy Disneyland's success. They were often doomed from the start because they were run by amusement park managers simply trying to clean up their act. There were some good ideas, but very little inspiration. Walt was passionate about what he did. The 'me too' guys couldn't see happiness beyond the gate admission price," Van once related. And Van didn't have to be drinking to tell things the way they were. He was direct to his point in every respect, but the twinkle in his eye kept people from ever taking offense. Jiminy Cricket was his favorite Disney character and over the years he took on aspects of the character as his own.

Van eventually returned to Disneyland and worked for Dick Nunis. Van was always proud to say, "Be kind to the gofer you hire. Someday he may be your boss." Van went on to establish Club 55 – for cast members who worked Disneyland's opening day and remained with the company – and The Disneyland Alumni Club for all former employees.

Memories of getting Disneyland launched and working with Walt Disney were fond ones for an otherwise non-sentimental guy. His recollection on how Walt would saddle up a horse for a ride through his park in pre-opening hours and his love of horses in general were pointed out as my son and I received Van's private Disneyland backstage tour. We were in the recently remodeled facilities behind Toontown as the stable master showed off features of the new stainless-steel stalls. "Walt would have loved those," Van said in response. Like so many of Walt's key people in park and studio operations, they knew what he liked and they continued to do things his way unless otherwise directed by newer management.

Van France was one of the few people to write about how difficult the first year of Disneyland's existence really was. The weather was a major factor. The temperature was over a hundred degrees the first 10 days the park was open. Then the rains that plagued construction came back and ruined most of August, the period the Stanford Research Group predicted Disneyland would do the most business during the first year.

"Employees were asked to hold their checks for a few days and the food was C.O.D. Early visitors never knew the money collected at the front gate was being used to buy the food they would purchase at lunch," Van reported. "Labor Day was to be the big payoff and we had an office pool to predict the crowd size. The media had warned people about long lines and traffic jams. I'm sad to say I won the pool with my estimate of around 10,000."

When kids went back to school after Labor Day the panic began to set in. "One guy figured out a way to save $10,000 with some cheaper looking umbrellas. Walt chewed him out in a way he would never forget. Walt would never sacrifice on quality," Van reported, "In any way, shape, or form."

Operation cost overages and sluggish attendance at Disneyland affected the entire company. To conserve cash, cartoon production ground to a halt and *Sleeping Beauty* was postponed. Television revenue picked up part of the slack, but one of the biggest shots in the arm came from the sale of Davy Crockett merchandise. Even though the episodes aired on TV in black & white, Walt had them filmed in color. In an unprecedented move, he ordered the three one-hour segments edited together and released theatrically. Never before had the public been asked to pay for something most of them had seen for free on TV. The film did exceedingly well at the box office and rekindled the Davy Crockett phenomenon all over again. So Davy played a major role in keeping the studio and Disneyland from the threat of financial ruin.

Disneyland attendance was better than expected the first winter. Several additional attractions were operational by the second summer when people began to arrive as expected. Walt once said, "We did it (built Disneyland) with the knowledge that most people I talked to thought it would be a financial disaster – closed and forgotten within the first year." As far as this author could find, he never publicly commented on how close his critics came to being right.

Van's favorite Walt Disney quote reguarding Disneyland was when the press asked about $900,000 of costs that were discovered having no paper trail. These costs were incurred during the crush of activity to get Disneyland constructed and in operation for the first several months. When questioned about this problem, Walt calmly replied, "Well, if you do Big Things, you make Big Mistakes." Getting a handle on all the operational procedures took some time, but in the end, "Walt's Folly" number two turned out to be an even bigger success than his first predicted disaster, *Snow White and the Seven Dwarfs.*

In his book *Window on Main Street,* Van France enumerated what contributed to Disneyland's eventual success. They were –
"Walt's reputation and dedication
The Disney Studio backing
The Disneyland TV program – called by some 'an
        hour long commercial
The lessees – both the 'fast buck' participants and the
        institutional lessees who also helped finance Walt's dream
The people who worked there and felt that what we
        were doing was – IMPORTANT
and – most important – Walt's world public who wanted
        to share his dream"
Van often commented that Walt Disney was a man of real class. Van never gave much thought to the fact that a big part of the Disney success was the fact that Walt surrounded himself with other men of real class like Van France.

The people Van wrote about sharing Walt's dream included individuals like Wally Boag, the top banana and Pecos Bill in the long-running Golden Horseshoe Revue. Starting in 1947, he traveled the world in vaudeville, playing such venues as Radio City Music Hall and the London Hippodrome. He did five shows a day in the Golden Horseshoe for 27 years. In between, he would do shootouts with the Sheriff of Frontierland. Wally also wrote the original Enchanted Tiki Room show and did all of Fred MacMurray's stunt work in *The Absent-Minded Professor.* Walt Disney loved the Golden Horseshoe Revue and normally visited it about once a week. "One time he came backstage and said to me, 'I'm doing a show for the Winter Olympics at Squaw Valley,'" Boag recalled, "'and I want you to produce the final show night...and be sure to remind me to give you a raise.'" That was the way Walt did things. He got to know his people so well, he put them in charge of major activities seemingly out of the blue knowing

Panoramic postcard views of Main Street U.S.A., Frontierland, and Tomorrowland as they appeared shortly after Disneyland opened around the fall of 1957.

full well they would knock themselves out to vindicate his faith in them.

And the quality of personnel permeated throughout the Disneyland organization. Everybody had a special rapport with Walt. Ticket seller and one-time Arcade manager Mary Van Thyme recalled how Walt had a passion for all of his toys. "He loved to play the Arcade...the music box and especially the big organ," Mary remembered. "One day something wouldn't work for him and he came up to me and wanted a refund. I told him that I couldn't do that and he said nicely that he had other ways to get his money back. I thought Walt was a pretty neat person."

Maintenance worker Chris Christopher recalled his encounters with Walt. "I'd see him after midnight walking around and in the early morning, too. He'd stop and talk about different things in the park. He was kinda quiet and he'd let you talk when he asked you a question."

One night Dominic Cente was mounting new speakers on the Jungle Cruise boats to replace the megaphones the pilots had been using. A man in a corduroy jacket, Levi's, and Stetson hat approached and asked him what he thought of the park. "As long as people have babies, this place will go on for a hundred years. It was about 1 A.M. and that was my first meeting with Walt Disney," Dominic remembered. "He was very, very interested in small details. He was a simple man, but he was a genius! Whenever Walt came around and we wanted to impress him, something would always go wrong. One time there was a press program at the Tomorrowland Railway Station. When Walt started to speak, no sound came out. George Short looked down and saw that the microphone had been unplugged and calmly plugged it back in." Walt realized such things happened and turned it into a positive, rather than reprimanded anyone.

Scotty Gribbes from the mill shop stated, "Walt was a gentleman. He was a man you didn't shy away from...a man you wanted to meet."

Pete Crimmings, a Disneyland operations supervisor, thought back over his many encounters with Walt, "The first three times he saw me, I was sitting down. I had the feeling he felt I was always on my fanny. But, he never said anything...just asked questions about the attractions, and went on his way. The stories about insisting on perfection are true. Two days before the opening of the (New York) World's Fair, he looked at a big steel canopy and felt it was too high. He wanted it lowered 18 inches and we lowered it."

Walt Disney was recognized all over the world as a major entertainment figure, yet he never stopped searching out the smallest details to improve his enterprises. His employees, down to his most menial worker, felt free to address him as Walt and convey what was on their minds. In a way, Walt's was a collective genius. Roy Disney operated much the same way. The people at Disneyland didn't see as much of Roy as they did Walt, but they respected him. Several old-timers at Disneyland Alumni banquets reported Roy was just as inquisitive as Walt, but Walt spent much more time at the park as he dreamed and planned on how to make it better.

Disneyland was an important part of Walt's life. Perhaps it was more of a personal achievement than his other ventures. It also turned out to be the most lucrative.

Roy felt the success of Disneyland increased Walt's vulnerability to lawsuits, so when his contract with WED Enterprises came up for renewal, Roy demanded changes. It caused the biggest rift between the two brothers in their long association. They didn't speak to each other for some time. The studio was divided into Walt's people and Roy's people. A very few were trusted by both and worked as diplomats between the two brothers. The WED contract allowed for Walt to produce one motion picture outside the studio. When Walt's lawyer threatened to have him do so, everything came to a head. Roy's advisors advocated a get-tough policy. Roy chewed them out, reminding them not a one of them would have a job were it not for Walt. Word got back to Walt and it broke the ice. Soon thereafter, Walt appeared at his brother's office with a peace pipe.

The rift was ended. Walt Disney Productions acquired WED Enterprises and RETLAW (Walter spelled backwards) was reorganized to allow Walt to continue to own the railroad (plus the Monorail, which was installed after the initial agreement) and all rights to his name. Walt Disney died still owning RETLAW. His family and estate received 818,461 shares of company stock (around $300,000,000 at the time) and all his personal possessions in return for Disneyland assets owned by RETLAW, except the Walt Disney name. The Walt Disney Company received use of the name for 40 years as part of the deal. The RETLAW entity survived and was used as a television station and real estate holding company. All remaining divisions of RETLAW were later closed into the Walt Disney Family Foundation in 2005. The foundation has founded a museum in the San Francisco Bay area to exhibit Walt's personal effects.

Disneyland offered Walt an opportunity he never had before. "That's what I like about Disneyland," he once remarked. "I can always keep plussing it. I'll never be finished with it. Now when I finish a picture, I ship it off and I'm done with it. I can never bring it back and fix it, no matter how much I want to."

The additions to Disneyland have continued to the present day, as Walt promised they would. Other Magic Kingdoms have continued the concept of "plussing" Walt's original. Still there is only one park where Walt measured, studied, and oversaw the improvements. Only one where he rode a horse on morning inspection tours to personally make sure the park was ready for guests. Only one park where he spent pensive nights after closing, walking the lands to determine small improvements or the location for a new attraction. This was Walt's park and no matter how many Magic Kingdoms eventually come to pass, there will still only be one Disneyland.

Chapter VIII – Walking With Walt

*"People often ask me if I know the secret of success and
if I could tell others how to make their dreams come true.
My answer is, you do it by working."*

—*Walt Disney*

Thus far, Walt's career has been traced through his major objectives to achieve realistic animation, live-action production, television programming, and the creation of Disneyland. He was now a creative and financial success. But wealth didn't change Walt. He still functioned as he always had. Disneyland only escalated his activities. It was truly his "happiest place on earth." His personality, by the accounts of those interviewed, was more friendly to Disneyland cast members than to studio storymen and animators.

Walt Disney often prowled the studio and Disneyland alone. His night and weekend visits afforded him the solace to evaluate his dreams and how they were progressing into reality. His dreams were big, but he concerned himself with the smallest details. "If we lose sight of the details, we lose everything," he once preached to his staff.

It would be fun to go back and walk with Walt to get answers to questions about his life and motivation. Unfortunately, that's not an option available to a Monday-morning researcher. The best available sources are the interviews Walt granted while alive and the experiences of those who did have the opportunity to walk and talk with Walt.

Art Linkletter tells the story about a big press conference being set up in San Francisco to launch *Fantasia* in 1940. Linkletter, a freelance news reporter back then, had arrived early with his cumbersome refrigeration size disk recording machine (tape recorders didn't become available until the 1950s). There was only one other worker in the room moving the tables and chairs around to get ready for the event. When Linkletter was finished setting up his equipment, he approached the man and asked if he knew who to speak to about getting a personal interview with Walt Disney once the formal presentation was finished.

"Well, I'm Walt Disney," came the response. "I always like to set up the room to suit the presentation I'm making."

"That's the kind of guy Walt was," Linkletter related during several talks at the 50th Anniversary of Disneyland's Happiest Celebration on Earth.

That San Francisco meeting began one of Walt's most personal relationships. Linkletter eventually had three of the hottest shows on radio – one each on each network – NBC, CBS, and ABC. Walt Disney was the undisputed leader in animation and later a producer of an increasing number of live-action films and TV programs. They were both powerful entertainment executives, but the Hollywood party circuit wasn't for them. Instead, their two families socialized together, did family camp-outs, and often traveled with or without their children. Their 26-year friendship lasted until Walt died.

One day at the office, the Tomart receptionist's voice came over the intercom, "Bill Justice is on the phone."

"Have you read *Walt Disney and Assorted Other Characters*," (by Jack Kinney) came Bill's excited voice over the phone. "You are always asking me about how things really were at the studio. THIS is how things were!"

Jack Kinney had been with Walt for 27 years, starting as an inbetweener in 1931. His book provided a candid look at how difficult and rewarding it could be working for Walt. In it, he relates brief anecdotes about hundreds of people who worked at the studio up until Walt became more interested in projects other than animation. The Kinney book not only told and illustrated how things were, but it broke the ice with Disney myth protectors. Subsequent books about Walt presented a more candid picture. It changed the direction of Bill's own book, *Justice for Disney*. His stories became more vivid and he too reasoned drawings would help illustrate them.

Fess Parker remembered one occasion when Walt kindly reminded him he was the boss. "There was a writer named Stan Jones who was a former park ranger. He became a composer and did a lot of the theme songs for John Ford movies. He wrote a little song called 'Ringle Rangle'. He and I used to sit around with a bottle of Jim Beam and our guitars. I enjoyed listening to Stan's music and learning his songs. One day I asked if I could see Walt and took my guitar in and I sang 'Ringle Rangle' for him.

"He said, 'We will just put it in the movie.'

"So we put 'Ringle Rangle' in *Westward Ho the Wagons*. It was the first film I did after Davy Crockett and the song sold half a million records. At some point, Buddy Epsen and I formed an ASCAP company called Musicland Publishing. This was Buddy's idea, but I became aware that the publishing rights were valuable. Walt came onto the sound stage one afternoon and I asked him, 'Do you suppose we could share 50/50 publishing rights of this song?'

"He said, 'No.'

"I said, 'Why not?'

"Well it is company policy."

"Who makes the policy?"

"I do."

Many sources report how tough it was in the Disney story department. If Walt wasn't pleased in a story meeting or pencil-test screening, silence was the first clue as he thought over what he saw and changes he might order. Often his thumb thumped the arm of the chair during this process. If he thumped slowly, he was contemplating changes he wanted to make. If the thumb pace was fast, he didn't like what he saw. When Walt spoke he enunciated with the skill of an accomplished actor. He was aided by piercing brown eyes, plus the arms and hands of an excited Italian. He made his point with passion in his voice, punctuating his thoughts with "Ya know, ya know." And you had to make sure you did know when he ended a sentence with, "Is that clear?" He had very expressive eyebrows and the left one typically shot up as he cogitated. In rare instances when he just didn't feel right about the story presentation, he would tell the story group to shelve the project, or just get up and leave the room. On the other hand, he gave his story teams the time they needed to come up with story developments. Walt was a firm believer in collaboration. Ideas and gags were the lifeblood of cartoons.

Ideas and constructive criticism were welcome, but everyone quickly learned not to criticize Walt's ideas even when asked. Everything started with getting the story right. Walt understood creative people. He knew pressure deadlines weren't always the way to get the best work from good people. He allowed time to do the job right, but there was always time to "fix" things. While his control might have been read as lax at times, he always knew what was going on. His after-hours and weekend inspections of work in progress were legendary. A sure sign Walt had been there in the early years was a trail of his Chesterfield cigarette butts. Later, they were distinctive dark brown hand-rolled cigarettes. Artists interpreted these clues as something only they picked up on, but Walt was smart enough to remove them had he not wanted the artists to know he was there. The main thing that counted with Walt was getting the job done the way he wanted.

Walt's persistent smoker's cough was the signal he was near during regular working hours. Everyone on the lot has a story about how that cough saved them for an embarrassing moment, often more than once. Ralph Kent was fond of telling how, "Whenever Walt visited Disneyland, the gate guard sent out a call to supervisors who passed the word along." When Walt stayed all night in his apartment above the firehouse, park cast members had only a short cough warning of his impending presence. It wasn't that employees feared a visit from Walt, they just wanted to have a few moments to collect their thoughts and anticipate what might be on his mind as to give a good account of themselves.

Walt wasn't very good at sports, but social and business aspects got he and Roy involved in polo with other Hollywood celebrities. Walt was in it more for his lifelong love of horses than the sport itself, but Roy always felt it was too dangerous for a person so important to the studio. Walt finally gave up polo after a serious injury that plagued him the remainder of his life.

Much has been written about Walt's railroading hobby and his Carolwood & Pacific one-eighth scale Lilly Belle steam train built at his Holmby Hills estate. The half-mile layout was built much to the dissatisfaction of Walt's wife, Lilly, who considered it a noisy eyesore in her personal Magic Kingdom of flower gardens and landscaping. The railroad only operated from around 1951 until it jumped the track in a tunnel and went out of control through the newly redecorated Disney living room wall. The line was closed down in 1953, but Walt soon had full-size locomotives to run at Disneyland.

Little mention has been made of Walt's lifelong interest in collecting miniatures. A middle room in his animation building office suite was filled with them. He constructed quite a few rooms precisely decorated with the correct scale miniatures. When furniture or accessories didn't exist, he made them. He was a stickler for detail and his rooms are a work of art in themselves. This hobby became a major factor in the development of scale models for set designs and theme park projects.

Walt Disney's demeanor was a mixed bag. There were days when it was best to keep out of his way. This type of day came to be described as one in which he "had his bear suit on." He could be very preoccupied as his mind worked through problems or ideas. One reason for his bear suit was to let people know he didn't want to be interrupted. Other times he was angry or worried. These traits were constant throughout his life as affirmed by all my close contacts from Ward Kimball to Ralph Kent.

Walt was big on developing gags, but not much for telling jokes. The studio was full of wild and wacky writers and artists. The atmosphere was loose enough that the "inmates," as employees called themselves, often pulled pranks on Walt. The Jack Kinney and Bill Justice books are full of them. They could often get Walt going, but being a smart guy, he'd eventually catch on and have a good laugh himself.

Ralph Kent tells the story about how his boss, Jack Olsen, got Walt to review work done the way he thought it should be, rather than the way Walt had requested. When Walt would stop by Olsen's office at Disneyland, Jack would leave enough of his version showing on his desk to make sure Walt could catch a glimpse of it. Olsen would then present the drawing as Walt had suggested and they would discuss it normally. When Walt asked about Jack's version on the desk, Jack would respond like it was nothing he needed to see, just some preliminary ideas he needed to get out of his system. Walt, of course, then demanded to look at the work Olsen wanted him to see. Had he presented it initially, Walt might have dismissed it right off or asked why he hadn't done as he directed. This way, he did what Walt

(Continued on page 113)

Photo courtesy of the Tomart Archives

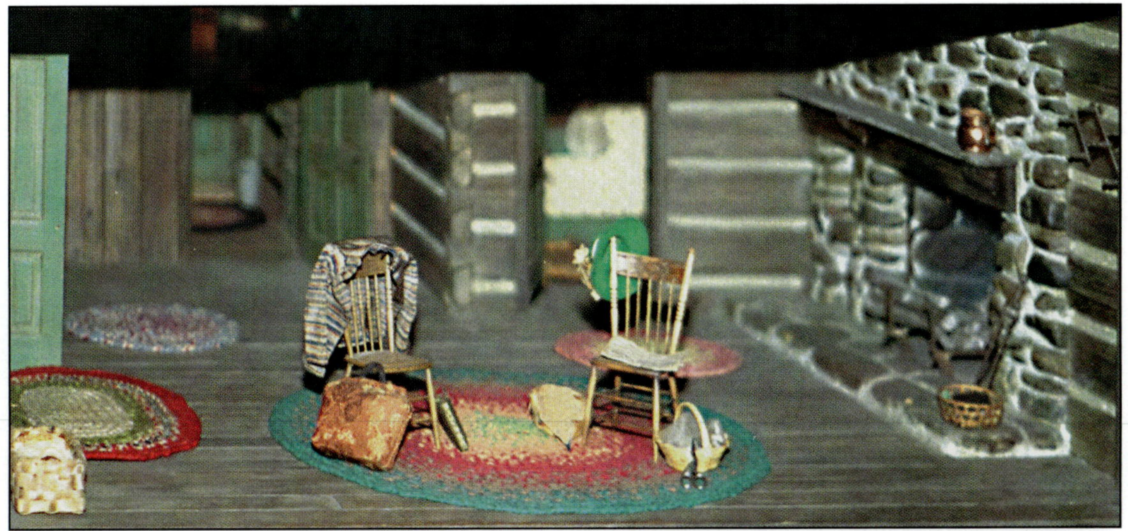

Above – Walt Disney's lifelong hobby was collecting miniatures. They were on display in one of his private offices at the studio and were used to construct rooms to scale. Every piece had to be exact. When Walt didn't own the correct piece he needed for a miniature room, he made it in his home workshop. The detail in his miniature rooms was often adapted to a detail in a film or at Disneyland. A collection of Walt's miniature rooms has traveled to museums around the world and are permanently housed at the Walt Disney Museum located in San Francisco's Persidio.

Below – This large print of the Walt Disney World plan was on the wall of every Contemporary and Polynesian Hotel room when the resort opened on October 1, 1971. They were removed as rooms were remodeled eight to ten years later and sold at Property Control for five dollars each.

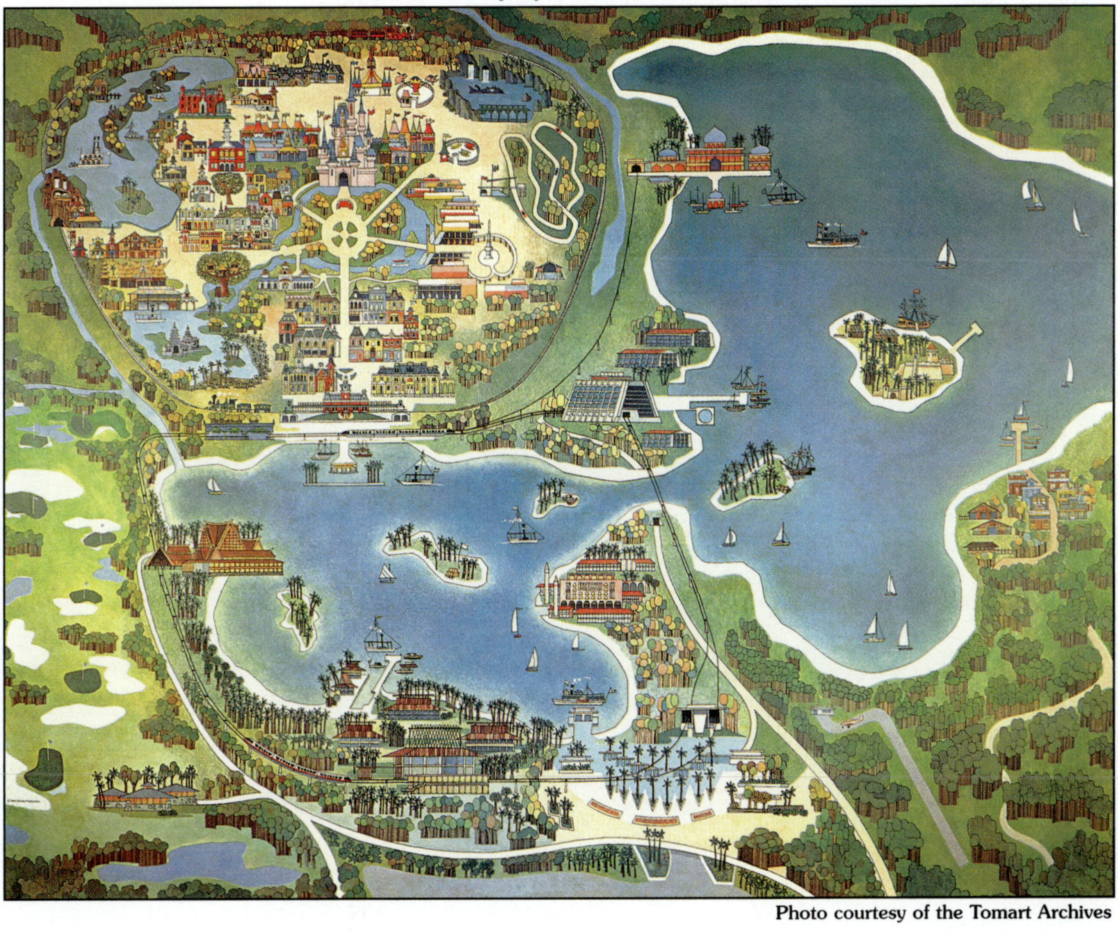

Photo courtesy of the Tomart Archives

All photos are from the Tomart Archives.

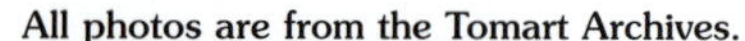

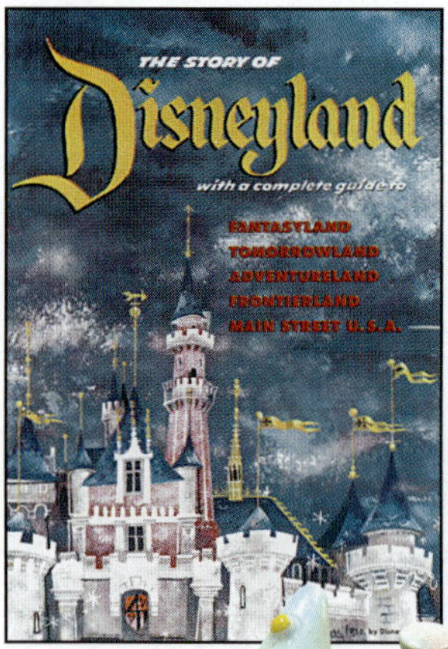

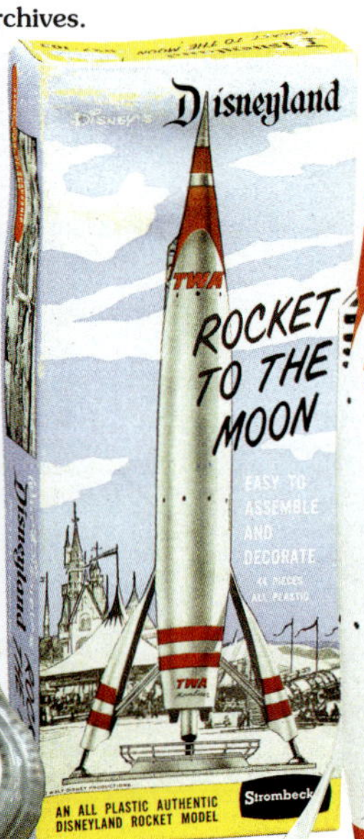

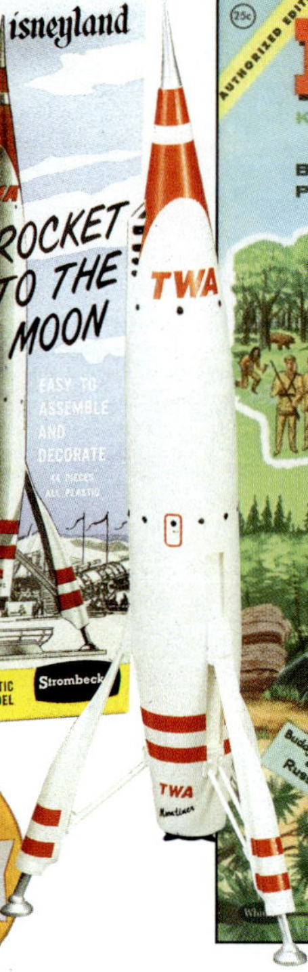

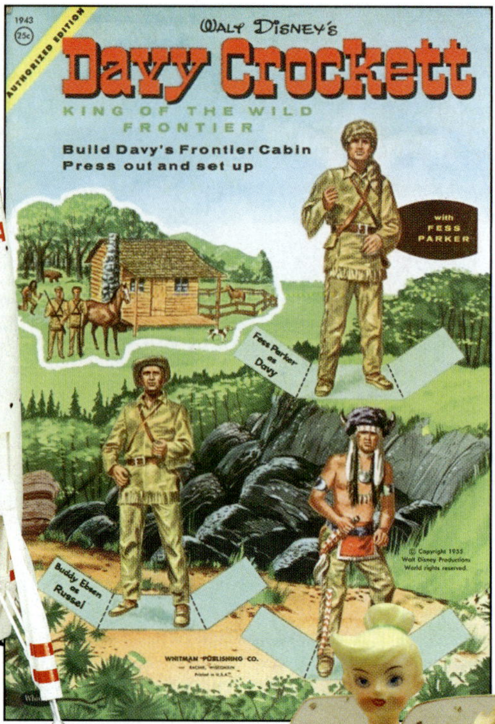

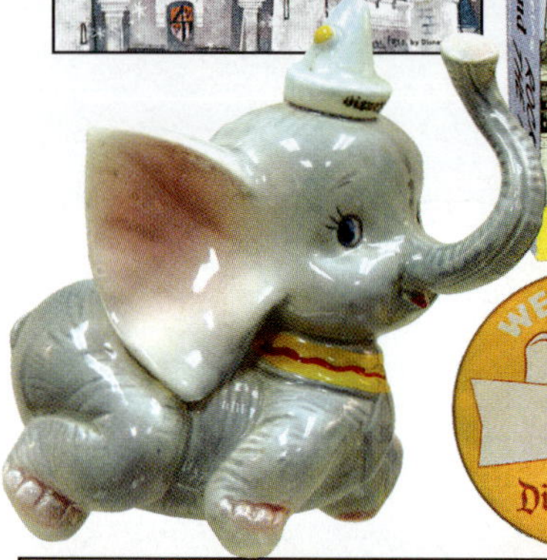

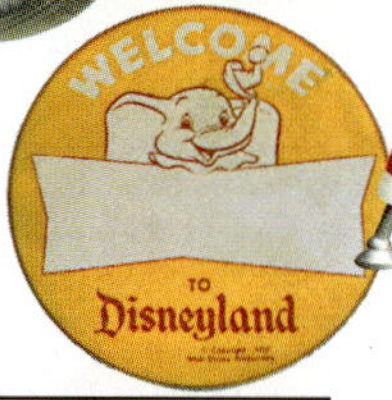

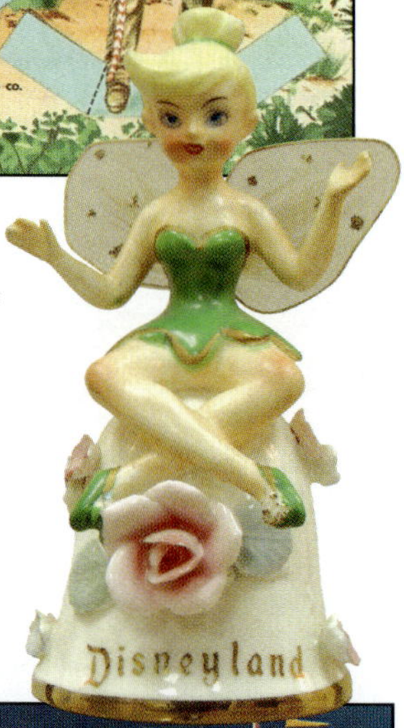

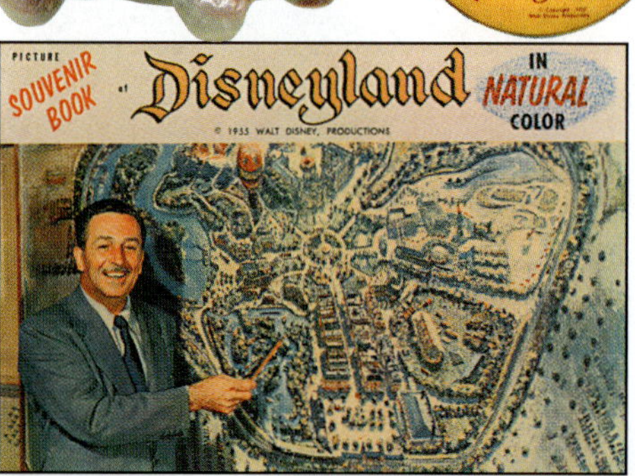

Exclusive park merchandise has played a vital role in the sucess of Disney theme parks since Disneyland's opening in 1955. Here is just a sampling of the souvenirs available in the very early years. A collection of this valuable memorabilia pieces together a facinating history of Walt's Disneyland.

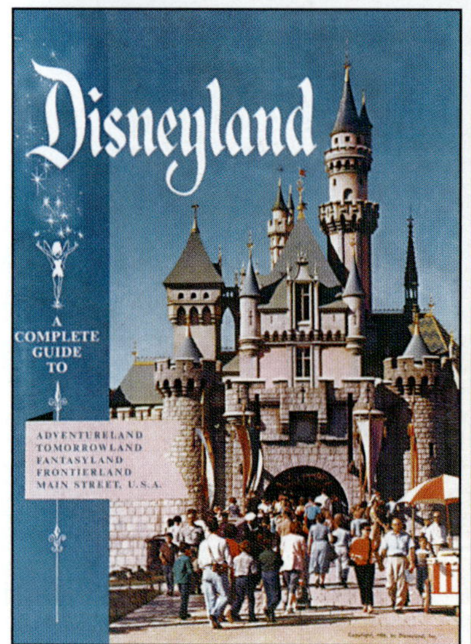

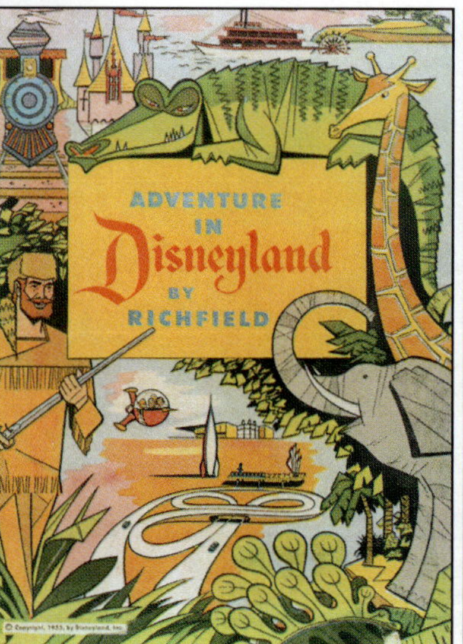

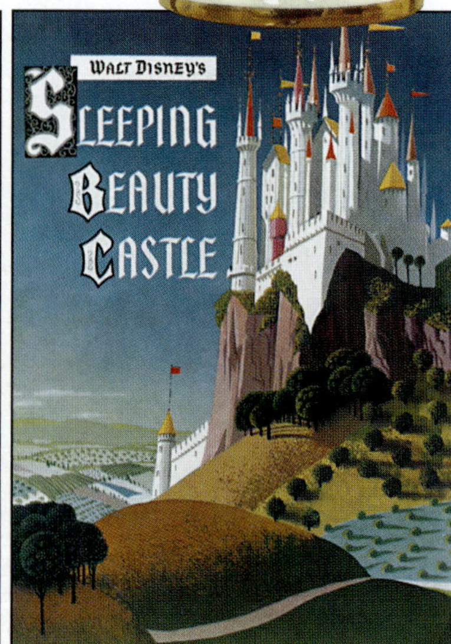

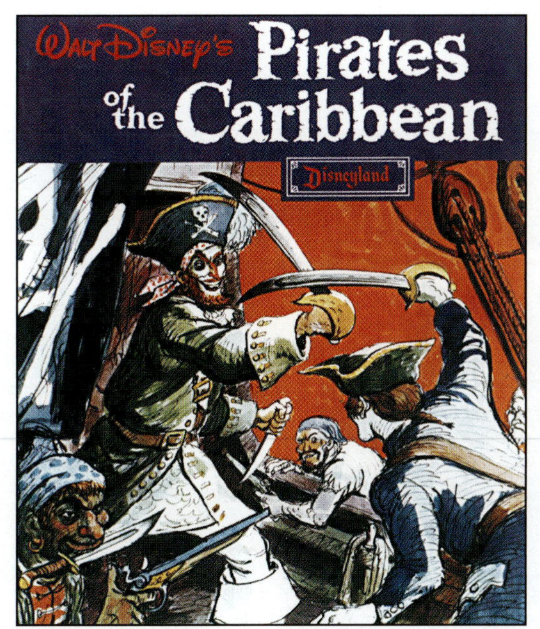

All photos are from the Tomart Archives.

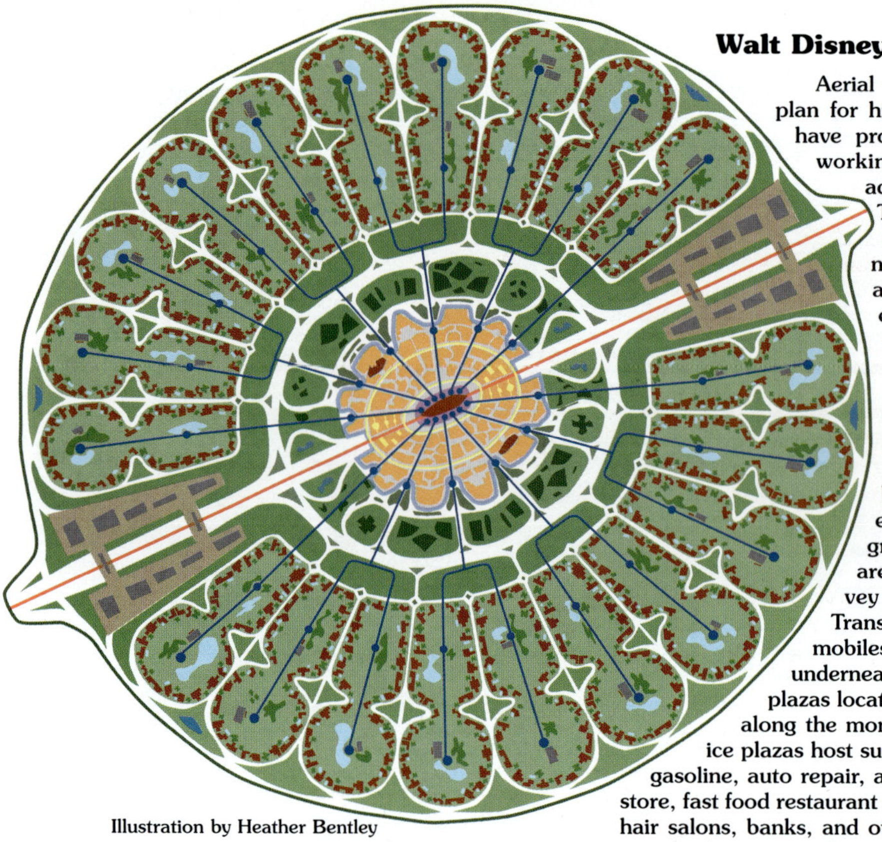

Illustration by Heather Bentley

Walt Disney's Concept Plan for His

Aerial view of Walt Disney's radial pod plan for his City of the Future that would have provided the most modern living, working, shopping, and recreation activities for 20,000 inhabitants. The light orange area is an environmentally controlled core business and international shopping area. On the edges of this enclosed center city are apartments for those who would want to live close to their work. A green belt surrounded these high-density living quarters. Schools, churches; health and recreation facilities dot the green belt. Pods of single-family homes encompass the core city and green belt in all directions. They are served by PeopleMovers to convey residents to the core Transportation Lobby. Personal automobiles can travel around each pod, underneath the center city, and to service plazas located at each end of the community along the monorail beam. These drive-in service plazas host supermarkets, discount stores, plus gasoline, auto repair, and tire centers. There is a bookstore, fast food restaurant farm, fitness center, dry cleaners, hair salons, banks, and other personal services and shopping facilities normally visited by car.

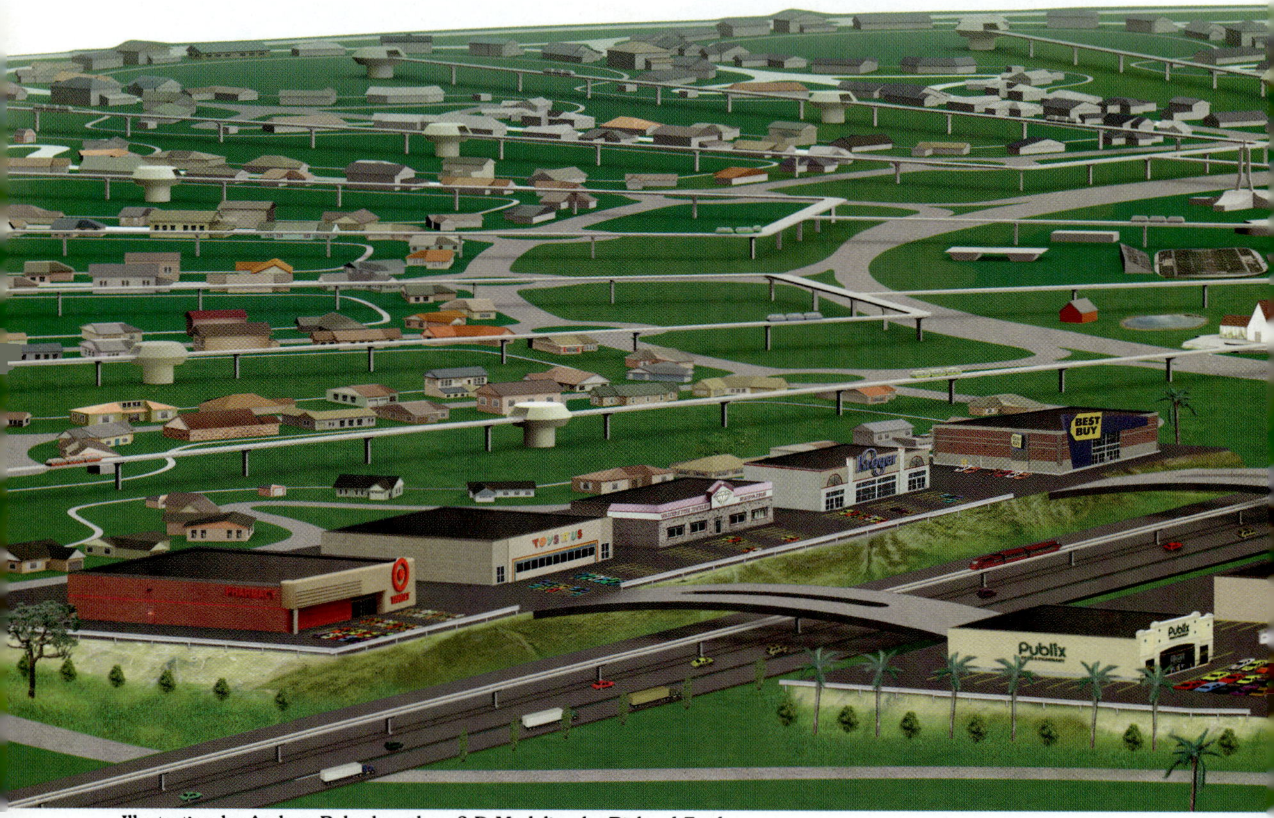

Illustration by Andrew Bako based on 3-D Modeling by Richard Zryd.

Experimental Prototype Community of Tomorrow

The architectural rendering at the bottom of these two pages provides a three-dimensional look at Walt's City of the Future. The center piece is the enclosed environmentally controlled business and international shopping district. This was to be a high-end mall with a 600 room hotel at the center. The latest fashions, technologies, and newest designs for household goods, and similar products would be available there. A wide variety of office space, a civic center, restaurants, and roving entertainers would be found throughout. Connected to this core city would have been several apartment buildings over-looking the green belt. No cars would be needed to travel from any living unit in EPCOT to the central Transportation Lobby for access to the monorail system or PeopleMovers to reach any other pod in the community.

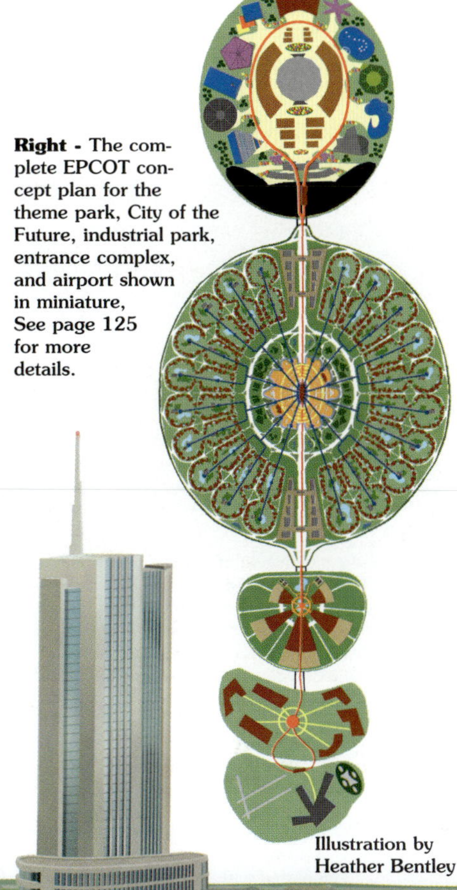

Right - The complete EPCOT concept plan for the theme park, City of the Future, industrial park, entrance complex, and airport shown in miniature, See page 125 for more details.

Illustration by Heather Bentley

Above - Transportation Lobby Hub where to Monorail converges with PeopleMover Stations and the center city hotel entrance.

Photo by Tom Tumbusch

Above – Universe of Energy pavilion in EPCOT's Future World is a prime example of Walt's plan for his city of the future. It incorporates roof-top solar energy panels to provide the electrical needs for the ride transportation, audio-animatronics, projection systems, and lighting throughout the building.

Below – The Horizons pavilion in EPCOT's Future World before it was razed to make room for Mission: SPACE .
Right – Giant mural displayed in the lobby of Horizons. Unfortunately, this large work was eliminated with the pavilion.

Photo by Tom Tumbusch

Photo by Tom Tumbusc

Dreamfinder and Figment as they were seen in the original Imagination attraction at EPCOT Center.

The World Bazaar at Tokyo Disneyland that replaces the Main Street shop district at other Disney theme parks. The challenge of a colder-climate location was solved by Walt Disney Imagineering.

Mermaid Lagoon "land" at Tokyo DisneySEA, the second Japanese theme park located adjacent to Tokyo Disneyland.

Photo by Amy Stelmack

Photo by Barry Koper

Tokyo Disneyland dancer appearing in the 15th Anniversary Celebration. Parades and shows at this first Disney theme park outside the United States are changed every four to six months to add new excitement and attract guests from a smaller geographical area.

Photo by Amy Stelmack

Walt Disney's commitment to excellence has been reflected in the manicured grounds of the Burbank Studio, his motion pictures, theme parks, and character merchandise. The traditions he and Roy Disney established have been carried on in new theme parks around the world, the highly sucessful Disney Cruise Line, and many other facets of the Walt Disney Company. Rarely have two brothers and their staff done so much to entertain so many millions of people all over the globe.

Photo by Hugo Stevens

Pin of Sleeping Beauty's Castle from Disneyland Paris, which opened as EuroDisney in 1992. The name was changed in 1994.

Opening day Hong Kong Disneyland September 2005.

The Disney Magic, flagship of the Disney Cruise Line, sailing in the Pacific Ocean.

Photo from the Disney Cruise Line press kit © The Walt Disney Company

Photo by Tom Tumbusch

(Continued from page 104)

requested and still got his personal ideas across. "Jack and Walt were a lot alike," Ralph Kent reported. "They had tremendous respect for each other."

"Mr. Disney is my father. Just call me Walt," was the normal response to anyone calling him anything formal. Annette Funicello told me she could never bring herself to call her boss Uncle Walt as did the other Mouseketeers. He was always Mr. Disney to her.

Key employees I got to know casually spoke of Walt Disney with guarded words. They remained protectors of his image long after his death. The perception of what one person considers a negative often is nothing more than a clue to the person's human nature. Eventually, true feelings came out. No Walt Disney employee interviewed disliked or thought anything ill of their boss. Most related tales about Walt's moods and Walt's perceived need to keep things unbalanced and how that made working at the studio more complex.

A reporter interviewing Walt once asked him how many people worked for him. He thought for a moment and replied, "About half." He was quick on his feet in response to questions, but Walt's personal sense of humor was characterized as "rural" by a group of employees in a media interview. It was a polite way of saying it wasn't very sophisticated.

The Disney staff of key personnel was almost exclusively male. This fact has led some to call Walt sexist. Many women worked in the Ink and Paint Department, and as secretaries, assistants, color stylists, background painters, costume designers, and in similar positions. There were few women doing actual story, design, and animation, but mainly women filled lower paying jobs. The animation building's Penthouse Club was open only to men. So the evidence points to some bias toward men. This, however, was not a trait exclusive to Walt Disney or his organization. During the '30s very few women worked. Society and the majority of women themselves viewed their place as taking care of children and the home.

World War II brought dramatic change. "Rosie the Riveter" became the icon of the women who worked to support the war machine at home while the men went off to do battle. They filled many other roles, too, and it became fashionable for women to work. Hazel George, the company nurse, was one of Walt's most trusted studio confidants. He had two long-time secretaries whom he also valued highly, but as a businessman he knew a woman could be expected to have an interrupted work history to have children. His personal family values understood their first priority was to the home. As society adjusted, so did Walt and his organization.

Ken Anderson, an art director on *Snow White and the Seven Dwarfs* and many other important Disney animated films, was also a gardener. Walt came into Anderson's office one day and asked him to ride down to Disneyland to discuss Walt's ideas for living bonsai trees and miniature plants in what turned out to be the Storybook Land attraction in Fantasyland. Interstate 5 was not yet complete and the roads were similar to rural country highways that you still find off the beaten path today. "Walt was driving his green Cadillac and sitting half turned toward me in the driver's seat describing his horticulture vision for this new attraction." Anderson recalled. "Without any malice, Walt ran another driver off the road. The guy was steamed and came racing after us and purposely cut in front of us, almost causing an accident.

"Come on Walt, let's go after that guy and get this thing straightened out. We meant him no harm."

"No need of that, Ken. Besides he may be a Disney customer."

Walt was more than just a casual boss. He got to know his people, their hobbies, likes, and dislikes. He cast his people to animate characters befitting their own personalities. He separated artists into background painters, story developers, animators, and eventually, Imagineers. He grouped animators into teams or units and often remarked how one unit was doing better than another. It was his way of giving praise without doing it directly and another way he kept his staff on its toes.

Animator Bill Tytla once related a story about his work on *Pinocchio*. He had been assigned the job of animating scenes with Stromboli. "It was a character I was excited about and was pleased with my work. I showed my drawings around to other animators. They all thought they were great and gave their praise. In the sweatbox later, with Walt, he commented it was a helluva scene, but that he expected better of me. He wasn't unkind and gave no specifics, just that the work wasn't passed. I was crushed and couldn't draw for days. Then it hit me and I started over. When I showed the new animation to Walt he said, "Great! Just what I was expecting." Tytla resigned from the studio shortly after the animation strike and regretted his decision to walk out for the remainder of his life. He loved working for Walt and the roles he played in Disney films.

Harvey Kamins worked in the print shop at Universal. The Disney Studio was gearing up for a big promotion and asked other studios for help as has been a long-standing Hollywood tradition. Universal loaned Harvey and another worker to the Disney lot for the two requested weeks. Soon after they arrived, Walt was there in the Disney print shop to greet them. Walt introduced himself. They chatted for a while before Walt said, "If you guys need anything while you're here, just call my secretary and I'll see you get whatever you need. Thanks for helping us out." Kamins was subsequently loaned to other studios and production companies as he rose up through the ranks of Universal, "But nothing like Walt's visit ever happened anywhere else."

Walt's attention to detail was aided by a great memory. Ralph Kent wrote to Walt Disney when he was only eight years old. It was back when he lived in Buffalo, New York and was known as Ralph Kwiatkowski (he had his name officially shortened when he was discharged from the military). Walt happened to see the letter on his correspondence secretary's desk and decided to reply himself. Many years later on a company plane flight to Denver, Ralph Kent mentioned he once wrote to Walt as a child and he had answered personally. Walt responded, "Are you that kid from Buffalo with the long name? Why in the hell didn't you tell me before this?" Many people interviewed remarked about how Walt could recall the smallest details years later.

You never knew when another chance meeting would lead to more insight to Walt Disney. At a special preview for Disneyland's Toontown a voice came out of the shadows; "Hey Tom," Paula Lowery, formerly of the Disney Archives, called from the Trolley. "I want you to meet someone. This is Richard Sherman." Most readers know of the prolific music work he and his brother, Robert, did for Disney films, World's Fair attractions, and theme parks. For the next hour or so, we bumped along on that Trolley talking about how we missed meeting each other in New York when the Sherman Brothers were doing *Over Here!*, a musical they had written for the Andrews Sisters. New York is big, but the theatrical district is small. We knew many of the same people, but our paths never crossed. The conversation got around to working with Walt and Sherman related several interesting stories.

When asked how he and his brother came to work for Walt, Sherman flashed a broad smile and related how Jimmy Johnson, head of Disney's music operations, had hired them to write a song for Annette to sing in a live-action film, *The Horsemasters*. "We had no idea we would be presenting it to Walt Disney for approval. When we met him, he started to tell us *The Parent Trap* story. Jimmy Johnson was as confused as we were. My brother finally broke in and mentioned we had been working on a song for *The Horsemasters*. 'Why didn't you stop me earlier, let's hear what you got,' Walt replied without missing beat. We thought we were dead, but played the 'Strummin' Song.' Walt just looked out the window. When we finished he said, 'That'll work!' Then he called to his secretary, Tommie Wilck, to give us a script for what became *The Parent Trap*. 'Since I spent all that time telling you about this one, why don't you try to come up with a title song for it?' Walt said as he handed us the script. It was an interesting first meeting. We weren't quite sure it went over that well. I guess we expected more than 'That'll work,' but we later learned that was Walt's way," Sherman added.

"Walt also changed how we were credited for our work. Before our Disney days we were always known as Bob Sherman and Dick Sherman. One day Walt suggested we should become Robert and Richard, because 'It's more dignified!' We added our middle initials and have been known as Richard M. Sherman and Robert B. Sherman ever since."

The most poignant of Richard Sherman's stories was the fact that Walt Disney would actually get tired. Often at the end of the day, he would ask the Sherman brothers to come to the piano in his office. He had them brief him on their current projects but then there was always a musical request. They knew the request without asking. It was "Feed the Birds" from

Mary Poppins – Walt's favorite song. On occasion, he would have us in and simply say, 'Play the song' and we knew what he meant.

"Walt was such a delight to work with. If Walt liked it and said it would be in the movie, it was in the movie. Nobody else could change his decision. You knew you had a winner when his face would light up with child-like appreciation. It was a joyful collaboration," Sherman added.

Chuck Jones, once a Disney animator, who became a leading creative force behind the Warner Brothers cartoon studio, described the working conditions at Warner as a "termite-infested old house" in his book, *The Life and Times of an Animated Cartoonist*. Walt tried to get Jones to stay at Disney, but gave up when Jones admitted the only job that would keep him there was Walt's. Walt replied, "That job is already taken."

Walt's mind worked all waking hours. An inspiration would prompt a phone call to employees from wherever he was with little heed to the clock. Ward Kimball, and undoubtedly many others, became irritated at receiving calls at all hours. So after a while whenever Walt called, the conversation began like this…

Kimball: "Hello"

Walt: "Hello. Ward, this is Walt."

Kimball: (easily recognizing the voice) "Walt, who?"

Walt: (agitated) "Walt DISNEY! Who else do you know named Walt?"

Ward reported Walt would get a little miffed at times, but then he seemed to get the message and magically the calls began to decrease.

One day in the late '40s the phone rang in Ward's office. It was Walt, but this time he didn't give Ward the chance to pull his standard gag. "Hey Kimball, do you have a train depot for the backyard railroad of yours?" "No," came Ward's response. "Well, you do now," and Walt hung up. The next day a studio crew unloaded the disassembled train station set from *So Dear to My Heart* in Ward's driveway. Ward had to add a roof and a back wall when he reconstructed it in his backyard, but this gift from Walt remained one of his most prized possessions. He used it to display old railroad memorabilia such as signal lanterns, switch keys, old photographs framed on the wall, a potbellied stove, conductor badges, and hats.

Ward enjoyed a special place among Walt's animators. Walt chose Ward to travel to the 1948 Chicago Railroad Fair with him…the only time he selected a single animator to travel with him on a strictly pleasure outing. Ward and Walt's intellects seems to mesh on most subjects. Yet, there were still occasions when Walt had to prove he was the boss. For instance, Ward was set to direct *Babes in Toyland*, but when Walt suggested Annette and Tommy Sands for the lead roles, Ward hastened a spontaneous reaction – "Oh no, Walt, not them." The next day Ward Kimball was removed from having anything to do with the picture.

Walt Disney was the undeniable boss of the studio, but he leaned heavily on Roy's financial and business expertise. Both drew decent salaries all through the thirties and forties, but neither sought publicity like other Hollywood studio heads. They remained simple mid-westerners all their lives.

Once Disneyland was a success, Walt could have dined in fine restaurants every meal. His whole family preferred eating at home. Walt traditionally took the girls to school in the morning and arrived home around 7:30 for a late dinner. Chili and beans were his favorite meal and a good supply of it traveled with him on business or pleasure trips.

There were occasional dinner parties at the Disney home for a small circle of family and friends. The annual Motion Picture Academy and Television Emmy Awards almost always had Disney Productions in nomination. Walt and sometimes Lilly routinely attended these major events along with those responsible for the nominated work. Walt's normal workweek included a lighter workload on Saturday, frequent studio visits on Sundays, and script work at home many evenings. The family also enjoyed many opportunities to travel and always went first-class.

When Walt traveled, he was presented with awards and tributes from all over the world. Artisans went to great lengths to create special awards to please a man they admired so much. A sampling of these awards were once on display in the Walt Disney Story attraction at Walt Disney World and are now on perminant display at the Disney Family Foundation museum in San Francisco.

In retrospect, Walt was more simple than complicated. He could envision what he wanted clearer than most. He was committed to the collaborative approach to story development and production within his vision. He was the boss, one who grew to manage individualistic creative types better than any formal education could teach. Studio hiring practices were strictly defined to employ people who could function and grow within the structure Walt's research and experience found to work best. Finances for the first 35 years the company existed were extremely tight. Still, the quality of the Disney hallmark was always the absolute best that talent and technology could provide.

The person who met with Walt most often; the person who knew and understood him best of all was his brother, Roy. They didn't "walk" together much. Each had his individual path to travel…Walt the creative wrangling; Roy taking care of all the business details. Walt took home the awards; Roy led the applause.

Roy's staff marveled at the perfect casting for the role Roy elected to play. He also had a creative flare as he proved when making the decisions to complete Disney World after Walt's death. He loved his brother and respected all that his brother went through to accomplish what he achieved.

Walt's life was in the spotlight. Roy was content to operate in the background. Newer employees often didn't know about Roy or that they had formed the company together. The result is a great Roy story. It is reported in different ways by people who knew Roy. The various tellings have a common thread which goes something like this: Roy is out walking on Disney property and encounters an employee unfamiliar with him. He offers a suggestion regarding the task that he was performing, to the point where the person asked if he thinks he is god. He replied, "No...I'm God's brother!" It's a great story and a great line. There was probably more than one opportunity to use it. Roy's response is not only funny, but says a lot about the way he viewed his relationship and esteem for his brother.

There are statues of both brothers at Disneyland and the Magic Kingdom at Walt Disney World. The bronze life-size sculpture of Roy sits on a bench beside a statue of Minnie under the flagpole in Town Square. People rush by up Main Street toward Sleeping Beauty's or Cinderella's Castle, but pause to have their pictures taken in front of the statue of Walt and Mickey. Roy and Minnie together – they had the supporting roles, but in this book they are all stars.

To this day, Walt still holds the spotlight; one Roy Disney gladly yielded his entire life. After his death Roy summed up his brother's career this way, "In everything he did, my brother had an intuitive way of reaching out and touching the hearts and minds of young and old alike." And no matter how much risk and financial aband Walt could dish out, Roy remained his partner and biggest fan.

Chapter IX – Project X

*"There's enough land here to hold all the ideas and plans
we could possibly imagine."*

—*Walt Disney*

"There will never be another Disneyland," was the standard reply to requests or suggestions regarding a second Disney theme park.

Privately, Walt was always bothered by what he called all the "Las Vegas honky tonk" developments that sprang up around Disneyland. The Disneys had sanctioned the Disneyland Hotel built by the Wrather Corporation, but had no control over the motels and shops built along the adjacent streets of Harbor Boulevard and Katella Avenue.

Entrepreneur Jack Wrather was a personal friend of Walt Disney and the Disneys owned land across West Street, on which they permitted Wrather to build a number of two-story motel buildings (since removed) and eventually the three existing tower buildings. The monorail ride was extended to the Disneyland Hotel in 1961 to make it the preferred hotel for visitors. Over the years, many of the offending buildings have been purchased, displaced by the development of the Anaheim Convention Center, or remodeled to meet stricter zoning standards imposed by the City of Anaheim.

However, little changed during Walt's lifetime and the subject remained a constant irritation. That discontent sowed the seeds that eventually grew into the decision to proceed with some type of Disney theme park located east of the Mississippi River.

Once Disneyland's Tomorrowland expansion was completed in 1959, plans began to be laid for a second park known at the time as Project X. The path to the announcement of a second U.S. theme park may appear convoluted at first glance, but every step was calculated toward its achievement.

Up to that point, the Disney organization took on several special event presentations including major football game halftime shows, Olympic events, and Rose Bowl festivities to help prepare for bigger events to come. In 1958, the General Electric Company approached the Disney organization to develop its pavilion for the 1964-65 New York World's Fair. The company wanted to demonstrate the progress electrical energy had contributed to everyday living conditions for the American family over the previous generations. The concept they described clicked in Walt's brain. Back in the early planning stages for Disneyland, he conceived ideas for animating human figures with some success. One of WED's earliest projects was to create a miniature dancing man. Walt had filmed Buddy Ebsen tap dancing in front of a measured grid wall to study the dance movement they needed to replicate in robotic action. The system was purely mechanical and a bit rough, but it worked. Work proceeded on a miniature barbershop quartet. It was also successful, but the synchronized mouth movement was not life-like enough for Walt's satisfaction. Rapid wear on the thin rubber face masks available at the time was also a problem.

Robotics continued to be studied and simple mechanical cam and lever systems were used to animate the creatures inhabiting Disneyland's Jungle Cruise and Nature's Wonderland attractions.

Long before land purchases began, Walt had been considering attractions that would make Disneyland East different from the original. One prime location being considered was around Washington, D.C. due to the area's high population density and proximity to Philadelphia, Baltimore, and New York. The location prompted the idea for a robotic Hall of Presidents. President Abraham Lincoln was selected as the experimental prototype for the project. The solenoid, invented during World War II, came to the attention of WED Imagineers. The device allowed electrical energy to be converted into mechanical energy. This, plus more durable rubberized plastics now available, eliminated problems with thinner latex face masks. Work on Walt's Audio-Animatronics system finally moved ahead at full speed.

The Disneyland Enchanted Tiki Room birds and plants were the first to use the system in 1963, but the human form was yet to be perfected. An attempt at a Confucius figure for a proposed Chinese restaurant at Disneyland was scrapped along with the project.

Robert Moses, organizer of the 1964-65 World's Fair, visited WED in 1963 and was shown the prototype of Lincoln. He stated he wouldn't open the fair without it and convinced the State of Illinois to sponsor the exhibit. There were still glitches in the Lincoln figure, but Walt and WED Imagineers vowed to have it ready in time for the Fair's opening. They did, and Lincoln functioned flawlessly at WED's Glendale headquarters. Audio-Animatronics also became the basis for the G.E. exhibit, named Progressland, as well.

When Lincoln was set up in New York, he stubbornly refused to move. It took weeks of troubleshooting to discover the source. The nearby Tower of Light was causing sudden and unpredictable power surges. WED Imagineers were among the first to discover how the rapid on/off electronic cycles of copiers, computers, and the increasing number of other electronic gadgets were beginning to corrupt the formerly steady flow of electrical power. Once this problem was resolved, Lincoln worked perfectly.

Moses' enthusiasm for Walt's audio-animatronics system helped Disney sell two more World's Fair exhibitors.

The company ended up providing four pavilions for fair participants – The State of Illinois sponsored "Great Moments with Mr. Lincoln"; "The Magic Skyway" carried visitors back to prehistoric times in a new car for the Ford Motor Company; "The Carousel of Progress" retraced the use of electricity in the American home for General Electric; and "It's a Small World" captured the spirit of children around the world for the Pepsi-Cola Company and UNICEF. These sponsor-paid attractions were all moved, in whole or in part, to Disneyland following the close of the fair. A fifth attraction was a result of the Ford exhibit. The "WEDway Peoplemover" was created to move the 160 new Ford convertibles along the Magic Skyway and a modified system was installed in Disneyland's Tomorrowland.

Ralph Kent remembered how the World's Fair also affected the Pirates of the Caribbean attraction already under construction at Disneyland, "It had been planned as a Madame Tussaud's Wax Museum type walk-through presentation. The steel had already been erected, but the success of the Small World boat ride at Flushing Meadows prompted Walt to order the ride systems for Pirates switched to the boats currently used."

Walt had concerns about his East Coast audience. A lot had happened since he made the cover of TIME Magazine in December 1937, and many of his East Coast intellectual supporters had abandoned him. His strong anti-communist activities hurt him as well.

The New York press was also against the World's Fair promoter, Robert Moses, and published negative stories about the fair during its entire New York run. Providing exhibits for the World's Fair gave Walt the opportunity to showcase the Disney family entertainment and study his East Coast audience. Despite all the negative publicity about the fair, visitor polls revealed that the Disney pavilions were extremely positive. Walt always ranked higher with his actual audience than with the critical press. Any reservations Walt may have had about Disneyland East were dispelled by the Disney experience at the 1964-65 New York World's Fair.

The Florida Project was top secret. Planning, done under the code name Project X, had been in the works for several years. Many sites for a second theme park were considered. An area around St. Louis received strong consideration. Niagra Falls was studied, as was the previously mentioned, Washington, D.C., before the planners zeroed in on central Florida near Orlando. Several dummy companies were set up to buy the land needed. Real estate agents, then the banks and newspapers tried to find out who was buying so much land. Unsuccessful, they began to speculate. Once the Disney name surfaced during a studio press junket, the company became the first choice as the logical buyer. No other company or developer seemed to have the wherewithal or the reason to acquire over 43.5 square miles of land. The land, however, was only optioned contingent on certain zoning, code, and regulation changes. Disney's plan called for the creation of The Reedy Creek Improvement District, excluding it from other county zoning, building codes, and government regulations. Reedy Creek would collect state and local sales taxes and contribute to certain infrastructure improvements, but it would be largely free of other governmental control. This required special state legislation, but Florida saw what Disney could do for the state and the company got what it wanted. Reedy Creek was one of the smartest moves the Disney brothers ever pulled off and it became highly controversial in later years. The land purchases were then concluded.

There were a few isolated parcels within the 43.5 square miles that refused to sell. One in the heart of the property near Downtown Disney was developed as a hotel resort not owned by the company. Others are still maintained as private residences in isolated areas.

Staffing up for the Florida Project was a major undertaking. The Disney Brothers prepared by buying a huge entertainment complex in Denver called the Celebrity Sports Center. It was built as an investment by Art Linkletter with Jack Benny, Burl Ives, and Joan Crawford. The complex had an inside Olympic-size swimming pool with a glass wall providing a spectacular view of the Rocky Mountain peaks. There were 48 bowling lanes which Disney eventually expanded to 90. Food was supplied by a gourmet restaurant, lounge, and a pizza and beer cafe, plus small snack shops throughout. Disney also expanded the video arcade area and installed the largest slot-car racing tables ever built by Aurora. This was the training ground for a large team of operational managers preparing to move to the Florida Project when the time came.

Walt Disney was personally involved in testing various aspects of the Celebrity Sports Center. Ralph Kent was made art director on the project and accompanied Walt on many flights to Denver on the company's Grumman Gulfstream airplane. "Sometimes Walt just wanted to get away to think for awhile," Kent remembered. "He'd do some work on the plane, but usually we would just talk. Businesswise, we discussed Project X a lot during the site-selection process. Walt was big on St. Louis and Washington, D.C., but the better year-round climate and existing tourism of Florida became the deciding factors. EPCOT was the main topic on our trips once the site was chosen.

"We always stayed at the Cherry Creek Inn located next to the Sports Center," Kent recalled. "Walt would register as Mr. Smith or Mr. Jones. The desk clerks knew who he was and just winked at him. Can you imagine the most creative guy in the world registering as Mr. Smith or Mr. Jones?

"Many of Walt's plans for EPCOT were used in the design and construction of EPCOT Center. World Showcase derived concepts from Walt's planning. The World's Fair influenced Walt regarding the World Showcase. It always bothered him that the big rich countries had the larger pavilions at Worlds Fairs, while the smaller poorer countries had little ones. He wanted them all to have equal façades in his EPCOT plans. Each was to have the same size piece of the pie in front so as not to overpower any other country. They could develop as much as they wanted behind the frontage. His desire was for each individual country to display the latest technology unique to that country.

"I remembered a project Walt had me working on while I was still working at Disneyland," Kent stated. "It was 1963 and Walt asked me to get the Disneyland Main Street elevations from Engineering and cut silhouettes for all the buildings. The instructions were to start at the railroad station and end at the castle. I was to lay out the silhouettes so each building was a little higher. A whole story level had to be gained in the distance to the castle. Walt took my work to Engineering and they analyzed everything in scale. I had no idea what it was for and Walt didn't explain. Later, I learned he was planning what became the basement level at Walt Disney World – two years before the project was announced. The idea was to have guests walking uphill without realizing it. A study revealed they may have not have realized the climb, but guests, particularly older ones, would feel it and get tired. Instead of the gradual adjustment, there is a faster climb at the base of the monorail or when departing water transportation. The hill is gotten quickly out-of-the-way in the distance to the railroad station. The whole Main Street area is on the second level with the main tunnel running under the street. The East Coast Victorian architecture is also subtly different from Disneyland. The buildings are taller to accommodate office space or storage areas on a third level.

"Walt also picked the location for the Magic Kingdom at the deepest part of the property. He said he knew its success was a given," Kent added.

Walt Disney had envisioned two major components for what he called Disney World's Magic Kingdom or a second Disneyland and EPCOT, his Experimental Prototype Community of Tomorrow. The two main reasons he wanted so much land were to keep the Las Vegas honky tonk far away, and to allow for EPCOT, his City of the Future. The remaining land in the master plan was set aside for a shopping center and future development.

Disney World formally became public knowledge on November 15, 1965. The countdown began for the announced opening October 1, 1971. Only the theme park and surrounding hotels were presented and discussed at this time.

Early in 1966 Walt made his position clear to his top executives, artists, and other key employees: he was confident in their ability to carry on with animation, live-action productions, TV, and theme park operations. His heart was now in the Florida Project.

The Magic Kingdom was the easy part. It would be larger than Disneyland and have some exclusive attractions and many modifications. The single entrance, Railway Station, and Main Street USA would remain much the same. Cinderella's Castle would be much larger and elevated. The central hub would have a Crystal Palace to the left and a major approach to

Tomorrowland on the right. All the lands would be larger as well. Liberty Square would be the first land of its type added to a Disney theme park. A huge Space Mountain (an indoor roller coaster in the dark) was in the master plan, but was not completed until the third year of operation.

The Magic Kingdom was to be linked to resort hotels and the main Transportation and Ticket Center via high-speed monorail trains. An armada of ships, the 7th largest navy in the world, was planned to shuttle guests around Phase One recreation areas. Unseen by guests were elaborate systems to provide invisible delivery of food and merchandise and to literally suck all the waste to a central treatment plant. It was to be a vacation kingdom of the future and it ended up happening almost exactly as Walt planned.

Much of the planning for Project X had been done secretly at WED Enterprises before the public announcement. In another locked room, at the rear of Walt's suite of offices at the studio, planning of a different sort had been taking place. Only Walt's secretaries, two confidants, and invited guests sworn to secrecy were admitted. The two men Walt selected for his top secret, yet unnamed project, were Marvin Davis, a planner who caught Walt's attention, and William E. "Joe" Potter, a retired Army general and former governor of the Panama Canal Zone, who was Robert Moses' second in command for the New York World's Fair. No one at the studio was to know what was going on in that room, especially Roy Disney. Walt knew what his brother's response would be and he needed time to gather all the facts and do preliminary planning before inviting his brother in to learn the second reason they purchased so much land in Florida. One of the reports Davis prepared on the project included the phrase "experimental prototype community of tomorrow." One night in the summer of 1966 Walt found it difficult to sleep. Suddenly a light bulb clicked on in his head. He sat up in bed and exclaimed out loud, "EPCOT!"

His plans for a "city of the future" had a name. The final pieces fell together for his presentation to Roy. As usual, Roy thought the idea was too vast and unworkable, but a press conference was held in early fall of 1966 to detail Walt's plans for EPCOT. On his deathbed, Walt made Roy promise his exact plans for EPCOT were to be completed. And Roy did try. In 1967, he published a booklet entitled *Project Florida / A Whole New Disney World*. It explained the second Magic Kingdom using photos of Disneyland attractions to be repeated in Florida, but mainly it showed Walt's planning for EPCOT to which he devoted the majority of his time the last months of his life. The booklet began with this quote: "With the technical know-how of American industry and the creative imagination of the Disney organization, I'm confident we can build a living showcase that more people will talk about and come to look at than any other area of the World." – Walt Disney. His urban plan for a whole new way of living within a totally planned community was designed for 20,000 people, plus tourists. It was a radial pod design built around a central city hub similar to the central plaza at Disney theme parks. The focal point was a 600 room high-rise hotel built atop a transportation lobby connecting the community to a 1,000 acre industrial park, entrance complex, jet port and second theme park. PeopleMovers radiated out from central monorail stations to various pods within each major complex. The need for automobiles would be largely eliminated.

There were several different types of living options. Spanning out from the central city of shops, restaurants, and businesses were high-density apartments, then a green-belt for schools, churches, and recreation, and finally low-density residential housing grouped in pods away from busier areas.

The central city would be completely enclosed and climate-controlled. Trucks and deliveries would be made on the lowest underground level, automobile traffic would operate on the next subterranean level above, free of any traffic lights, while pedestrian traffic would be completely separated above all motor vehicle movement on the same level as the transportation lobby. Shops and businesses would have been constructed in international themed areas. The EPCOT plan called for a British Square, Scandinavian and Asian market places, and South American plazas. There would be roving entertainers like you find at the World Showcase at EPCOT today. Walt's goal was to achieve the first accident free, noise free, pollution free city center in America. He felt these amenities would attract the families he wanted to live and work there in leased housing. He figured such a unique living experience would draw tourists from around the world to see and vacation in such a marvelous environment.

EPCOT was massive. Developers normally are required to put in streets, sidewalks, and basic utilities. The EPCOT plan called for an infrastructure that would have cost perhaps

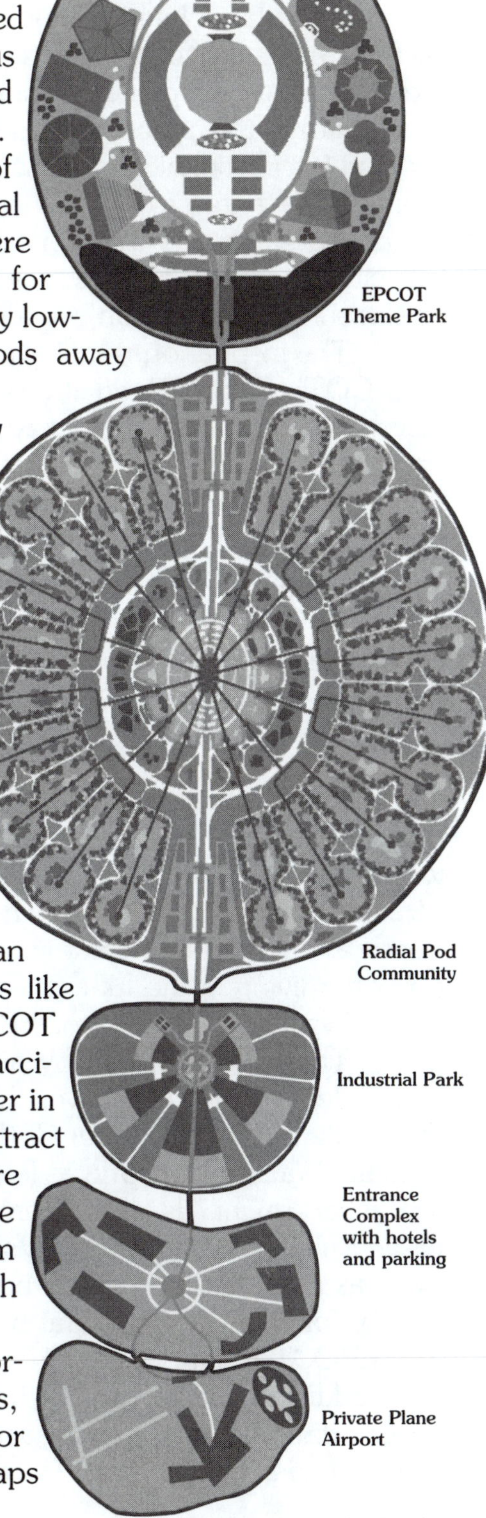

Illustration by Heather Bentley

a hundred times as much for all the underground development and enclosed environment controlled center-city hub. This author knows of no actual budget estimates or development phases for the EPCOT plan, but the cost would have been in the billions for total execution. The construction costs alone would have been staggering without any consideration for expenses such as trash collection, transportation, maintenance, the cost of government and other normal operating expenses. The EPCOT plan was still mostly a dream at this point. Walt probably had a plan for tourist income, industry, and international support. He figured he could also tap into government grants and wanted to use the profits from the Florida Magic Kingdom and the proposed second theme park in the EPCOT plan to construct the futuristic city concept. He shared his ideas with Roy, but the Magic Kingdom and its surrounding "Vacation Kingdom of the World" had to be completed first.

The inspiration remains and many of the ideas have been put to work at EPCOT's Future World and World Showcase. It opened as EPCOT Center eleven years after the Magic Kingdom on October 1, 1982. The "Center" part of the name was dropped in 1994. Its Future World demonstrated many up-to-the-minute technologies and the World Showcase provided the international shopping and dining experiences Walt had envisioned for his Experimental Prototype Community Center City. EPCOT has an outer access road servicing all the Future World and World Showcase pavilions just as Walt planned for other types of EPCOT pods.

In his 1966 press conference, Walt declared there would be no retirees permitted to live in the original EPCOT, because everyone had to have a job within the community, but he also talked of a second planned development where people could own their homes instead of just paying a reasonable monthly rate; a place where anyone could live. This development was realized as the city of Celebration. Just off Interstate 4 on State Route 192, it is a thriving model of what the residential part of EPCOT might have become. This planned community has already used many ideas Walt forecast for better living in the future.

Was Walt's dream for EPCOT even possible?

The management of Walt Disney Productions spent eight years after Walt's death trying to answer that question. Certain voices wanted to scrap the whole EPCOT idea, but CEO Card Walker felt a deep commitment to try to make Walt's plan work; at least to get the second theme park built and to see what might develop from there. Walt knew the kind of revenue Disneyland generated. Studies showed Walt Disney World would do at least twice as much business. Walt had planned to use this money as the start-up money for EPCOT. The total project would have had to be done in phases. The EPCOT theme park would have probably been done first to help generate additional cash followed by the very center of the urban hub hotel and transportation lobby. The pods were modular and could have been developed on an as-leased basis. Getting the entire climate-controlled center totally completed, leased, and in operation could have taken many years had the original plan gone forward. So much would have depended on the industrial, business, and perhaps government support, plus the workforce needed to live in and operate such a unique undertaking.

Walt just may have been way ahead of his time once again. His EPCOT blueprint promised a different style of utopian living that may never fully come to be, but as crowded population centers continue to become more unlivable, it is entirely possible that Walt's dream of living in the future may indeed be tried. It is full of good ideas, certainly not all unique to Walt Disney, but a dream others in the future may yet make come true.

In modern battles over proposed changes to the Reedy Creek Improvement District, it has been argued the purpose of the special legislation was Walt's promise to build his futuristic community and it never happened. The charges simply are not valid for three reasons. The Disney brothers made it clear they would not come to Florida without Reedy Creek and concluded no land purchases until it was passed. The state legislators approved the deal to attract the company and the benefits the state has reaped far exceeded all forecasts at the time. Second, there was no mention of EPCOT in the November 15, 1965 press conference. Even Roy Disney never heard the term and was vague about the planning at that time. EPCOT was not formally revealed until a press conference in the fall of 1966. Third, while the plans for EPCOT changed, a substantial number of the concepts originally proposed have been developed. What plan doesn't undergo changes? Look at most government programs. And the promises of EPCOT continue to be found fulfilled not only in Florida, but in other communities around the world.

Had Walt Disney actually completed final EPCOT Center planning, some things would have probably been different, but his Imagineers undoubtedly did it much the same as Walt. The Spaceship Earth ball is the "weenie," but it is the very first thing inside the Park, not the draw to get the people away from the single entrance. Still, it funnels the crowd to one of three different directions and it all seems to work. Many guests choose EPCOT as their favorite park. No Disney characters, except Figment, were associated with this second park for the first twelve years of its existence because managers felt that's the way Walt would have wanted it.

EPCOT Center did encounter some major problems on opening day. Key among these was the mile-plus walk around the World Showcase. Older guests had trouble making it around the lake. Two boats and some surface vehicles were installed for those who needed help.

New attractions seem to be more difficult to establish and maintain at EPCOT. Every exhibit has traditionally been sponsor driven. Two of the best have been revised, Journey Into the Imagination (twice) and Ward Kimball's outstanding theme park contribution, The World of Motion. General Motors wanted a Test Track to better sell their products, but Test Track could have easily been built around The World of Motion. It is a change Walt would have probably never permitted. He was always for improvement. Both these attraction changes were steps backward.

Horizons, the one Future World pavilion to be replaced, was a fascinating trip into life in the future. Some of its prophetic innovations have been realized...large, flat-screen TVs, and hands-free phones, but farming under water and in space are still futuristic. This ride-through exhibit gave guests three different ways to return to the present. It was a very interesting attraction to many, but not enough. Attendance was always less than other Future World adventures. When the show lost its sponsorship, Disney started to look for a replacement. The attraction was completely razed and Mission: SPACE was built on the site. In The Land, Kitchen Kabaret was replaced by Food Rocks until it too was removed to make room for Soarin'.

EPCOT is more educational than other Disney theme parks, but none of its elements have ever been copied in Japan, Paris, or Hong Kong. Still, it is the third most visited theme park in the United States behind Walt Disney World's Magic Kingdom and Disneyland, according to the Theme Park Insider website. Other rated theme parks in order of 2006 attendance estimates were Disney/MGM Studios, Disney's Animal Kingdom, Universal Studios Orlando, Disney's California Adventure, Sea World Orlando, Universal Studios Hollywood, Busch Gardens Tampa, Sea World San Diego, Knott's Berry Farm, Paramount's Kings Island, Cedar Point, and Six Flags Great Adventure Chicago. This data shows Walt's attention to detail and the way he built his organization has continued to pay off over 50 years after his first theme park revolutionized the industry.

Location obviously plays a vital role in attendance figures. Disney's California Adventure ranks as high as it does simply because it is located across from Disneyland. It was built in deference to many things Walt wanted for family entertainment and provides an interesting contrast to Walt's approach to business. Creation of DCA was in the hands of a cost-cutter. Imagineer Sam McKim once related, "When all the cost estimates were in, we were ordered to cut them line by line by 20%. We had to make everything cheaper to make budget. It was not the Disney way and it will cost them much more in the long run."

Walt believed in good value; quality for a price the average family could afford. After the Walt Disney World opening in 1971, our family made annual visits. In 1972, the cost of a garden room in the Contemporary Hotel was $18.75 per night plus tax. Fourteen adventure ticket books for two days cost $14.95 for adults and $7.95 for children under 12. There was a marching band on Main Street, a Fife and Drum Corps in Liberty Square, and two horse cars traveling up and down Main Street. Visitors marveled at the wonderful time they had and told their friends. Attendance soon surpassed projections. The success of Walt Disney World under Walt's policies paved the way for unprecedented corporate growth. Despite trouble at the box office for Disney films and a downturn in TV revenue in the early '80s, the theme parks continued to thrive for 20 years after Walt's death. People visited often and were happy to pay the price.

In the next 20 years, admission prices more than tripled. The amount charged for food and lodging seemed to grow faster. Conversations about a trip to Disney World began to focus on high costs rather than the great time had by the family. Visits the average family could afford became less frequent. The average expenditure per Disney theme park guest has always been highest in the industry, but the amount of merchandise items purchased has dropped as other prices have risen. Millions of dollars are now spent on advertising and promotion, whereas little was required under Walt's policies. Only Disney accountants can compare and figure which way was best in today's dollars. If there is a way to compare the past, present, and future, my money would be on Walt's way.

The Disney/MGM Studio and Animal Kingdom theme parks are both successful and enjoyable. It is hard to know if Walt would have added them. Unlike Disney's California Adventure, both are true to Walt's blueprint for a successful theme park and extend Walt's dreams into the 21st Century. They fit nicely even if they were not originally foreseen as part of the Florida Project.

When Disneyland was created, it was envisioned as a place that families would come to visit for a day. National television coverage drew crowds from a much larger area and they wanted to stay longer. As the park expanded, there was more to do than a single day permitted. Disneyland graduated from a 12-hour destination to a multi-day resort.

The Florida project was planned as a multiple resort "Vacation Kingdom of the World" from the start. The monorail connecting the Magic Kingdom to the Contemporary and Polynesian Resorts was as much fun as any theme park attraction. Golf, tennis, horseback riding, boating, swimming, camping, and other sports and outdoor activities were featured, along with fantasy and thrills. A large staff of sports pros was available for instruction in the early years. A third hotel, the Golf Resort, was not on the monorail beam, but provided an alternative for dads who enjoyed playing a first class golf course. Three other hotels – the Asian, Venetian, and Persian – were in the original master plan. The hotel construction was innovative. Disney had contracted with U.S. Steel to build the Contemporary and Polynesian Resorts using steel framework and slide-in pre-fabricated rooms. When U.S. Steel announced they couldn't meet the deadline for the Polynesian rooms, the resort was redesigned and Disney managed to use available modules to build 492 rooms in time for the opening. It has since been expanded.

Many of Walt's Disneyland construction staff handled building the opening phase of Walt Disney World. Admiral Joe Fowler oversaw construction. General "Joe" Potter, who joined the company after Disneyland opened, played another vital role, largely replacing C.V. Wood who got the first theme park operational. A core group of only 30 managers were in charge of getting the massive project operating according to schedule. The Denver Celebrity Sports Center proved its worth, contributing many executives to the opening effort. Roy Disney managed it all, adhering to Walt's plans to the best of his ability.

Financing the huge project was easier than getting Disneyland from a dream into reality. The biggest chunk came from convertible debentures. The public was so anxious to back the project the offering was oversubscribed. Several issues were made as finances required...and the company called the bonds years early. Roy O. Disney dedicated the Florida project in his brother's name on October 1, 1971.

The insect infested swamps had been converted to lakes, highways, hotels, and a Magic Kingdom larger than the California original. The Florida theme park had a substructure underneath. It was Walt's way of testing his plan for EPCOT. Trucks delivered via rear entrances to underground loading docks. Food came up to on-site kitchens. Trash went down. The telephone service, power generation, water purification, and sewage treatment were all run under Disney supervision using the most modern methods. Attractions previously controlled mechanically were now run by computers. The Florida Project's environment was a major concern long before national awareness became a buzzword at executive cocktail parties. The backstage show was every bit as impressive as the magic guests came to experience.

Project X was made public in 1965, a reality in 1971. The first phase of Walt Disney's crowning achievement was completed not quite five years after his death. Art Linkletter tells how many people come up to him and remark how sad it was that Walt did not live to see it finished. His standard response is, "He saw it, that's why it's there."

Indeed, Walt Disney had superior visionary power. It drove him to create things never before imagined. He predicted his 43.5 square miles of Florida could "hold all the ideas we could possibly imagine," but his imagineers are still using ideas he left behind...and will be for the foreseeable future. Those ideas are being used all around the world as Disney theme parks are built in countries never thought possible during Walt's lifetime.

Walt believed in collaboration, but realized one person had to make the final decisions. He did not believe in committees and was never good at delegating; even worse at grooming a creative successor. After his death, a committee of seven executives was chosen to run Walt Disney Productions and nearly ran it into the ground. The course to complete the Florida Project was well charted and work on several good pictures were in development before Walt died. But when all were completed it was clear the committee was a problem. The retirement of most of the team Walt built during the '30s complicated the situation. The ironclad hold Walt Disney once had on his studio had all but faded away.

Chapter X – What Would Walt Do?

"In this volatile business of ours, we can ill afford to rest on our laurels, even to pause in retrospect. Times and conditions change so rapidly that we must keep our aim constantly focused on the future."

—Walt Disney

Marty Sklar, long-time company Vice President and head of Walt Disney Imagineering, the organization that plans and develops Disney theme parks, once said, "Walt Disney lived with one foot in the past and the other in the future." A turn-of-the-century Main Street USA wasn't any more relevant to the kids of 1955 than the kids of 2007. Yet, Walt Disney believed the past was important. The contrast provides a striking difference from the real world just exited to his Disneyland of entertainment and adventure.

History was used time and again in Disney films and TV shows to set up or provide a background for something futuristic. The past fascinated Walt as much as the future. He felt lessons were to be learned from what has gone before. It grounded him. Flubber wasn't put to use in the latest hot sports car, rather an old Model T Ford. Even though the film has been updated in color, there is still a timeless charm in the original.

An animated history of aviation was used to set the stage in *Victory Through Air Power* and reused on TV as an introduction to Disneyland's "Man in Space" series. The EPCOT Center producers used history extensively in Future World's Spaceship Earth, Universe of Energy, and the sadly missed original World of Motion attractions. Walt Disney may have had a hand in some of these designs. If not, they were designed by people who had worked with him and were still asking, "What would Walt do?"

Disney theme parks celebrated the 100th anniversary of Walt Disney's birth in 2001. A survey of 76 children at the time determined few knew he was ever a real person. Only two kids in a fifteen-year-old and under study group knew he died of lung cancer. Some thought he was just another fantasy character. One boy knew he was the man in the statue holding Mickey Mouse's hand, but didn't know anything else about him.

That information comes as quite a shock to those of us who were so influenced by the man himself. It's sad because the lessons of Walt Disney's life teach a valuable education from which more children could profit. The pop-culture kids of today thrive on the idea of getting rich quick as a rock musician, sports hero, or TV/movie star. The concepts of Horatio Alger or Walt Disney have fallen through the cracks of today's up-tempo, activity laden life. Any type of work ethic often isn't introduced until a child's late teens. There's a world of knowledge on the Internet if you know what facts you seek, but the distractions along the information superhighway are many. The salvation of future generations lies in the rare inquiring minds like that of Walt Disney.

Today's child, despite all the technological advances, suffers not from the sparse information encountered by Walt Disney in the early 20th century, but rather from a deluge of facts, figures, surveys, opinions, and telegraphed story segments.

The situation a century after Walt's birth finds the average young adult starting from scratch in his or her late teens or early twenties versus a boy or girl of ten with a newspaper route. They will have a better chance of a productive life if they have a college diploma; perhaps an advanced degree. Those without a degree have to scramble for a decreasing number of manufacturing jobs. In a way, these young people are more like Walt Disney when he first started to find his way in the world. Too many, however, are without a clue on how to find their niche, or more importantly, what to do about it once they establish a goal. Winning the lottery is the biggest fantasy of all. The odds of winning in the Ohio Mega Millions jackpot are about 175,700,000 to one. Odds are a little better to become a rock, sports, or movie star. Those winning the celebrity lottery, however, will average only one to three years basking in the light of fame and fortune. A few college graduates will become CEOs or establish a winning business. More will capitalize on their course of study. The rest will settle for whatever job they can get. They don't realize success is in their own hands until it is too late.

Knowing how Walt and Roy Disney persisted in digging out opportunities and capitalizing on them is a rare lesson. Their attention to hiring practices, product quality, business integrity, and customer satisfaction will still be important to success a hundred years from now.

The biggest success Walt Disney achieved was finding something he enjoyed doing and figuring out how to do it better than his competitors. Furthermore, he found new challenges and opportunities along the way. His education came from the real world and was still incomplete the day he died. His knack for putting his accumulated learning to work matched that of a Benjamin Franklin or Thomas Edison, who were also intrigued by questions of their day and set out to answer them.

Did Walt have a superior mind? Was he just stubborn in his convictions? Was he unbelievably lucky? Did he somehow know the right thing to do? Perhaps all those elements came into play at certain phases of his life, but first and foremost Walt Disney was in control of his own destiny. When an important decision had to be made, he was the one to make it. Roy Disney normally went along, sometimes after considerable wrangling, because his brother's track record was uncannily correct. When Roy was opposed to what Walt wanted to do, Walt did what he had to do to convince his brother first. Above all, he knew he was limited without Roy's financial expertise behind him. His artists and imagineers were never as difficult as Roy on rare occasions, but Walt, however frustrated, was always wise enough to take the time to get Roy behind his ideas 100%.

While improving animation entertainment, Walt was just one of the guys. It was an era of great experimentation and discovery cumulating in *Snow White and the Seven Dwarfs*. It would be interesting to see what would have happened without the interruption of the animation strike of 1941 or World War II. Those events put the studio on its ear for nearly ten years. Would the studio have gone into live-action production earlier or not at all? Circumstances dealt the cards it did and the studio survived into the 1950s, its most important decade of growth and development. Live-action, television, and Disneyland corrected the studio's tight cash flow and made operations and expansion easier for the next twenty-five years. It was the achievement of Roy's dreams, if not Walt's. The availability of money, and lots of it, got Walt dreaming again. The 1964-65 New York World's Fair gave Walt the opportunity to test Disneyland concepts on East Coast audiences. The successful reception of the four attractions Walt Disney's Imagineers created for this otherwise money-losing venture was all the proof Walt needed to go forward with his Florida Project.

Walt Disney turned everything else over to his trusted staff of artists, animators, and Imagineers to concentrate on Florida and its Experimental Prototype Community of Tomorrow. Tomorrowland had always been the most difficult land to keep relevant at Disneyland. Technology develops too fast. Perhaps the Tomorrowland experience should have been a warning as to the fate of Walt's EPCOT plan. It is hard to believe Walt didn't take it into consideration, but whatever his vision for achieving this final goal died with him.

There are now five Magic Kingdoms in the world. Out of all the millions of guests visiting Disney Magic Kingdoms and other parks, some inquiring minds are sure to ask how it all came about and who was Walt Disney? He wasn't the normal corporate executive concentrating on the bottom line. He was keenly aware of his audience and his employees because he was constantly out among them, asking questions, and finding answers. In some answers, he found gems of truth that guided his decision making. The stature he gained in the 1950s made it possible for Walt to get anyone on the phone. Top experts were eager to help. Walt had access to the best advice available and distilled it down to shape his final products.

What would Walt do?

After his death, the surviving directors, animators, artists, and Imagineers who knew Walt so well, were often chided for asking, "What would Walt do?" The products they turned out continued to mirror Walt's standards. He had already made the decision to let these proven and trusted employees run their operations while he concentrated on the Florida Project. What they produced in the ten to fifteen years following his death were much the same as if Walt had lived all those years.

Problems started to develop when the people he put in place as far back as the 1930s began to retire. The new people who took over didn't have as much direct experience under Walt. They didn't always know what Walt would do. At times, they could have benefited from such knowledge, particularly when it came to problems where the Walt team had previously figured out sound solutions. The company had a successful surge of animated hits beginning with *The Little Mermaid* in 1989. *Who Framed Roger Rabbit?* had been a previous success in 1988, but it was largely the work of outside companies under the direction of Steven Spielberg, a longtime student of Walt Disney's animation and production techniques. This resurgence included *Beauty and the Beast*, *Aladdin*, and *The Lion King* before some good, but lesser hits followed. The animated feature catalyst, *The Little Mermaid*, was begun by Walt during World War II and maybe it sparked someone to once again ask, "What would Walt do?"

The Walt and Roy Disney success story is the genesis of the Walt Disney Company history. Not to go back and study that success would be a grave error. Those who badgered Walt survivors for asking, "What would Walt do?" were the misguided. "Brainstorming" and similar techniques have often led to trouble for more contemporary Disney managers. Walt would do the research, ask questions, and test until he figured out the correct answer. That's the basis for everything he did. Yet, all he concluded was based on the principles of honesty, integrity, sound planning, quality, and a knack for recognizing or crafting a good story. Certainly the fact that he and Roy could sell their ideas was a big help. Their sales abilities, however, rested in their convictions and the soundness of their proposals. Their ideas were always attention-getting and were backed with solid research. When either man made a presentation on behalf of the studio, they were well prepared and thoroughly convinced they had a winner. Dick Nunis once commented they were "such good salesmen because they didn't know they were selling."

Too many decisions made in modern times by the corporate Walt Disney brand have not been because people asked, "What would Walt do?" Rather they have been made for the lack of asking. Press guests at the opening of Disney's California Adventure were politely asked to judge it on its own merit and not compare it to any other theme park. When personally asked by a pert Disney guide, "What do you think?" this author's response was simple, "Other than being against Walt Disney's basic principles, it's professionally done and clean." The alternative could have been DisneySea which is currently thriving in Japan. Apparently, the Japanese Oriental Land Company, owner of both Tokyo parks, has greater respect for the achievements of Walt Disney than some of the successors in his own company.

In 2006, The Walt Disney Company, which now includes the ABC Television Network, ESPN and other cable channels, book and magazine publishing, and many other business enterprises in addition to film production facilities and theme park operations, employs thousands of people worldwide. "It all started with a Mouse" is a favorite corporate quote used early on by Walt himself. In reality, it was all started by a man who had a loving brother who joined in partnership in 1923. Their collective brains and those of their talented staff became the corporate Walt Disney. Hard-earned policies were learned, not dictated. Together, they molded the new animation industry into a brand unique to Disney. Building on this solid base, the company expanded into live-action motion pictures, TV, and theme park innovations.

The eye of this entertainment tornado was the man, Walt Disney. Largely self-taught, nobody could tell him what he couldn't accomplish until he tried. Even when others told him *Snow White* was a folly or that Disneyland was such a dumb idea it would close within a year, he charged ahead anyway. To be sure, few people have proven the experts wrong as often or to the magnitude of Walt Disney. He was an independent individualist with the conviction of the biblical Job. He was a man of his time, always keen to the latest technological advancements and which ones to employ in his own enterprises. And when new technology wasn't there, his people developed innovations like the storyboard, multiplane camera, Fantasound, audio-animatronics, and "blue screen" moving-matte technologies. There were hundreds of small developments along the way, like how to get different colors of "water" to flow side-by-side without mixing in Rainbow Caverns. Walt sincerely believed if he could dream it, he could figure out a way to do it. The phrases "I can't" or "It's not my job" were not permitted in his vocabulary.

Knowing he couldn't do everything himself was impressed on him early on at the Pesmen-Rubin Commercial Art Studio. He quickly learned other artists had a talent greater than his own. That didn't deter him from finding his own niche in animation and the role he could fill best. He constantly found opportunities, but he had such strong convictions on how he wanted things done, it's doubtful he could have ever worked for anyone other than himself.

Money and financial matters held little interest for Walt. Once he linked up with his brother Roy, he was largely free from such concerns and was able to focus on the creative side where he excelled. Their collaboration will be recorded as one of the greatest partnerships in corporate history.

Some scientists tell us we only use a small part of our brain capacity. Maybe Walt was wired in such a way to allow him to use a greater percentage than other humans. His first advertising job started him on a path to animation and entertainment. His inquiring mind took over from there to generate questions and ideas. He was compelled to seek answers for his own gratification. Finding those answers was fun. His fun was infectious. When others found personal satisfaction in his brand of fun, it became an organization doing the work of creating enjoyment for others. His key people also enjoyed monetary rewards at a time so many others were out of work.

The studio produced cartoon shorts. Walt knew, however, this type of product was at the mercy of the theater booking agent. People paid to see features. They expected a newsreel and cartoon. They may have even preferred a Disney cartoon, but they still paid to see features with their favorite stars. If the Disney Studio was to firmly establish itself, it too would need to produce features. Today, animated features are common. Computer animation makes it possible for anyone to produce an animated film. Most have taken their lessons from Walt Disney.

Back in the mid-1930s, an animated feature had never been done. *Snow White and the Seven Dwarfs* was a big risk. No one even knew if a audience would sit through a "long cartoon." That's precisely why Walt made it different than a normal cartoon. His version of this popular fairy-tale fantasy was calculated more to the story than a string of gags found in the standard cartoon. *Snow White* had some great laughs, but it also generated real fear, surprise, charm, sadness, joy, and tears upon Snow White's "sleeping death." In short, it had everything people paid to see in a live-action feature of the time. Walt had studied audiences. He chose the story because he had seen a silent black & white version as a young boy and remembered how the adult audience had reacted. His version made it fun and exciting for the whole family. The brand of "Walt Disney Presents" was now engraved in the minds of the film-going public.

Pinocchio was a logical follow-up to *Snow White and the Seven Dwarfs*. It had a lot of the same European charm and look. The story was much darker, but in sync with the feature versus cartoon concept. *Fantasia* was a bold experiment, an animated classical music concert. Walt had to know this was a stretch for his normal family audience, but he never limited himself until the limit was established by his audience.

Then came the animation strike of 1941. Walt took it personally. It was the one time being the best in the business worked against him and his studio. He had plenty of bad advice. The studio didn't deserve what it was put through. Walt was well within his rights and made a prudent management decision in his stand for a National Labor Relations Board election. President Roosevelt, however, was pro-union and the election got put off.

The studio desperately needed to complete *Dumbo* to get the animation income stream back on track. Roy wavered in fear of secondary boycotts and agreed to a plan to get Walt out of the way so the strike could be settled. Had Roy not acted when he did, the studio could had been caught in the war before *Dumbo* was completed. At least *Dumbo* was a success and the future seemed bright.

Less than two months later, Pearl Harbor was attacked and the studio went into survival mode for the rest of the decade. The studio's momentum was lost. No one knew how long the war would last or if the Allied Forces would win. It looked bad for several years. The casualties were in the hundreds of thousands. There was scarcely a family untouched. It was a golden time for the major live-action studios. People attended theaters in those pre-television days as much to see the war newsreels as the feature films. Radio news broadcasts provided the most up-to-the-minute coverage, but pictures were vital to everyone's understanding of the Allied Forces wins and defeats.

Disney adapted war themes to cartoons. It was the subject on everyone's mind. Walt supported the war effort every way possible despite the deleterious effect it was having on the studio. He produced *Victory Through Air Power* at a loss to provide support for the strategic-bomber concept because he felt it was a logical solution to turning the tide of war and limiting the deaths of Allied ground troops. The studio and remaining employees supported the USO, the non-profit private organization providing entertainment to military service personnel away from battle fronts.

During the war, Walt Disney began to formulate ideas for new animated features and a Mickey Mouse park where the whole family could go and enjoy themselves together. But there wasn't enough income to follow through on any ideas of substance. It had to be a frustrating time for Walt. He was poised for a giant leap forward with nowhere to go. The remainder of the 1940's after *Bambi* was released in 1942 was spent treading water. *Cinderella* provided the needed breakthrough in 1950. While his animation teams focused on *Alice in Wonderland, Peter Pan,* and *Lady and the Tramp,* Walt spent more and more time on live-action, TV, and Disneyland.

When asked about his greatest achievement, Walt Disney replied, "Everything." Those close to Walt felt it was Disneyland. The theme park couldn't have existed without the cartoons, animated features, and TV shows that preceded it, but it was obvious to all who knew Walt...Disneyland was special. Maybe it was the fact every friend he consulted about this dream told him, in all sincerity, to forget it. Art Linkletter, who had invested his entertainment income into many different enterprises and became a multi-millionaire, thought Walt "had lost it" when together they visited the Anaheim orange groves. Linkletter said he was even more emphatic when the two flew over the swamps of central Florida, the future site of Walt Disney World, "I couldn't possibly see how that swampland could be turned into anything usable. I reminded Walt how I was against Disneyland, but that it was special and should remain the one and only as to not deter from its uniqueness," Linkletter added. But Walt had already figured out how to solve the swampland problems and was just as sure about Florida as he was about Disneyland.

Risking everything when you start out is one thing. Risking a prosperous multi-million dollar movie studio to build a dream everyone else thinks will fail is something else again. That takes a man who is an ultimate gambler or one with the convictions of Walt Disney. He certainly wasn't a gambler. His outside research pointed to key factors favorable to a new family entertainment concept and confidence in the Disney name. Walt was sure others were guided by past experience while his eyes were fixed on a developing opportunity.

Looking back and seeing how Walt did it can be misleading. Most business people can relate stories about individuals who were equally convinced their ideas would succeed, but failed. What made Walt different? Ward Kimball felt Walt had timing on his side. The lack of formal education probably served Walt well. He was never taught what he couldn't do and was persistent…a workaholic when zeroing in on an idea. Walt asked questions and developed other techniques until he was convinced he had the answers he needed…and used the information to figure out how to accomplish his goal and simply didn't give up. When the research results were in, he didn't just charge ahead as others might do. Then he double-checked them with concepts like pencil-tests, scale models, more outside research, and prototypes to see how improvements could be made based on what he learned…then often repeated his checking process. Walt would let experts work on a problem until they felt they had an answer, then point out other directions for study. His personal approach was to learn as much about his goal and then look at it with a fresh eye for ways to simplify or make improvements.

When lung cancer took Walt Disney without public warning on December 15, 1966, the world was shocked. Front-page news stories appeared on nearly every major newspaper in the free world…and some that weren't free. Even though he was, as Van France used to say, "a staunch conservative with red, white, and blue in his eyes," the public Walt Disney knew no political boundaries. Writers and cartoonists worldwide mourned his passing. The printed tributes alone fill 21 oversized scrapbooks in the Disney Archives.

Art Linkletter was one of the few people Walt told when he was diagnosed with lung cancer. In recalling the moment at the 50th Disneyland Alumni Club banquet, Linkletter quoted Walt as saying, "Look at all the things I was able to accomplish in my life, but the one thing I could never do was to quit smoking."

Walt Disney's death cost us much more. Walt's dream of EPCOT was never fully realized. Many say the concept died with him, but the foresight to fight for the Reedy Creek Improvement District, the planning for the 43.5 square miles that became Walt Disney World and the EPCOT elements built into the Florida Magic Kingdom were all put on paper by Walt. Extensive plans, drawings, and paintings for the Experimental Prototype Community of Tomorrow were also done before his death. The only missing ingredient was Walt's risk-everything-for-a-dream mentality.

After Walt's death, Roy Disney became the keeper of Walt's dreams. The last years of his life were dedicated to two projects closest to Walt's heart: getting the faculty and operations mess at Cal Arts straightened out, and opening the Florida Project. Accomplishing both goals with great flair seldom seen in the years spent in the shadow of his younger brother, Roy Oliver Disney died on December 20, 1971, less than three months after he dedicated Disney World in his brother's name.

Walt knew Disneyland would grow. To capture the "before" look, he had film crews shoot footage of Disneyland during 1955 and 1956. This film didn't record any special event, just guests enjoying the park during normal operations. Nearly two hours of this footage was shown to Disneyland Alumni Club members Wednesday afternoon July 26, 2005. There was mention that some of the footage was used in a *People and Places* film, a series similar to the True-Life Adventure films, but featuring different human cultures. Many eliminated attractions like the stagecoach, Conestoga wagon, and the mule-pack tour were recorded. The Rainbow Caverns Mine Train through the Living Desert of falling rocks and mechanical snakes and other desert creatures, added in 1956, was thoroughly documented. The "before look" was undoubtedly filmed to serve as a benchmark for improvements to be made in subsequent years. However, the film also shows how Disneyland was the way Walt created it. The 60-plus attractions added to the park in the 52 years since proved the "after" Walt knew would show as the park developed. Missing, however, are so many enjoyable things that simply disappeared: the large Main Street marching band, the horse cars passing at just the right moment, the artists doing caricatures, newspaper boys selling the *Disneyland News*, and other festive entertainment. If Disneyland ever truly wanted to restore itself to original splendor, little brick and mortar would be required. All they need to ask is, "What would Walt do?" and put back the people Walt felt were so important to the success of his dream. Where else can children be exposed to a barbershop quartet, horse-drawn streetcars, Dixieland bands, street comedians, and the music of John Phillip Sousa, all in a three-block area? You can argue they are not relevant all you want, but you can't escape the fact they remain entertaining and were unique to the Disneyland success. It seems someone is already thinking back and some of these things are already being reactivated.

What would Walt do?

The question is more important today than after Walt's death. Back in 1966, he had hand-picked successors in place and already operating almost completely on their own. They knew a lot about what Walt would do and carried on with his dreams. Unfortunately, today's Disney studio employees and theme park cast members are far removed from Walt's personal guidance. They all get a brief education on Disney Traditions, but few really know the details of Walt and Roy Disney's struggles. The principles that figured so strongly in the success of the company have been blurred by a succession of management styles and changing corporate goals.

Walt and Roy Disney built what has become The Walt Disney Company from the film Walt brought to California from Kansas City and what was left of $40 in cash when he boarded the train. It became a multi-million dollar empire by the time the Disney Brothers died. The Disneys prospered through the years of the Great Depression of the '30s and survived through World War II to emerge as an unqualified debt-free success by the end of the 1950s. The lessons they learned are documented in much greater detail than most other corporate successes. The company virtually wears its "trade secrets" on its sleeve. Anyone who cares can figure out "What Walt would do." Like it or not, what Walt would do remains a ghostly yardstick of the Walt Disney Company's performance years after the co-founders deaths.

"Walt Disney wasn't a buddy, but didn't act like a boss either," Fess Parker remembered of his Davy Crockett years.

Walt was motivated by the creative process rather than money, but operated in a tight cash position in all but about eight years of his career. Roy Disney was the primary keeper of the company purse strings, but Walt was an astute businessman as well. They rewarded their income-producing people well, but still watched every dollar; a common trait of businessmen who operated through the Depression years.

On the other hand, Walt Disney was the biggest kid at Disneyland. He had real steam trains and monorails to operate on a whim. Quite a contrast! Maybe his ability to lead pressure-packed meetings or negotiate a tough deal and then have fun driving a train at Disneyland prompted people to consider him complex or unusual. Then again, not too many people have the opportunity to do all those things.

Walt and Me – Epilogue

"My adventure with Walt Disney has been lifelong. It has been personal and influential. He has been a good friend and true."

—Tom Tumbusch

Bambi ended and the house lights came up. My mother and I were filing out of the Salem Theater with the crowd. As we passed the small coat-check booth, I spotted a man standing in the window and loudly, as a five-year-old is apt to do, asked my mother, "Is that the man who killed Bambi's mother?" That visit to our neighborhood theater is my oldest recollection of anything Walt Disney.

Getting to know Walt, as I have, has allowed me to dream bigger dreams and see those dreams become reality. In doing so, I have enjoyed meeting many name personalities from the Broadway, business, and political worlds. Early on, I was able to realize these celebrities were just human beings like me pursuing different dreams.

This book wasn't researched in terms of months or years. In fact, it didn't start out as a book project at all. The work is the result of a rewarding friendship – a story about inspiration and making dreams come true. Over a sixty-years period, it became a book. It is about how Walt Disney has personally influenced one person. Even though he didn't know me or most other members of his audience, he treated us with respect and carefully shaped his products to maintain our friendship and loyalty.

The Disney Studio didn't give guided tours when I first visited there in 1977. In fact, it was difficult to find back then. Mickey Mouse wasn't painted on the water tower and there were no signs on the building. The wall around the studio grounds looked the same as St. Joseph's Hospital across the busy thoroughfare. Just the address, 500 S. Buena Vista Street, was a visitor's only guide. The Roy O. Disney building had recently been completed, but the rest of the studio grounds remained much the same as when Walt was alive. Parking lots and the old Zorro set still stood where the Team Disney, Frank G. Wells, and multi-story parking garage structures are now found. Studio merchandise could be purchased in a small area in the commissary before it was remodeled and all the historical artifacts from famous Disney motion pictures were removed. Only photographic blow-ups remain. The art deco architecture was still predominant. I can still picture my first walk down Mickey Avenue and encountering the sign at Dopey Drive. Seeing the manicured grounds and strolling the halls of the animation building where classic cel set-ups lined the walls was an unforgettable experience. Like Walt, those cels are gone. They have been replaced by photographic reproductions because the originals are too valuable.

There have been many trips to the Disney Studio over the years. One research visit lasted four days and it was my good fortune to meet about fifteen ladies from the old Ink and Paint Department...or the Nunnery as it was named back in the '30s. The oldest had worked on *Pinocchio*. The youngest has started with *Alice In Wonderland*. It was sometime in the early 1980s. They had been rehired to produce over 4,000 hand-inked and painted Limited Edition "Gallery Cels" Disney was selling at the time. We became friends at lunch and they took me on a tour of their department. The working quarters were tight; not cramped, but every inch of space was put to good use. They worked from copies of the original drawings and color keys with paints made from the original formulas. Finished painted cels were hung on wire lines to dry. Images were traced with color inks on the front of the cel and painted on the back, just like the ones used to produce cartoons and animated features before the Haloid-Xerox process became widely used in 1960 for the production of *101 Dalmatians*.

The girls of the Nunnery were a lively group. More than one could have fallen in love with Walt Disney given the chance. They all had known him and characterized him as "good-looking." He would stop by regularly to see how they were doing and joke with them. They spoke of him as a kind man...a genius...and all felt privileged to have known and worked for him. Walt always had questions, too. Whenever a problem with the work was expressed, he could come up with a suggested solution. Their job was menial and tedious. Yet Walt had a way of making it rewarding. He was careful to convey how their job gave his pictures color. All felt they were doing more than tracing and painting between the lines. They were helping to bring beloved characters to life. Like everyone else at the studio, they were aware of Walt's moods. Those who spoke on the subject figured it was a by-product of his genius...or he had good reason to be of foul temper. All felt his true nature was good. None had ever feared him like some animators and storymen did. They looked forward to his visits and were not only employees, but fans. Each one smiled when talking about her contribution to this picture or that. Those four days and the wonderful girls of the Nunnery gave me a true sense of what it must have been like to work at the studio under

Walt. It was an exceptional trip unlike any other to the famed Burbank citadel.

The Disney Studio grounds mirrored the quality Walt Disney demanded in all his enterprises; the same quality we expect when we see a Disney film, travel to a Disney theme park, sail on a Disney cruise ship, or buy Disney character merchandise. None of that started with a mouse. It was started by a man who drove himself harder than any of his employees.

Walt Disney was, as Ward Kimball pointed out years ago, the right man in the right place to do the first sound and color cartoons. Technology presented the opportunity, but he, rather than any of his competitors, seized that opportunity. Disney was the first Hollywood studio to embrace television. True, his real motive was to finance his Disneyland dream, but again he led the way in taking advantage of TV acceptance to advance his own agenda. His zeal to capitalize on new ideas puzzled some of his longtime animation staff as cartoon production ended, but it was time to move on. Key animators like Freddie Moore, Norm Ferguson, and director Jack Kinney left the studio. Walt's hands-on leadership, however, helped retain key people who were ready to move forward with him.

It wasn't my good fortune to be in the right place to personally know Walt Disney. My contribution to the Disney tradition has been to salvage the merchandise history of the company before some of the key players passed on. Seven books have resulted from what I've learned. Tomart's DISNEYANA Update magazine continues the work presented in those volumes. I've written on the subject in other magazines, including *The Disney Magazine* before it was discontinued.

There has been personal appearances as well. When I speak to Disney enthusiasts, I'm frequently asked what Disney character is my favorite. The Mickey, Donald, Goofy, Disney villains, or Winnie the Pooh fans seem to hope I will name theirs. My standard response is, "Walt Disney." And when I say Walt Disney, I'm speaking about the brand, not just the man. Walt had a right to be the focus of it all, but his brother Roy and the creative forces they mustered were an inseparable part of making it all possible.

Walt had his flaws. There is a certain comfort knowing he was human like the rest of us. His drive to follow his dreams was compulsive beyond the point few of us are willing to travel. It made him a different and interesting person to study. Learning to understand the many facets of Walt Disney through personal friendships and acquaintances gave me a unique opportunity to ask questions, do research, study the results, and ask more questions. I've read the books that praise Walt Disney and those that drag him through the mud. Fortunately, there were those whom I could question personally to form my own judgments, which I have presented here. My mission has been accomplished, because I feel I truly got to know Walt Disney and how he managed to do all the things he did.

In the process, I realized how heavy was the head that wore the Magic Kingdom crown. Not from the traditional problems facing a leader who influenced the entire world. Rather a head so full of dreams there wasn't enough time to see them all through. Many of those dreams have been passed on to others in the Disney organization and still continue to be realized. New faces at the studio seem to be reverting back to the things Walt would do. And I think that's a good thing.

Having a dream and figuring out how to make it a reality provides a powerful sense of accomplishment and satisfaction. My friend, Walt Disney, showed me it could be done. Doing so has been a life-changing experience, and his friendship continues to be rewarding.

Thanks Walt!

Disney Research Library at a Glance

"Walt Disney – The American Dreamer" only seeks to convey the author's personal experiences with people who worked directly with Walt Disney and the resulting impression of how he and his brother Roy made the Disney organization the success it became. The information was assembled over many years. During this time most of the books and other reference materials listed in this section were acquired and read. This knowledge provided the source for questions asked of those who worked with Walt. The body of published work is vast. Hopefully, this different approach to a bibliography will help readers sort out the materials available on Walt Disney and the work of the Disney Studio. Entries are listed in the traditional way. Book covers usually have a photo of Walt, a character, or a castle, plus the title cited. Since many covers are similar, a photo is provided to help readers recognize familiar works. Comments have been added to guide readers so they may distinguish works of specific interest.

Books

Arseni, Ercole; Bosi, Leone; and Marconi, Massimo. WALT DISNEY'S MAGIC MOMENTS. Arnoldo Mondadori Editions, Milan, Italy, 1973.

Published on the 50th Anniversary of the founding of the Disney Brothers Studio in 1923, this interesting venture provides highlights of Disney and studio history. Four pages are dominated by Salvador Dali's sketches and paintings for the then never completed Destiny *or* Destino *collaboration. The main interest is the way ten Disney animated shorts are presented. Following a page of the title header scenes from each, the story unfolds much like a storyboard. Each extreme is described below the printed composite frame for the entire length of the film. The films shown in this fashion are:* Plane Crazy, The Gallopin' Gaucho, Flowers and Trees, The Orphans Benefit (Color), Pluto's Judgement Day, Mickey's Rival, Don Donald, Donald's Nephews, Brave Little Tailor, *and* Ferdinand the Bull.

Ashman, Howard. THE NEW MICKEY MOUSE CLUB BOOK. Grosset & Dunlap, New York, 1977.

This book introduces the second TV Mickey Mouse Club *format devised for the Disney Channel cable network. This attempt to totally revise the winning formula of the '50s version was perhaps the least successful attempt of the TV versions. The old black & white shows were re-released to syndication by the SFM Media Service in the years immediately preceding the New MMC with great success. The cast was chosen more for political correctness rather than talent, the name of the days were changed, and the production staff couldn't approach the professionalism of Bill Walsh. None of the Mouseketeers went on to achieve further fame like the '90s version that produced Britney Spears, Christina Aguilera, and Justin Timberlake.*

Bailey, Adrian. WALT DISNEY'S WORLD OF FANTASY. Gallery Books, New York, 1982, 1987.

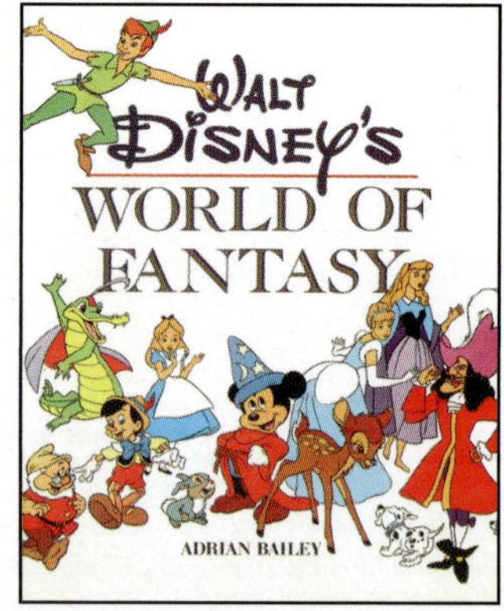

This book begins with a standard biography of Walt Disney and develops into a studio history with the usual mix of well used and exclusive photos. The studio's history deals with Oswald, Mickey Mouse, and Silly Symphonies before taking each feature in order of release. This book does a better job showing animators, story, and production people than most historics which focus the credit on Walt Disney. There is also some exclusive art and other artifacts used for documentation. Live-action films, True-Life Adventures, Disneyland, Walt Disney World, and EPCOT Center are also covered.

Barks, Carl. WALT DISNEY'S DONALD DUCK. Abbeville Press Inc., Publishers, New York, 1978.

The "best of" Donald Duck stories by Barks, except for the first "Pirates Gold" story, are reprinted in excellent, detailed color. There is a brief history of the character, and Carl provides the introduction with art from films, books, and newspaper comic strips by others. Like similar books in this series, the body of the book reprints famous stories written and illustrated by Carl Barks. Included in this volume are Frozen Gold (1944), Lost in the Andes (1949), Maharajah Donald (1947), Luck of the North (1949), Land of the Totem Poles (1949), The Magic Hourglass (1950), A Christmas for Shacktown (1952), Only a Poor Man (1952), The Golden Helmet (1952), and The Gilded Man (1952).

——. WALT DISNEY'S UNCLE SCROOGE. Abbeville Press Publishers, New York, 1979.

This book reprints Disney copyrighted comic book stories drawn by Carl Barks. The introductory material, written by Piero Zanotto, features background on Carl Barks, some of his famous book covers, and samples of his non-Disney oil paintings. A special introduction to the Uncle Scrooge character, using non-Barks art, was written by Carl himself. The remainder of the volume reprints some of his most famous stories, starting with "Christmas on Bear Mountain," the first appearance of the character in 1947. It's followed by the second Uncle Scrooge story – "The Old Castle Secret", printed a year later. His appearances became more frequent and the Uncle Scrooge comic book was launched in 1952. Sixteen other Barks Uncle Scrooge stories also appear in this volume.

Barrier, J. Michael. FIFTY YEARS OF ANIMATION – BUILDING A BETTER MOUSE. Library of Congress, Washington D.C., 1978.

This publication was prepared in conjunction with a Library of Congress exhibit of material filed to obtain copyright protection. The occasion was the 50th anniversary of Steamboat Willie and Mickey Mouse. It contains a condensed Disney Studio animation history. The exhibit was enhanced by material loaned by the Disney Studio, but the books, comics, sheet music, record albums, and perhaps the model sheets were from the Library's collection. There are some Walt Disney quotes not found elsewhere. This book was not intended to become an important reference, merely a companion booklet for the casual visitor to the exhibit.

Beard, Richard, with introduction by Marty Sklar. WALT DISNEY'S EPCOT CENTER – CREATING THE NEW WORLD OF TOMORROW. Harry N. Abrams, Inc. Publishers, New York, 1982.

This is the most complete book published on EPCOT Center as it was on opening day. Horizons is covered in great detail even though it was not yet operational. It has since been raised to make room for Mission: SPACE. The Living Seas is included by illustration only because it was being

reduced in size due to lawyer liability concerns. The spectacular features designed for but eliminated from this under the sea exhibit were used later in several non-Disney theme parks. The World of Motion, the Dreamfinder and Figment version of Imagination are preserved here in the form they should have remained, as is the original spirit of CommuniCore before it was overly commercialized. There is no mention of the Wonders of Life as no sponsor had yet been found. In the World Showcase the coverage of the American Adventure is exceptional, providing large-sized photos of the pavilion and the paintings used in the film segments. Deals on Norway and Morocco were not yet concluded, so there is no mention of them, but there is coverage of Equatorial Africa, which failed to conclude its intend to build. Some historic illustrations show the plans for this never-constructed country exhibit. Interesting facts, construction photos, and models of the still existing pavilions round out this colorful and now historic volume.

Blitz, Marcia. DONALD DUCK. New English Library (Times-Mirror). Harmony Book division of Crown Publishers, Inc., New York, 1979.

A comprehensive "biography" of Donald Duck from the "Men behind the Duck" and his first 1934 film appearance in The Wise Little Hen *to his feature appearances in* Saludos Amigos, The Three Caballeros, *and others. Coverage of his World War II shorts and '40s endorsement of a wide range of food product reflect the era when Donald was the number one cartoon character in America. His extensive appearances on merchandise, in newspaper comic strips, and Carl Barks comics round out his value as a top Disney star. Donald's international appeal and complete filmography complete this work. Good for initial research of Disney's second most known cartoon character.*

Bright, Randy. DISNEYLAND INSIDE STORY. Harry N. Abrams, Inc., Publishers, New York, 1987.

The story begins around 1940. After a brief history on how Disneyland went from ideas to a solid project, the tale gains momentum as construction begins. The text is illustrated with well over 200 photos, drawings, plans, and models depicting how the various plans progressed from concept to concrete. Readers are given a peek at Walt's private apartment above the firehouse, the backstage and warehouse areas, plus photos of many world leaders and celebrities who have visited Walt's wonderland. An appendix lists each new attraction and the year they were added or deleted. The end sheets are reproductions of the 1958 Disneyland souvenir map – the park's first. This is one of the more important works done on Disneyland, preserving the way Walt meant it to be.

Burnes, Brian; Robert W. Butler; and Dan Viets. WALT DISNEY'S MISSOURI – THE ROOTS OF A CREATIVE GENIUS. Kansas City Star Books, Kansas City, 2002.

This book is a treasure chest documenting Walt's early life, mainly his years in Marceline and Kansas City, with some coverage of his time in Chicago. The descriptions, vintage photos, and interviews with citizens who knew, worked with, or hired members of the Disney family provide the heart of this volume. School photos, invoices for Walt's used camera and photo supplies, old postcards and other artifacts document every major event in Walt's Missouri life. Stories on his boyhood friend Walt Pfeiffer and A.V. Cauger, the man who hired Walt and Ub Iwerks at the Kansas City Film Ad Co., include photos of them at work in 1919 and Cauger's visit to the Disney Studio in the mid-1940s. There is background information on Virginia Davis, Walt's first Alice in Cartoonland star, who was still alive when this book was written, plus write-ups on most of his early Kansas City animators and his musical director, Carl Stalling. Elias Disney's failed farming experience

and his Star *newspaper distribution route are additional subjects. Walt and Roy Disney returned to Marceline in 1956 and were treated as stars. Many old acquaintances, particularly some who helped Walt through rough times, were still alive and local Kansas City newspaper reporters covered every angle. Candid scenes and interviews conducted in connection with that visit gives this book a fresh flavor. Those familiar with Walt and Roy's early years were amazed at how many details from the era stayed with both Disney brothers and influenced their later lives.*

Canemaker, John. BEFORE THE ANIMATION BEGINS – THE ART AND LIVES OF DISNEY INSPIRATIONAL SKETCH ARTISTS. Hyperion, New York, 1996.

John Canemaker's fascination with Disney's story department has resulted in this intriguing book on the unsung artists Walt hired to feed ideas to other story planners, animators, and background painters. There is a chapter dedicated to the careers of each individual artist covered and his or her art. Presented are Albert Hurter, Ferdinand Horvath, Gustaf Tenggren, Joe Grant, James Bodrero, Kay Nielsen, "the Fantasia group," Bianca Majolie, Sylvia Moberly-Holland, Mary Blair, Tyrus Wong, David Hall, Eyvind Earle, and Ken Anderson. Photos of the artist accompany each chapter. The chapter on Joe Grant recounts his tenure as head of the Character Model Department and the use of three-dimensional maquettes. The final chapter covers some of the modern-day inspirational artists.

——. PAPER DREAMS – THE ART & ARTISTS OF DISNEY STORYBOARDS. Hyperion, New York, 1999.

The Disney Studio invented the storyboard and was the first animated film production company to have a Story Department. Walt Disney believed as Canemaker quotes, "If the story is good the picture may be good, but if the story is weak, good color, music, and animation cannot save it." Walt felt a good story was the backbone of every picture. Getting it right was essential to success. Canemaker makes the point Walt also felt a storyman "was only as good as his last story" and therefore expendable. Canemaker documents the Disney Studio before the storyboard innovation when Walt simply thought of an idea and paid $5 a gag to build an Alice Comedy or Oswald the Lucky Rabbit story…down to modern times in the story department. Leading storymen from Ted Sears, the first head of the story department, through the careers of Webb Smith, Albert Hurter, Pinto Colvig (also the voice of Goofy), Harry Reeves, Homer Brightman, Carl Barks, T. Hee, Earl Hurd, Roy Williams, Bianca Majolie, and the legendary Bill Peet are all included. Musical boards are the subject of a special chapter. Other story artists, old and new, are also mentioned. Accompanying the background of each artist is story art featuring his or her work with special emphasis on the early animated features – Snow White, Pinocchio, Fantasia, and Dumbo.

Childs, Valerie. THE MAGIC OF DISNEYLAND AND WALT DISNEY WORLD. Mayflower Books, New York, 1979.

This photo-essay book compares the Magic Kingdoms of Disneyland and Walt Disney World in a subtle way. The best of both are shown without a preference of one against the other. In fact, you would have to have some knowledge of both parks in the late 1970s to know where some of the photos originated. The large photos, however, are useful in comparing the parks then versus now – the character clothing on guests, eliminated shows, bands, and attractions. One could easily play a game called "What's Now Missing From This Picture?" Skull Rock, the Pirate ship, the Skyride, the entertainers, the flower market, the canoe rides, old-style monorails, and so much more. A real treasure hunt for park enthusiasts.

Cotter, Bill. THE WONDERFUL WORLD OF DISNEY TELEVISION. Hyperion, New York, 1977.

This is the most complete record of Disney television shows written up to the copyright date. The author has researched background material from the point where the Disneys refused to give up television rights to their film distributor, United Artists, and switched to RKO in 1937. He points out how Walt started to consider what to do with those rights near the end of World War II, when it became evident the time for television to be introduced to the mass market had finally come. The real value of this work is a description of every individual production done for broadcast or cable television, complete with cast and production credits. Histories of famed series like the Disneyland *anthology,* The Mickey Mouse Club, Zorro, *and up to prime-time adult comedy strips like* The Golden Girls. *It was obviously a labor of love as so many books about Walt have been. As one reviews the volume of programs done during Walt's lifetime and considers all of Walt Disney's other projects, it becomes hard to imagine how one man could have supervised so much work. This 628 page volume transfers a large part of the Disney Archives into a home library.*

Culhane, John. WALT DISNEY'S FANTASIA. Harry N. Abrams, Inc., Publishers, New York, 1983. Reprinted with a new cover, 1999.

This modern take on Fantasia *is much different than the 1940 Deems Taylor book. There is less on the composers and their inspirations for each musical selection and more regarding The Making of* Fantasia. *There are many more color plates and black & white drawings, some truly striking, as are the behind-the-scenes photos of Disney, Taylor, Stokowski and the principal animators, sketch artists, and background painters. These help the reader understand the tremendous complexities of the* Fantasia *undertaking. The story and inspirational sketches for characters and segments not used show some of the difficult choices required. A serious effort has been made to track down and give full credit to all parties involved in the production on a sequence by sequence basis. A master source book for this outstanding Disney Studio masterpiece.*

——. *FANTASIA 2000*. Disney Editions, New York, 1999.

Most listings in this bibliography are limited to those covering Walt Disney and his contribution to the body of studio work during his lifetime. Fantasia 2000 *is listed because it does contain a remastered edition of* The Sorcerer's Apprentice *and it confirms the original concept of* Fantasia. *Walt's idea was to replace* Silly Symphonies *with an even-growing repertoire of classical numbers that could be released in different combination in subsequent years. Several segments were already in development when* Fantasia *failed at the box office and World War II closed down feature production.* Fantasia 2000 *proved the concept was sound even though it wasn't produced until sixty years later.*

Dunlop, Beth. BUILDING A DREAM. Harry N. Abrams, Inc., Publishers, New York, 1996.

Walt Disney supervised the design and construction of the Hyperion Avenue and Burbank studios, Disneyland, and did substantial planning for Walt Disney World's Magic Kingdom and EPCOT. His Philosophy for space usage, functional design, and dramatic details has been carried forward by Walt Disney Imagineering and outside architects to provide the theme park buildings, hotels, and other structures needed for the ever-growing Disney Worldwide empire. This fine art treatment offers superb photography and even includes some coverage of structures found in Disney animated films.

Eliot, Marc. WALT DISNEY HOLLYWOOD'S DARK PRINCE. Carol Publishing Group, New York, 1993.

The author baits the reader with scandalous charges against "Uncle Walt" based on the thinnest of evidence, easier disproved than substantiated, before launching into a fourth-rate biography full of factual errors. There are more holes in this work than an electric shaver screen; strictly supermarket tabloid stuff. Walt was not born ten years earlier as numerous photos with his baby sister Ruth (whose birth certificate was recorded properly) so prove. Walt did believe, as did many others, communist party sympathizers were behind the animation strike of 1941. His resulting anti-communist stand and testimony before the House Committee on Un-American Activities did not make him a "domestic spy." Walt was not anti-Semitic. He valued many key Jewish employees and, as the author quickly skips over, was named Man of the Year for 1955 by B'nai B'rith. It is common knowledge Kay Kamen, Ltd. was an outside company and shared 50% of merchandise royalties income from 1933 until his death in a 1949 plane crash. He was not an "inside" rep as the author describes. Donald Duck's first "official" appearance was in 1934, not 1935. Walt Disney did welcome Ub Iwerks back to the studio in 1940 and they remained lifelong friends. He even paid many of Ub's debts, much to brother Roy's displeasure. Walt Disney Productions went public to raise money to increase the number of animated films per year, not to cover losses from Pinocchio due to Hitler invading Poland and cutting off the international market. The author sees a metaphor in every Disney fantasy, psychoanalyses every Disney action without ever having met the man, and cites very few sources who had direct contact with the man he chooses to attack. This book was nothing more than a commercial attempt to sell books by attacking a universally revered purveyor of wholesome entertainment. To anyone who has seriously researched the life of Walt Disney, Eliot has all the credibility of a fortuneteller trying to read the past in a bowling ball.

Field, Robert D. THE ART OF WALT DISNEY. Collins, London and Glasgow, 1942.

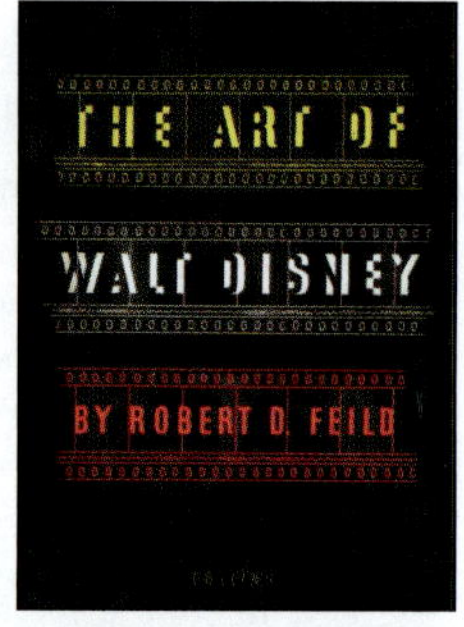

The base material for this work was collected between June 1939 and May 1940, making it one of the earliest works to try to describe the Disney appeal. The author's intellectual approach is a bit wordy as he tries to put the Disney audience connection into words. The author's social-impact statements about film, stories, ideas, music, images, human relations, and other theories, however, frequently drift from the book's title. Readers patient enough to wade through this thinking-in-print will find early photos and information on the Burbank studio right after it was built, model sheet photos, concept drawings, and dozens of color plates from films of the period. The book was very popular. It was reprinted several times and updated in 1947. It served Disney researchers until more factual and complete references were published. A lot to read through for a small amount of relevant material not found elsewhere.

Finch, Christopher. THE ART OF WALT DISNEY – FROM MICKEY MOUSE TO THE MAGIC KINGDOM. Harry N. Abrams, Inc., New York, 1973. Many abbreviated editions.

The first edition of this benchmark book is the most elaborate studio history/Walt Disney biography ever done. The gold foil-stamped title pages and full-color fold-outs underscore the Disney quality art displayed throughout the book. Historic photos, many printed for the first time (but used since), helped fuel the amazing interest in Walt Disney's life and prompted others to preserve segments of Disney history in books of their own. Finch's work established a pattern for updated studio histories and it remains essential reading for anyone interested in learning more about the life of the Walt Disney brand. Finch benefited from full access to the studio and animation art archives, plus the use of any material he chose to include. There are, unfortunately, many cut-downs and edited versions of this important book; both hard and softbound. If they are 9" x 11½" in size you have an edited edition lacking many of the elements which makes the full edition important and useful.

——. WALT DISNEY'S AMERICA. Abbeville Press, Inc, 1978.

Capitalizing on the success of his previous book, The Art of Walt Disney, Christopher Finch returned with this attempt to identify the man behind the history in greater depth. He compares the Disney role in developing animation and Disneyland to other great artists, events in cinematic history, and culture achievements. This intellectual approach leads the reader down many philosophic paths deftly illustrated with hundreds of photos culled from theme park and studio archives. The text rarely rises above East Coast cocktail party rhetoric while the illustrative material smack of items left over from Finch's highly successful first attempt. In the end, readers learn precious little about the man, but more about his history and work.

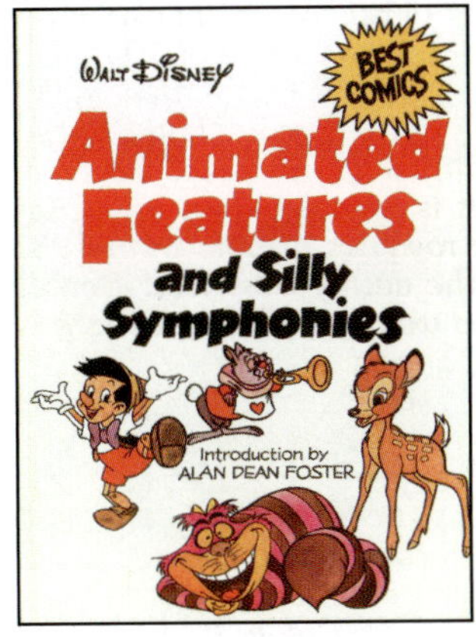

Foster, Alan Dean. WALT DISNEY ANIMATED FEATURES AND SILLY SYMPHONIES. Abbeville Press Publishing, New York, 1980.

Sunday newspaper color comic sections were the prominent household entertainment from the early 1900s into the 1960s. The golden age of such strips was from the '20s until TV captured home visual interest by the mid-'50s. This was the era of Mickey Mouse, The Silly Symphonies, and early animated features. Most older Disney fans are familiar with the Mickey Mouse and Donald Duck newspaper comic strips. This book preserves the Silly Symphony and animated feature strips. The Disney Classic series were actually re-run in newspapers each time an animated feature was re-released to theaters. Many of the strips preserved here include the cut-out play money and "Mickey Mouse Movies" animation wheels. The animated feature strips included are Snow White, Pinocchio, Bambi, Cinderella, and Alice in Wonderland.

France, Van. CLUB 55 – THE PIONEERS. Walt Disney Productions, 1975.

Club 55 was an organization founded by Van France and comprised of cast members who opened the park in 1955 and were still working at Disneyland 10 years later. This book was published in conjunction with Disneyland's 20th anniversary in 1975. It pictured all but a few remaining Club 55 members. It has the look and feel of a high school or college yearbook. Along with each picture are the edited results of interviews conducted by Mike O' Brien. The art director was Gene Camelot, with Pam Vadnais serving as secretary, and Reive Bardese as photographer. Each member was asked how he or she got hired, various jobs held, memories about being a Disneyland Pioneer, and favorite recollection of Walt and Roy Disney. It was a souvenir of the 1975 banquet and the print run was limited to attending members and a few archival copies. Overall it paints a totally different picture of Walt's relationship with the Disneyland cast members than the tremulous one he had with his artists and production staff at the studio.

——. WINDOW ON MAIN STREET. Laughter Publications, Nashua, NH, 1991.

Here is the inside story on building Disneyland, getting it open and the people who converted an orange grove in Anaheim, California to the world's first theme park in less than a year. The author relates what a hectic year it was, and traces how all the important elements came together. He is also the only author to tell how difficult the first year was and the impact it had on the entire Disney Studio. Every expert in the amusement park and film business predicted Disneyland would fail within its first year. Van France reveals how close they came to being right and how the skill of the Disney organization made the adjustments necessary to survive.

Funicello, Annette, with Patricia Romanouski. A DREAM IS A WISH YOUR HEART MAKES. Hyperion, New York, 1994.

151

This is the story of a shy, reluctant Cinderella who was plucked from a close-knit Italian family at age 12 to become a Mouseketeer and a Disney movie star. Approximately a third of the book is Disney related. It provides a unique view of The Mickey Mouse Club TV program, plus the '50s and '60s Disney live-action features in which she appeared. Walt could recognize individuals with whom the public could identify. Annette's story relates how the show changed the lives of the children chosen to be Mouseketeers and what it was like to live a Disney fantasy. She enjoyed a close relationship with the Sherman Brothers who wrote most of her hit songs. The balance of this autobiography deals with her two marriages, three children, and battle with MS with occasional flashbacks to her Disney experience. She takes special relish in the day she was no longer recognized as Annette and was referred to as "Hey, pizza lady" while working her son's Little League concession stand.

Geis, Darlene, Editor. WALT DISNEY'S TREASURY OF CARTOON CLASSICS. Harry N. Abrams, Inc., New York, 1981. Second Edition, Disney Press, New York, 1995.

The most popular Silly Symphonies are retold in storybook form. Cel composites or film frames are used to illustrate each tale. Nineteen stories have been selected from the Silly Symphonies produced. A brief uncredited introduction provides historical information on this series.

——. WALT DISNEY'S TREASURY OF CHILDREN'S CLASSICS. Harry N. Abrams, Inc., 1978. Second Edition, Disney Press, New York, 1995.

This storybook was done in the same format as The Walt Disney Treasury of Cartoon Classics, using animated features rather than cartoons as the source material. Seventeen stories appear including all the early animated classics excluding Fantasia. A brief story about the film's creation follows each featured production. Large blow-ups of film frames illustrate the story narratives.

Ghez, Didier – Editor. WALT'S PEOPLE VOLUMES 1, 2, & 3. Print on Demand, 2005-2006.

Each volume contains an average of 15 interviews with an important artist, animator, or other associate of the Disney Studio, particularly those of the 1930s and 1940s, plus later artists who worked on animated features and at Walt Disney Imagineering. The interviewees provide many references to working for Walt, but also cover aspects of the person's life before, and sometimes after, their years with the Disney Studio. The transcripts have been edited for grammar and correct speech. Otherwise, the interviews are great research data rather than polished text. Many of the interviews have never been printed before in English. International Disney scholar Didier Ghez has done an excellent job unearthing this interesting information.

Gordon, Bruce and David Mumford. THE NICKEL TOUR. Camphor Tree Publishers. Santa Clarita, California, 1995 First Edition; 2000 Second Edition.

The Nickel Tour gets its name from the postcards reproduced throughout the book to chart the growth and development of Disneyland. There are other photos too, and stories behind all the original and new attractions as they were added. It is an interesting concept that reveals how the park has changed as updated popular attraction postcards were issued. The postcards are cataloged according to a system developed by Roger Le Roque & Nick Farago in 1979 and serves as a checklist for those who collect them. The book,

Gottfredson, Floyd. WALT DISNEY'S MICKEY MOUSE. Abbeville Press, Inc., Publishers, New York, 1978.

Following a brief introduction to Walt Disney and Mickey Mouse by Gottfredson, this book reprints eleven of the artist's most famous newspaper comic-strip serials not appearing in the Walt Disney's Goofy volume. There are photos of Walt and his studio personnel, plus a guide to familiar Disney comic characters and how the style of the most popular ones changed over the years. There is also a translation of popular character names into nine different languages. The stories reprinted are Mickey Mouse in Death Valley (1930), Mickey Mouse and his Horse Tanglefoot (1933), Mickey Mouse the Detective (1933-34), Mickey Mouse and the Sacred Jewel (1934), Mickey Mouse and Pluto the Racer (1934-35), Mickey Mouse Runs His Own Newspaper (1935), Mickey Mouse and the Pirate Submarine (1935-36), Mickey Mouse and the Foreign Legion (1936), Mickey Mouse Adventures with Robin Hood (1936), Mickey Mouse and the Seven Ghosts (1936), and Mickey Mouse on Sky Island (1936-37).

Gottfredson, Floyd and Carl Barks. WALT DISNEY'S MICKEY MOUSE IN COLOR. Another Rainbow Publishing, Inc., Prescott, Arizona, 1988.

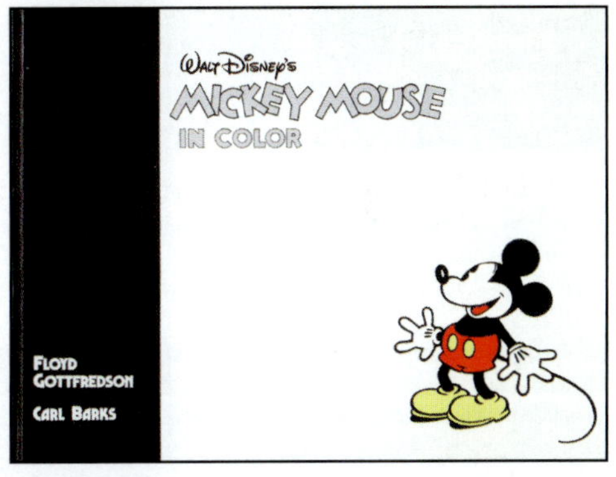

This book features the work of two outstanding Disney artists left mainly to develop stories and art on their own...Floyd Gottfredson to create the syndicated Mickey Mouse newspaper comic-strip and Carl Barks, famed Disney comic book creator. In 1930, Walt asked Gottfredson to take over the comic strip for two weeks after the departure of Ub Iwerks and Win Smith. He was never relieved and was in charge of the department for the next 45 years. Carl Barks worked at the studio's story department where he did the storyboard for the unproduced Mickey Mouse in the Northwest Mounted cartoon short which is reproduced in color. The story on how he left the studio and was recommended for the freelance job of creating stories for comics follows. In that capacity, he created the characters Uncle Scrooge, Grandma Duck, Cousin Gladstone, the Beagle Boys, and many others. His distinctive drawing style clearly identifies his work and, like Gottfredson, developed a large fan base on the quality of the art done. Neither one was personally identified until years later. The oversized book is designed to reproduce the color Sunday newspaper comic pages from several of Gottfredson's most popular serialized stories – Blaggard Castle, The Mail Pilot, and The Phantom Blot. There were two editions of this book – the oversized edition limited to 3000 copies, contained a record of a joint interview with Barks and Gottfredson. A reduced-size trade press edition was also published.

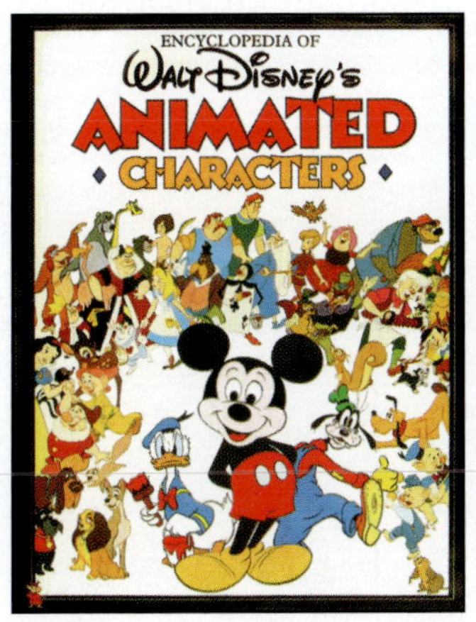

Grant, John. ENCYCLOPEDIA OF WALT DISNEY'S ANIMATED CHARACTERS. Harper & Row, Publishers, New York, 1987.

Major characters from Disney shorts and features are treated in the first third of the book. The named characters in the Disney animated features follow in order of release date – starting with Snow White and the Seven Dwarfs through The Great Mouse Detective. Updated versions have also been done to add more recent films. Each feature listed includes full credits, the film's background, and story synopsis before giving a picture and description of each character. A filmography for each character in the section on shorts makes it easy to find the films of favorite characters, even though their names may not appear in the title. Disney Archivist, Dave Smith provides the foreword in this book, produced by Justin Knowles. This work includes one of the most complete bibliographies on Disney magazine articles ever published.

Green, Amy Boothe and Howard E. REMEMBERING WALT – FAVORITE MEMORIES OF WALT DISNEY. Hyperion, New York, 1999.

This book paints a picture of Walt Disney through the eyes of family, friends, and associates as they remember small snippets from their encounters with one of the world's greatest communicators. Hundreds of photos, unfortunately unidentified, help the spirit of the presentation. The material was compiled from sound bites edited from hundreds of interviews conducted over the years for various publicity and research projects. They communicate a human sense of the man provided by those who made important contributions to the reputation and the identity of the Disney image, particularly his brother Roy, the silent partner in the Disney brand of family entertainment.

Green, Katherine and Richard. THE MAN BEHIND THE MAGIC. Viking/Penguin Group, New York, 1991.

This was the authors' first pass at a Walt Disney biography improved upon with their later 2001 work, Inside the Dream – The Personal Story of Walt Disney. This early work presents the material in a less coffee book style with more early black & white family photos. It reads a little easier without all the graphics flashing on each page. Both books are insightful within the different creative formats. The authors are true to themselves and Walt Disney in both styles.

——. INSIDE THE DREAM – THE PERSONAL STORY OF WALT DISNEY. Roundtable Press Book/Disney Editions, New York, 2001.

One of the nicer illustrated coffee table biographies of Walt Disney, with more family photos than most. It moves through the historical stuff rather briskly, aided by wonderful art direction and interesting sidebars. The photos are on point, aptly substituting for descriptive text. It is recommended as a first read for those interested in a more pictorial overview of Walt Disney's life. His major achievements are highlighted and an attempt is made to present more about the man in keeping with his historical image. One of the reasons so many books have been written about Walt Disney is there is so much to tell. This is a beautifully done book, taking advantage of modern publishing techniques to communicate its subject matter.

Holliss, Richard. WALT DISNEY'S MICKEY MOUSE – HIS LIFE AND TIMES. Harper & Row, Publishers, New York, 1986.

The anatomy of Mickey Mouse is covered in this volume. Most of his different looks as the character developed over the years are seen in drawings, posters, screen grabs, books, comic-strips, and merchandise. A running commentary threads through the different eras in his life, from his first cartoon shorts and Saturday afternoon theater Mickey Mouse Clubs to his TV and theme park adventures…and a new era of televised Mickey Mouse Clubs. His starring role in Fantasia and his World War II activities receive special notations. A filmography through 1983 is included in this concise "biography" of THE Mouse and his creator.

Holliss, Richard and Brian Sibley. WALT DISNEY'S SNOW WHITE AND THE SEVEN DWARFS & THE MAKING OF THE CLASSIC FILM. Simon & Schuster, Inc., New York, 1987.

Produced in conjunction with the 50th Anniversary of the first Disney animated feature, the book provides a concise look at the film that captivated Hollywood when it premiered in December, 1937. The development, original character designs, inspirational art, even some art from Ward Kimball's bed-building scene cut from the film, are included. Then the story from the film is synopsized scene by scene accompanied by layout, and camera direction drawings to support the full-color frames reproduced from the film. The music, voice actors, and a letter from Adriana Caselotti, the voice of Snow White, are also shown. Other memorabilia from the film

and a diagram of *Snow White's Scary Adventure* from Disney theme parks are referenced in an appendix along with film credits and a selected Bibliography.

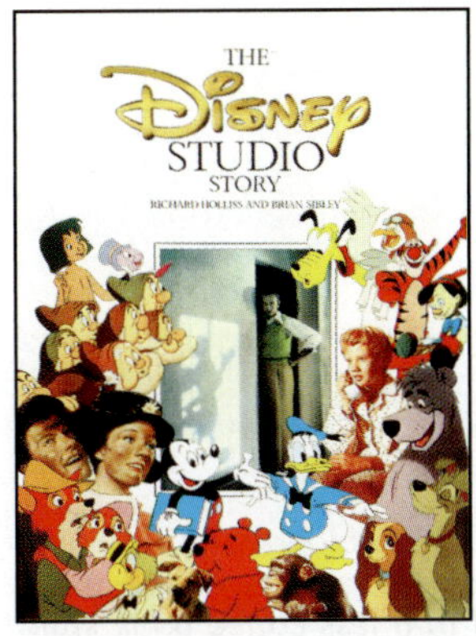

——. THE DISNEY STUDIO STORY. Crown Publishers, Inc., New York, 1988.

Another Disney Studio pictorial history from the Alice Comedies up through the 1987 production of the live-action film, Stakeout. The history of the company is compiled in a mixed bag of narration, thumbnail film reviews, and illustrations ranging from movie stills, fan cards, merchandise, studio personnel photos, and artwork. Designed as a coffee table book, it is one of several such books published periodically to update the achievements of Walt Disney, his staff, and successors.

Hurter, Albert. HE DREW AS HE PLEASED. Simon and Schuster, New York, 1948.

In the small introduction to this sketchbook, Walt Disney wrote, "Albert Hurter was a master creator of fantasy. In his whimsical imagination all things were possible. The sketches in this book testify not only to his rare sense of humor, but also to his genuine ability as an artist." Walt Disney recognized Hurter's ability to stimulate sight gags and put him to work in 1931. He helped pioneer the exaggeration technique and forever influenced the studio with his humanizing of inanimate objects. The characters in the Silly Symphony Musicland were designed by him, as were many of the details and backgrounds in Snow White. Virtually all the clocks and toys in Geppetto's workshop and the European backgrounds in Pinocchio were done by Albert Hurter. Nearly a thousand of his sketches are shown in this review of his work. The creative source for many scenes in Disney cartoons and features are revealed. More importantly, the value of this type of idea art at the Disney Studio becomes a clear testament to understanding Walt Disney and the success of his enterprises. Albert Hurter died in 1942 and willed money to Disney storyman Ted Sears to publish this book on his work. His drawings continued to inspire characters like Luminere in Beauty and the Beast and Marc Davis' work on the Disneyland Pirates of the Caribbean attraction, which in turn was the idea source for the Jack Sparrow movie series look.

Imagineers, The. WALT DISNEY IMAGINEERING – A BEHIND THE DREAMS LOOK AT MAKING THE MAGIC REAL. Hyperion, New York, 1996.

Walt Disney created a special group of artists, sculptors, engineers, architects and functional designers in 1952 to create Disneyland and the attractions it housed. The operation has since designed eleven major theme parks, plus World's Fair exhibits, water parks, shows, themed shopping complexes and just about anything a man can dream up. Originally called WED Enterprises, this group is now known as Walt Disney Imagineering. This book illustrates how they take concepts and ideas and turn them into reality. Just a small sampling of work done for theme parks all around the world demonstrates the wide variety of unique projects this organization has tackled. Art for proposed, but never executed projects, is sprinkled among the original concept art for familiar landmarks now found in theme parks and other Disney ventures, Great background for those who have never had the opportunity to tour the actual facilities in Glendale.

Jackson, Kathy Merlock – Editor. WALT DISNEY CONVERSATIONS. University Press of Mississippi, Jackson, 2006.

Here is a compilation of Walt Disney interviews with leading magazine writers, speeches made by him, plus a transcript of his testimony before the House Committee on Un-American Activities in 1947. The stories reprinted are as early as 1929 up until the year of his death in 1966 as reported in such publications as the New York Sunday News, Family Circle, The Ladies Home Journal, Newsweek, Look, The Toronto Star Syndicate, *plus transcripts provided by the Canadian*

Broadcasting Corporation and the Disney Archives. "The Amazing Secret of Walt Disney" by Don Eddy, published in The American Magazine, August, 1955 *is a particularly illuminating piece on Walt Disney the man.*

Johnston, Ollie and Frank Thomas. BAMBI – THE STORY OF THE FILM. Stewart, Tabori & Chang, New York, 1990. (Also see Frank Thomas)

Bambi has been named the favorite Disney animated feature by many animators, artists, and others, including Merchandise Division art director Lou Lispi, who cited the Bambi film and the character merchandise he created as the favorite of all his work. As Johnston and Thomas relate, Bambi was not typical Disney fare. It was more real than fantasy, portraying such heady subjects as a mother's death and a disastrous forest fire. Hardly a cartoon, Bambi dealt with serious subjects requiring special treatment. This book relates how those challenges were met with both story and art. The book itself is classified as a "gift book." The layout and art direction rise to a special level for this type of behind-the-scenes animated feature presentation. The storyline, how the changing seasons were animated, and sections on each character are illustrated with art pertaining to the text. Photos and coverage of all the principal storymen, artists, and animators are also included. A beautifully done book. A promotional flip-movie book with the same cover was sometimes used as a premium. The two were shrink-wrapped together for such promotional sales.

——. THE DISNEY VILLAINS. Hyperion, New York, 1993. (Also see: Thomas, Frank)

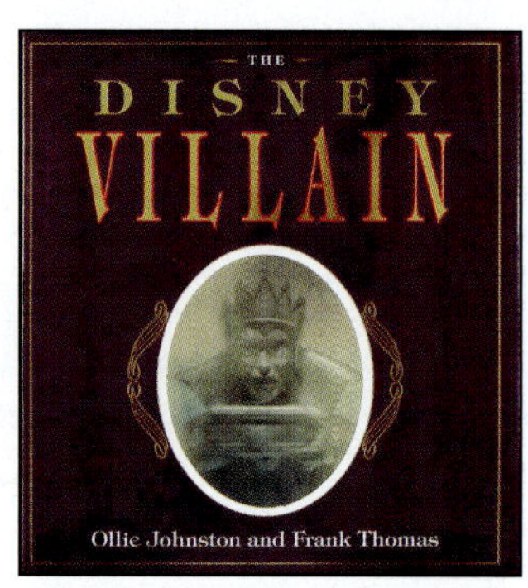

There can't be good without evil was the Disney Studio's premise for the creation of the villains audiences loved to hate. From Black Pete (AKA Peg Leg Pete) to the Evil Queen in Snow White *to the menacing Maleficent in* Sleeping Beauty, *the classic Disney villains are analyzed in this volume like no other. From the prince of nasties Chernabog to buffoons like Captain Hook and the henchmen in* 101 Dalmatians, *they are described by directing animators Johnston and Thomas who usually drew the characters being terrorized rather the villains themselves. The perspective written about, however, is that of Walt's and others at the studio who had a special knack for villains who never succeeded in killing anyone, as hard as they might try. Typically, their plans backfired and they were thoroughly throttled in the end.*

Justice, Bill. JUSTICE FOR DISNEY. Tomart Publications, Dayton, Ohio, 1992.

Disney animator and imagineer since 1937, Justice tells what it was like to join the studio in time to work on Snow White and the Seven Dwarfs *up through the opening of Walt Disney World. He retired in 1979, but continued with the company as a consultant on several special projects following his official departure. His words, drawings, and pictures provide an insider view of both studio and theme park operations. He animated all the Chip 'n Dale theatrical cartoons and was responsible for character animation for seven theme park audio-animatronics presentations – Pirates of the Caribbean, the Haunted Mansion, The Country Bear Jamboree, the Hall of Presidents, the Mickey Mouse Revue (which he created), the updated Carousel of Progress, and America Sings.*

Keller, Keith. THE MICKEY MOUSE CLUB SCRAPBOOK. Tempo Books/Grosset & Dunlap Publishers, New York, 1975, 1977.

This pictorial return to the '50s Mickey Mouse Club is a great source on the subject. It credits Bill Walsh, the first producer of the Disneyland TV show, and later many Disney feature films, for his outstanding work on the MMC. It shows the audition photos for the first 24 Mouseketeers and several that only lasted a few shows. The author paired 28 original Mouseketeers' photos to current publication date portraits, along with photos of the 1977 cast of the New Mickey Mouse Club kids, the first series to be taped in color. Many other aspects of the popular series are covered, including rehearsal and production photos, memorabilia, special guests, and animation done exclusively for the program.

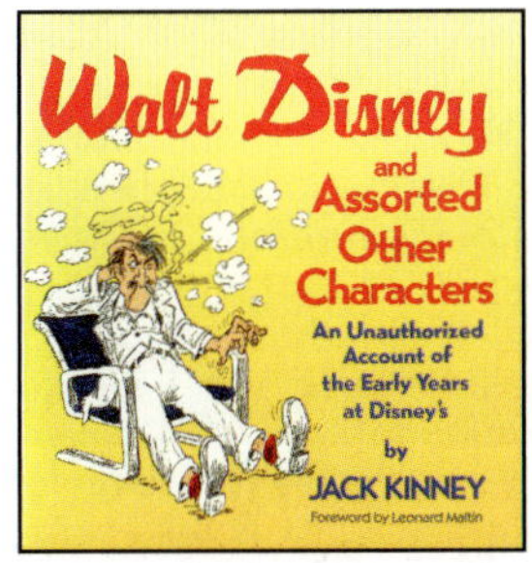

Kinney, Jack. WALT DISNEY AND ASSORTED OTHER CHARACTERS, AN UNAUTHORIZED ACCOUNT OF THE EARLY YEARS AT DISNEY'S. Harmony Books, New York, 1988.

The book Disney insiders love to read and talk about. Kinney writes evenhandedly about his up and downs at the Disney Studio, his employer from 1931 and for almost 27 years thereafter. His points are made in words and cartoons. Kinney's book was one of the first to pierce the protectionist wall surrounding Walt Disney. It is a history of the company conveyed in thumbnail sketches of the artists, musicians, and production people who helped build the studio, particularly from the time Kinney joined the company until he left Disney in 1957, with emphasis on the 1930s. A must-read for anyone trying to understand Disney operations during that period.

Knowles, Justin. WALT DISNEY'S DONALD DUCK – 50 YEARS OF HAPPY FRUSTRATION. H-P Books, Tucson, Arizona, 1984.

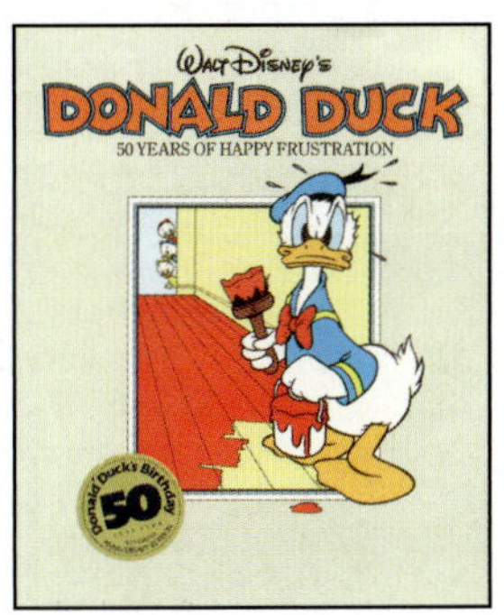

This biography of Donald Duck credits Walt Disney as his creator, even though Walt never could really get into the character. Mickey was his alter-ego and he may have resented Donald's success a bit. At the peak of cartoon-short production, Disney had six separate units producing them – two concentrated almost exclusively on Donald shorts. He was undeniably the studio's most popular character in the late '30s and throughout the '40s. The work traces Donald's career, with special sections devoted to Clarence "Ducky" Nash – the voice of Donald; Al Taliaferro, who drew the Donald Duck newspaper comic strip for over 30 years; and Carl Barks, who drew Donald Duck stories for Walt Disney Comics and Stories, Donald Duck, Uncle Scrooge, and other comic-book titles. The usual photos, art, and memorabilia are used for visuals in this illustrated treatment.

———. WALT DISNEY'S GOOFY – THE GOOD SPORT. H-P Book, Tucson, Arizona, 1985.

The transformation of Dippy Dawg from Mickey Mouse's barnyard years to Dippy the Goof, and finally to Goofy after Art Babbit took over the character is documented in story and pictures. Babbit was really responsible for developing the character who is the Goofy we know today. It was, however, the Jack Kinney "How To" series of cartoon shorts that further refined the character after Babbit left the studio during the 1941 animation strike. While Goofy became a Disney star, he never quite attained the stature of Mickey Mouse or Donald Duck. Still, he became a leading figure in books, toys, and other character merchandise as this book records in its illustrative presentation.

Koenig, David. MOUSETALES – A BEHIND-THE-EARS LOOK AT DISNEYLAND. Bonaventure Press, Irvine, CA, 1994.

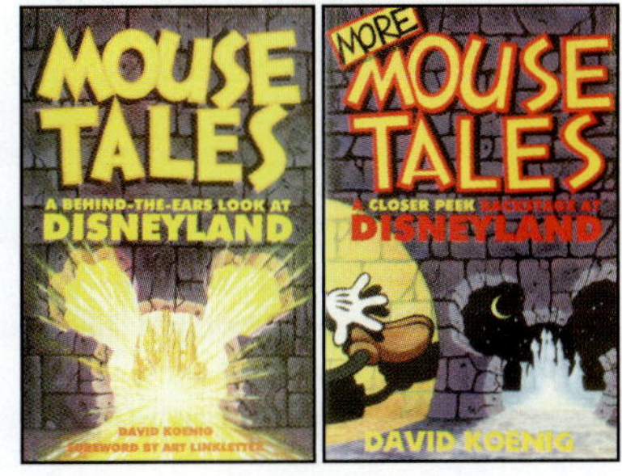

Rather than extol Disneyland's world-acclaimed virtues, the author presents a litany of non-secrets and supposed blemishes the real world has inflicted on the first Magic Kingdom. The book reveals pages of Disneyland statistics, largely lifted from the standard "Fact Book" provided by the park publicity office, and provides a "complete" listing of lawsuits filed against Disneyland, Inc. (most won by the company). The errors are large and many. The existence of the private Club 33 has never been "kept secret." The figures in Nature's Wonderland were not the first audio-animatronic creations. They were operated by mechanical cams and levers. The book is a sad attempt to air Disneyland's dirty laundry. Readers can take heart in how little dirt from the "real world" has managed to breach the berm surrounding "The Happiest Place on Earth" in its first 40 years of being open to all, except one Soviet Russian dictator.

———. MOUSE UNDER GLASS – SECRETS OF DISNEY ANIMATION. Bonaventure Press, Irvine, California, 1997.

This book provides the author's analysis of the "30 most popular animated features." The source book or story is compared to the Disney version wherever one existed. Plot holes, bloopers in the production, and hidden names, symbols, and other "secrets" about most productions are "revealed." The author is critical about Walt's "dictatorial" management of the studio, particularly the treatment of story developers in favor of the animators. He is correct in his assertion that the stories, gags, and character development were done by non-animators…and they were the essence of what made Disney films different. Walt's role as the creative director and visionary of what went into the studio's films is underplayed as is his overall track record. There are many curious sidebars. The author sees the studio's animated features different from official coffee table books presenting information on the same films.

Krause, Martin; Linda Witkowski, and Steve Ison. WALT DISNEY'S SNOW WHITE AND THE SEVEN DWARFS – AN ART IN ITS MAKING. Hyperion, New York, 1994.

The Indianapolis Museum of Art exhibited the Steve Ison animation art collection of Snow White and the Seven Dwarfs drawings, cels, backgrounds, and complete setups in 1994. This book was published in conjunction with that exhibit. The Ison Snow White collection is the most extensive in private hands and provides a perfect platform to tell about the creation of this classic film and the elements that went into its production. Ison's collection was made possible by the friendships he cultivated with the artists, animators, and others who worked on this historic feature film. Information he learned in his years of collecting is passed along to the readers as the art or moments from the film "frozen in time" retells the Disney version of the classic fairytale. The text and visuals provide one of the most detailed reports on the film available in print.

Kurtti, Jeff. SINCE THE WORLD BEGAN. Hyperion, New York, 1996.

Unlike the hardbound tourist oriented souvenir books sold at Walt Disney World, this work provides a history of the planning, land acquisition, and construction of the Florida Project. It contains one of the best descriptions of the vital Reedy Creek Improvement District available outside copies of the legislation documents. It shows how the efforts of Walt Disney with Disneyland, the 1964-65 New York World's Fair, and the planning for Florida's Magic Kingdom and EPCOT continues to influence development to the present day. Each major project on the 27,000+ acres of Walt Disney World from 1971 to 1996, plus planning for Disney's Animal Kingdom areas not yet developed, are covered. Areas like Discovery Island and River Country, plus eliminated attractions 20,000 Leagues Under the Sea and the Mickey Mouse Revue are included. Behind-the-scenes stories about research conservation and environmental projects are also covered. This is the most comprehensive, compact history of Walt Disney World from the inspiration of Walt Disney through its first 25 years of operation.

Lambert, Pierre. MICKEY. Demons & Merveilles, Paris, 1998.

This magnificently produced tribute to the film appearances of Mickey Mouse is written entirely in French. The language is no barrier to enjoying the pictorial history of black & white and color Mickey roles. The use of spot UV coating make featured illustrations look like real cel setups. The accompanying art and actual notations on each piece of art is still in English, so it is easy to follow the author's point of interest, even if you can't benefit from his full descriptive text. The full script/story drawings for Steamboat Willie are reproduced in a reduced, yet still readable, size. Other early story

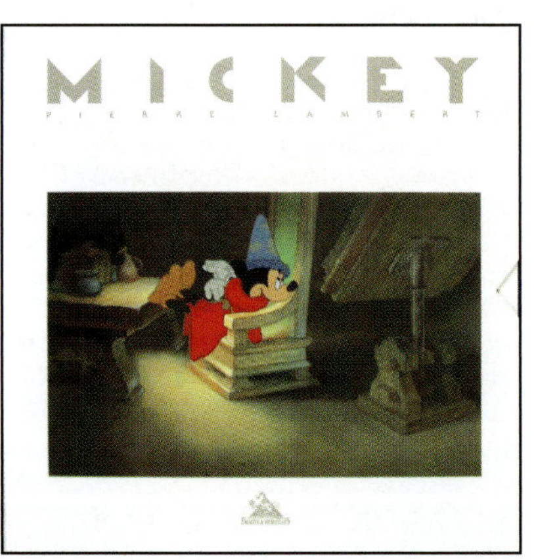

158

panels and model sheets are also shown. The book reproduces hundreds of art pieces as close as modern technology allows. Seeing historic actual-size cel setups in such vivid realism is both stimulating and educational. The frontispiece is a printed cel that lines up on a printed background to set the stage for the UV coated set-ups that follows. The technique is also used to make several photos appear to be originals. Walt always preferred good sight gags over narration or dialogue. This book underscores his philosophy with an added bonus if you can read French. (English edition also available.)

Littaye, Alain and Didier Ghez. DISNEYLAND PARIS – FROM SKETCH TO REALITY. Nouveau Millenaire Editions, Paris, Limited 2000 copies English Edition, 2002.

This is a masterful presentation on the creation of EuroDisneyland (later renamed Disneyland Paris) and all the attractions in existence on the occasion of the park's 10th Anniversary. Hundreds of color photographs detail the distinctive European flare of this unique Magic Kingdom and all the exclusive attractions found there. Frontierland is the domain for Phantom Manor and island location for Big Thunder Mountain. The Lucky Nugget Saloon, Western River Excursions, and field of geysers are also described. Adventureland, sans Jungle Cruise, offers a Bazaar styled after the Africa pavilion designed for EPCOT (but never built), the Aladdin Enchanted Passage, Indiana Jones and the Temple of Peril rollercoaster, and the Skull Rock/Capt. Hook's pirate ship, once a Disneyland attraction, plus the traditional pirates and Swiss Family Robinson attractions. Fantasyland, with its incredible Sleeping Beauty's Castle, Castle tour, Alice In Wonderland Maze, redesigned Small World attraction, and Old Mill Ferris wheel, set it apart from other Disney parks. Discoveryland provides a striking departure from Tomorrowlands found elsewhere. The huge Dirigible Hyperion, Le Visionarium, Le Mysteries du Nautilus, and Space Mountain examine the future from a mid-1800s perspective. The hotel village is also covered.

Maltin, Leonard. THE DISNEY FILMS. Crown Publishers, Inc., New York, 1973. Second Edition 1984. Third Edition, Hyperion, New York, 1995.

Film historian Leonard Maltin started with a list of Disney feature films, researched and screened them all, then wrote a review for each one. He also included all available credits: those that appeared on the screen and those his research unearthed. He talked with people associated with many of the films and recorded this background information under each feature film title. All Disney feature films up to the year of each edition are included. There are also summaries and lists of

cartoon short subjects and selected TV episodes. The real value of this work, however, is the information Maltin has compiled on each film and his evenhanded reviewing style that allows readers to judge for themselves if the film would be of interest to them.

Marling, Karal Ann, Editor with Foreword by Nicholas Olsberg, Chief Curator, Canadian Centre for Architecture and Introduction by Marty Sklar, Vice-Chairman and Principal Creative Executive, Walt Disney Imagineering. DESIGNING DISNEY'S THEME PARKS – THE ARCHITECTURE OF REASSURANCE. Flammarion, Paris, New York, 1997.

This book was published in conjunction with an exhibition of traveling Disney Architectural theme park art with showings at the Canadian Centre for Architecture (Montreal), The Wather Art Center (Minneapolis), UCLA at the Armand Hammer Museum of Art and Cultural Center (LA), and the Cooper-Hewitt Design Museum (New York). Over a hundred drawings, paintings, and models covering the first concept of a Mickey Mouse park near the Burbank studio to

Disneyland, and theme parks up through the opening of Disneyland Paris. Overall park layouts to building details are examined. Never-built attractions and lands are described. There is much to tell about theme park architecture and no book can do it all, but this one offers information, art, and photos found nowhere else. A valued publication for anyone researching Disney theme parks.

Merritt, Russell and J.B. Kaufman. WALT IN WONDERLAND – THE SILENT FILMS OF WALT DISNEY. La Giornate del Cinema Muto/La Cineteca del Friuli, Pordenone, Italy, 1993. English edition distributed by The John Hopkins University Press, Baltimore, Maryland.

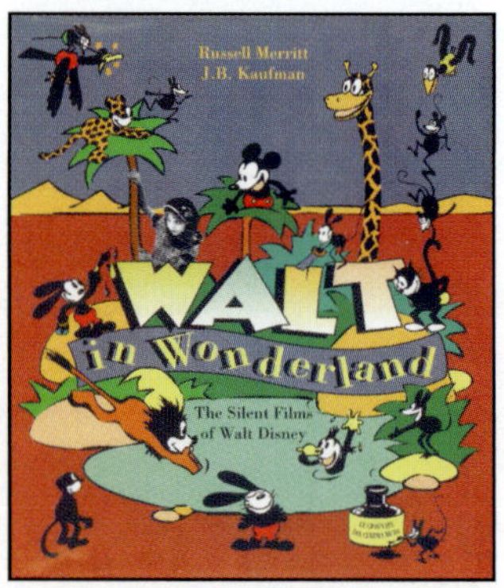

This is the most extensive printed work on Walt Disney's silent films from his first Laugh-O-gram one panel cartoons through the first two Mickey Mouse shorts. The bulk of the material features the Alice Comedies *and* Oswald the Lucky Rabbit *films. The selection is valuable because these are the least known of all Disney animated shorts. The author provides a detailed history of all the silent films documented with photos, layouts, storyboards, film frames, poster art, and other artifacts from this largely forgotten era. There is a silent filmography listing every silent film, credits as known, plus a synopsis or other background information.*

Miller, Diane Disney as told to Pete Martin. THE STORY OF WALT DISNEY. Henry Holt & Company, New York, 1957. Dell Publishing Co., Inc., New York, 1959 (Paperback).

This was an early attempt at a biography. It was written after the successful opening of Disneyland, but Walt had many productive years yet to live. The contents were serialized in The Saturday Evening Post. *The book was also sold at Disneyland. His daughter's perspective relates some insight to the man. The historical data, however, is covered in greater detail in subsequent biographical books.*

Mosley, Leonard. DISNEY'S WORLD. Stein and Days Publishers, New York, 1985.

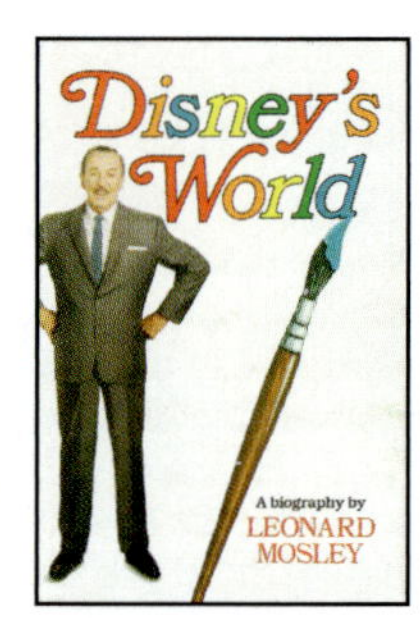

Mosley, film critic for the London Daily Express and professional biographer of international personalities, writes one of the more interesting biographies of Walt. Interest seems to be his main concern as his facts are found faulty in many cases. His reports of conversations with Ward Kimball are in direct conflict with my personal talks with him. Kimball interviews published in Walt's People *and other journals also fail to support Mosley's contentions. He misleads the reader with references to what Ward Kimball was paid as a beginning inbetweener when talking about the animation strike seven years later. He implies he was only making $50 a week when in fact he was paid around $200. He states Disney employees were underpaid when they earned substantially more than their counterparts at other Hollywood cartoon studios. Throughout the book he refers to the great wealth the Disneys took out of the studio during the '30s, when in fact they did not; as the 1940 annual report, going back to 1935 as the SEC required, and many other public documents clearly show. As an important international film critic, Mosley had interviewed both Walt and Roy Disney several times and must have established*

excellent rapport with Lillian Disney and perhaps Diane Disney Miller while preparing this work. My inside sources to Walt's life were more limited, but I found many of his conclusions and opinions, particularly about Roy O. Disney, to be in difference with my own findings. His suppositions about the root of Walt's problems in 1931 and other personal matters cited throughout the work I found to be unsupportable and totally unnecessary. He also gives space to the rumor Walt's body may have been frozen, which has also been disproven. These reservations aside, Mosley's book is nicely crafted and an interesting read, particularly for those versed in the actual facts of Walt's life who can ignore all the errors.

Palmer, H. Marion. WALT DISNEY'S SURPRISE PACKAGE. Simon & Schuster, New York, 1944.

This Giant Golden storybook provides a look at the most promising Disney projects in the works during World War II. Nine of the twelve stories were eventually made into Disney animated or par-

tially animated features, the most recent being Chicken Little. The stories were adaptations from the source material by the author assigned to the project, but the story art was all done by the Disney Studio. The book provides a rare look at these Disney works in progress. Many of the characters and art direction styles changed completely in the final produced versions. Some showed little change. Many art books show selected sketches of this type of development, but Surprise Package provides a glimpse at the body of work being developed by the Disney Story Department at a given moment in time. The twelve stories included are Through the Picture Frame, Brer Rabbit and His Satchel of Gold, The Emperor's New Clothes, The Little Fir Tree, Lady, Chicken Little, Alice's Adventures in Wonderland, The Wind in the Willows, Peter Pan and the Pirates, Peter and the Wolf, The Square World, and Happy Valley (Mickey and the Beanstalk).

Peet, Bill. BILL PEET AN AUTOBIOGRAPHY. Houghton Mifflin Company, Boston, 1989.

    Bill Peet joined the Disney Studio as an inbetweener on Snow White *in 1937. He was assigned to the story department for work on* Pinocchio *and then on to* Dumbo *where he contributed several sequences. He worked on World War II training films and* Victory Through Air Power *followed by the animated sequences in* Song of the South *and development of the mice and Lucifer for* Cinderella. *Peet worked on shorts, TV shows, and* Sleeping Beauty *during the '50s. He developed the entire story for* 101 Dalmations, The Sword and the Stone, *and the first part of* The Jungle Book *before leaving to write and draw children's books full-time. Two-thirds of his book recalls his roller coaster career working with Walt. He presents a candid view of Walt's uneven temperament and cameleon reaction to positive and negative story presentations. Early on he cites how storymen winning Walt's approval praised his judgement, while those rejected thought of him as* a bully. Peet stayed 27 years and was one of the most productive storymen, but his voice choice for the leopard in* Jungle Book *was twice rejected and Peet walked out of the studio never to return. Still he valued his years at the studio and often asked himself what Walt would have thought of his stories.*

Petersen, Paul. WALT, MICKEY AND ME. Dell Publishing Company, New York, 1977.
    The author, son of actress Donna Reed, was the first member of The Mickey Mouse Club to be fired for conduct unbecoming. He lasted only three weeks. Needless to say, he doesn't have much good to say about what Walt Disney expected from those he chose to be Mouseketeers. He is equally negative about child actors. The main value of his book is found in the quotes of children who succeeded on the show. The dismal picture he portrays about early life on a Disney soundstage conflicts substantially with my personal experience with the seven Mouseketeers I've known and how they feel about their experience on the program.

Price, Harrison "Buzz." WALT'S REVOLUTION BY THE NUMBERS. Ripley Entertainment, Inc., Orlando, 2003.

    The Disney brothers became convinced of the value in marketing research in the 1930's and it soon guided every stage of story development and production. In 1953 they hired "Buzz" Price, then of The Standford Research Institute, to study possible sites for Disneyland. His research led to Anaheim and what he calls in his book "Walt's Revolution" of the attraction industry. The work covers the research done for Disney theme parks, domestic and foreign, and jobs done for virtually every other theme park, museum, aquarium, and similar development since the success of Disneyland. It is also a management guide to the profitable operation of such ventures. The math, formulas, and statistics are all there for the business minded who want to understand the nuts and bolts operations of major entertainment ventures.

Rawls, Walton. DISNEY DONS DOGTAGS. The Abbeville Publishing Group, New York, London, Paris, 1992.
    The Disney Studio proved to be a valuable stateside asset during World War II. It did hundreds of training films, posters, and artwork of all types. The studio produced films to get U.S. citizens to pay their income taxes early to support the war effort, plus films to encourage the purchase of War Bonds and stamps. There were some propaganda films and support for the USO. Many cartoons had

war themes and Walt produced *Victory Through Air Power* to promote the development of a strategic bomber. This book touches on these and other war themes, but mostly it shows art and the finished products from many of the 1200 military insignia designed to help boost moral among Allied Fighting Forces. This is one of the best guides to studio efforts during this important time in U.S. history.

Rovin, Jeff. OF MICE AND MICKEY. Manor Books Inc., New York, 1975
This book is an assembly of bits and pieces from the first TV Mickey Mouse Club based primarily on interviews with

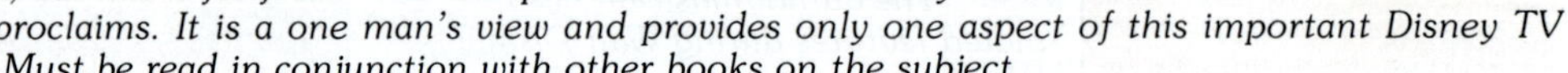

Mouseketeer Lonnie Burr. Many of the photos used were supplied by him. There are trivia tests, quotes from Walt Disney, and profiles of other Mouseketeers, especially Annette. Also included are brief historical references to Walt Disney (kind and unkind) and how little he had to do with the show. Producer Bill Walsh was clearly the man in charge. Each element of the MMC – special days, recurring series, featured talent – are discussed, but this is far from "The Complete Guide to the Mickey Mouse Club" as the subtitle proclaims. It is a one man's view and provides only one aspect of this important Disney TV venture. Must be read in conjunction with other books on the subject.

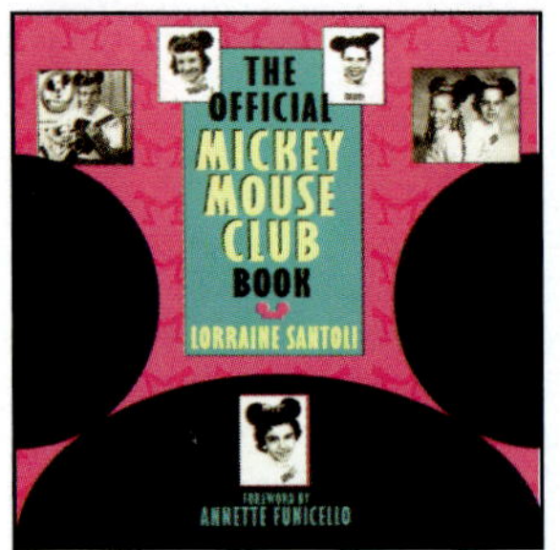

Santoli, Lorraine. THE OFFICIAL MICKEY MOUSE CLUB BOOK. Hyperion, New York, 1995.
The best history of the first TV Mickey Mouse Club. It provides background on the theater clubs of the early 1930s and the first Disney TV specials. Then it moves on to the concept, auditions, and final selection of the first Mouseketeers. Each segment of this popular ABC daily program – the special days, serials, featured Mouseketeers and other events — are all covered. Black & white photos and candid behind-the-scenes shots document the three years the show was in production. There are also photos of MMC memorabilia, reunion events, producer Bill Walsh and other show personnel. The MMC was a huge undertaking with original songs, stories, sets, and choreography for a whole hour, five days a week. The Club forced Howdy Doody, the NBC kid show leader since 1947, off the daily schedule to a Saturday morning slot.

Schickel, Richard. THE DISNEY VERSION. Simon and Schucter, New York, 1968.
This highly negative look at Walt Disney's life smacks of a work written by someone with an ax to grind. It purports to be an penetrating biographical work written for intellectuals. The author concedes his effort was based on some personal interviews, but mostly on the public record. It's obvious the interviews were conducted with Walt detractors like Art Babbit, and to some extent, Bill Tytla and Jack Kinney. The supposition, analogies, and conclusions are fiction devised by the author and come across as psychobabble to anyone with any first-hand knowledge about the life of Walt Disney. The biography information can easily be found in Bob Thomas' Walt Disney – An American Original, Diane Disney Miller's The

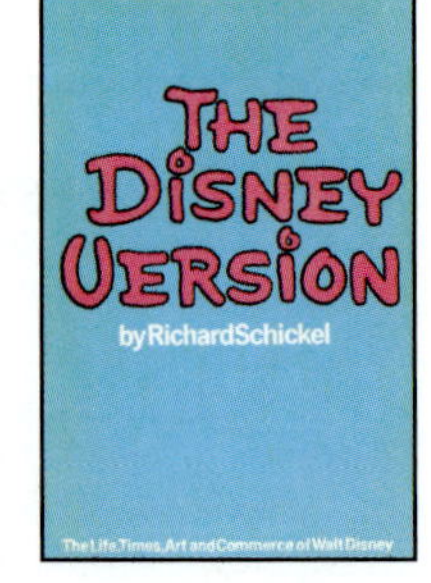

Story of Walt Disney, and numerous other titles on Walt's life and histories of the Disney Studio listed in this bibliography.

Schroeder, Horst with foreword by Steve Hulett. Walt Disney's Goofy. Abbeville Press Publishers, New York, 1979.
This book is about Floyd Gottfredson, who drew the Mickey Mouse newspaper comic strip from 1930 to 1975. Goofy is almost incidental to many of the stories reprinted here from the British Mickey Mouse Weekly Magazine. The introductory material provides a good history of the character and some merchandise memorabilia. It then reprints the following stories – Mickey Mouse and the Terrible Bandit Wolf Barker (1933), Mickey Mouse and the Great Ostrich Race (1936), Mickey Mouse Mighty Whale Hunter (1938), Mickey Mouse Outwits the Phantom Blot (1939), Mickey Mouse and the Dude Ranch Bandit (1940), Mickey Mouse on Cave Man Island (1940-41), Mickey Mouse in the Jewel

Robbery (1942), Mickey Mouse in Love Trouble (1941), and Mickey Mouse and the Black Crow Mystery (1942).

Schroeder, Russell. WALT DISNEY HIS LIFE IN PICTURES. Disney Press, New York, 1966.

A quick read published in sound-bite asides and captions to over 150 Walt Disney photos ranging from his baby pictures to those taken the last year of his life. It is an excellent photo-essay, often using multiple shots from the same photo shoot to capture Walt's personality at a given moment. There is heavy emphasis on his early life, the period of the 1930s as he inspired more life-like animation, and from his TV years. It's not a child's storybook, but reads about as fast. Those who like to study and compare photos will get much more from this fine selection.

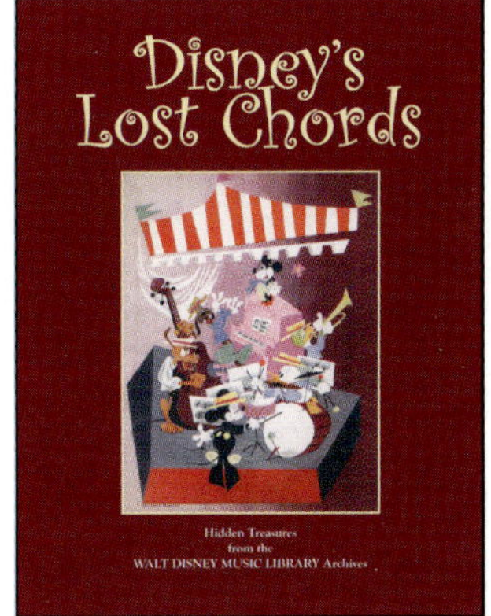

———. DISNEY'S LOST CHORDS. Voigh Publications, Robbinsville, N.C., 2007.

The author/musician has rescued 77 songs written for Disney animated features during Walt Disney life, but not used. These were songs Walt approved, but were cut from the film because of changes made during story development or production. Most are being published for the first time. Many are good songs, but the character designed to sing them was cut from the script. Many only existed as a melody line and chords, but the author developed the songs into standard sheet music format. Songs chosen are from Bambi up through The Jungle Book, the last animated film being prepared during Walt's lifetime. Songs from the unproduced films Rainbow Road to Oz, Chantecler, and Hansel and Gretel are also included along with 225 photos and illustrations, plus text giving the background on the songs and films. There is an interesting contrast between the songs Walt ultimately used and those discarded.

Shannon, Leonard. DISNEYLAND – DREAMS, TRADITIONS AND TRANSITION. Disney Press, New York, 1994.

This book traces the history of Disneyland from concept up through 1993 where it switches gears to address traditions and transitions into the future. The publication date is concealed to extend its shelf life at theme parks. It was written by a Disney Public Relations man who provided all the usual puff. What makes this book interesting is coverage of all the little details of the park largely overlooked in other books of this type...the windows on Main Street, the different figures found on popcorn carts, backstage workers, attraction posters, Imagineers building the model of Toontown, mostly exclusive photos from interesting angles, and photos of attractions removed over the years.

Sherman, Robert B. & Richard M. WALT'S TIME. Camphor Tree Publishers, Santa Clarita, California, 1998.

Walt Disney gave the Sherman Brothers their first big break, the opportunity to write a song for Annette to sing in The Horsemasters. They rewarded his faith in them with hundreds of songs for films, the 1964-65 New York World's Fair, and theme park attractions. They were a major creative force in the development of the story for Mary Poppins for which they won Academy Awards for the best original musical score. The book is done as a scrapbook loaded with photos, drawings, and artifacts documenting their illustrious careers. It covers all their Disney and other achievements on Broadway and Tin Pan Alley. Even after they left the studio payroll in 1968, they were called back many times for film, theme park, and Disney Channel assignments. They were named Disney Legends in 1990 and have made many personal appearances at Disney events. The stories behind Tall Paul, It's a Small World, One Little Spark (Imagination), I Wan'na Be Like You, and Supercalifragilisticexpialidocious are just a few of the histories revealed in the informative read. The book is also great fun visually!

Shows, Charles. WALT – BACKSTAGE ADVENTURES WITH WALT DISNEY. Wingsong Books/Communication Creativity, La Jolla, California, 1980.

The author joined the studio as it was expanding into television. His first assignment was the Man in Space series for the "Disneyland" anthology program. He worked with Walt for the next 12 years. There is a brief Walt history at the end, but mostly it's a book about the inner workings of the studio, its quirky personnel, and stories about Walt and happenings around the studio. It is much like the Jack Kinney and Bill Justice books, complete with cartoons. The accounts are all true, but the names and situations have been changed for whatever reason. For example, Ward Kimball is renamed Firehouse Fred. The book opens with the Tomorrowland TV team writing about the "Wheel" when the topic was really early aviation. The author's stated reason was to protect the privacy of his subjects. Most are thinly veiled, but it does make it difficult to understand who or what was really involved. It provides a humorous read, but it is not to be quoted with any confidence.

Smith, Dave. WALT DISNEY FAMOUS QUOTES. Disney Kingdom Editions, Lake Buena Vista, Florida, 1994.

This book is categorized according to the subject matter on which Walt was speaking. It is also cross referenced. The quotes are more extensive than the latter version published for general bookstore and mail order sales. This second version is more loosely organized and the quotes are briefer. In Walt Disney's Famous Quotes, Smith also provides more introductory and background material. The quotes selected are mainly inspirational. This version enjoys a nicer layout and photos of Walt throughout the text material.

——. DISNEY A TO Z. Hyperion, New York, 1996, 1998, Disney Editions 2006.

Disney Archives founder and Chief Archivist Dave Smith, set up most of the files and indexes from which this book was assembled. His knowledge of the corporate Disney is second to none. This book answers all the common questions about Walt Disney, his cartoons and motion pictures, TV, and other company facts and activities. This encyclopedia type coverage limits most citations to minimum facts, a small trade-off to widen its scope. There are plenty of other books to fill in the background and details. Always the best place to start when factual information is required.

——. THE QUOTABLE WALT DISNEY. Disney Editions, New York, 2001.

Walt Disney had a great sense of public relations. He sat for hundreds, if not thousands of interviews. He spoke with thoughtfulness and many gems of wisdom resulted. Dave Smith has gone through transcripts, magazine articles, production meeting notes, and other sources to put some of Walt's best one and two-liners into a handy, almost pocketsized recap including my personal favorite. "Somehow I can't believe there are many heights that can't be scaled by a man who knows the secret of making dreams come true. This special secret, it seems to me, can be summarized in four C's. They are Curiosity, Confidence, Courage, and Constancy, and the greatest of these is Confidence. When you believe a thing, believe it all over, implicitly and unquestioningly."

Smith, Dave and Steven Clark. THE FIRST HUNDRED YEARS. Hyperion, New York, 1999.

The book was published in conjunction with the 100th anniversary of Walt Disney's birth. It provides a year-by-year history of the major events in his life and studio. The copy is concise, working in just the more notable milestones. Hundreds of photos are presented in one of the nicest art direction jobs found in books of this type. Disney Senior Archivist Dave Smith is well-versed in the most often asked questions and covers the most popular subjects while providing some unexpected sidelights. An excellent premier in studio history and the biography of Walt Disney.

Soloman, Charles. THE DISNEY THAT NEVER WAS – THE STORIES AND ART FROM FIVE DECADES OF UNPRODUCED ANIMATION. Hyperion, New York, 1995.

This is one of the most fascinating Disney art books published along with a flood of others in the 1990s. Story sketches from abandoned Mickey, Donald, and Goofy cartoons are covered. The heart and major interest, however, comes in the art and descriptions of the dozens of animated features begun, but not completed. Besides cartoons, the entries are categorized in sections of Fairy Tales, Narrative Films, Fantasia and Successors, and the Rest of the Stories. Despite the segmentation, much of this work was done when the studio was stymied during World War II. It was perhaps the greatest period of story experimentation within the studio. Hans Christian Anderson and his stories, including The Little Mermaid *and* The Emperor's Nightingale, *Walt Kelly's* Goldilocks and the Three Bears, Navy Mickey, The Chanticleer, The Gremlins, *plus the additions to* Fantasia *(The Ride of the Valkyries, Clair de Lune, The Flight of the Bumble Bee),* The Baby Ballet Adventures in a Perambulator, Insect Ballet, Russian and South American Folk Tales, *and* Salvador Dali's Destino *are discussed with supporting art by some of Disney's leading creators. Other examples are included to demonstrate this vital time in studio history.*

Solomen, Jr. Jack/Steve Hulett. SNOW WHITE AND THE SEVEN DWARFS. Circle Fine Art Press, 1978 Deluxe Edition; The Viking Press, New York, 1979; Trade Edition.

This classic Disney story was edited by Jack Solomen, Jr. with The Making of Snow White and the Seven Dwarfs written by Steve Hulett. The story and other sections of the book are illustrated with storyboard sketches, animation drawings, layouts, model sheets, background paintings, and cel set-ups. The oversized book was designed as a coffee table book, and conveyed a sense of all the elements necessary to bring the story to life on screen. The color plates carry the storybook format, while the additional art captures details easily overlooked as the action unreels in the theater. The deluxe edition came with a bookmark of 35-mm film cut from a print of Snow White. The contents of different editions are identical.

Taylor, Deems with foreword by Leopold Stokowski. WALT DISNEY'S FANTASIA. Simon and Schuster, New York, 1940.

The second oldest art book published on a Disney film, this work takes each of the seven sequences (eight if Ave Maria, Part B of the seventh segment, is counted separately) and provides the Disney interpretation in words and storyboard sketches. Stokowski's brief "Foreword" stresses how different people visualize music and that the Disney artistic conceptualization is only one of many possible versions. Deems Taylor provides background on each composer and the storyline each had in mind when the music was written. This is followed by an explanation of the Disney artists interpretation. Musical staffs are used as fluid illustrations throughout this coffee table book of the period. The book is an excellent explanation of the actual film, done in a unique style of the period. Later books include more detail and art, but this book is a work of art in itself.

Thomas, Bob with the staff of the Walt Disney Studio. THE ART OF ANIMATION. Simon and Schuster, Inc., 1958.

This book is a primer on the history, techniques, and prominent examples of animation; plus what it takes to become an animator – Disney style. This educational book was also a promotion piece for Sleeping Beauty, the studio's then soon to be released animated feature. Walt must have been pleased with the result because as late as the 1980s, this book could be found in just about every office in the studio. It is profusely illustrated with drawings, cel set-ups, photos, diagrams, layouts, and whatever it takes to communicate each step of the animation process, plus it has one of the best explanations of the multi-

plane camera ever published. The first photo of Walt Disney's "Nine Old Men" also appeared in this book. It is outdated by copyright, but nothing quite its equal has been published since.

———. WALT DISNEY: MAGICIAN OF THE MOVIES. A Rutledge Book/Grosset & Dunlap Publishers, New York, 1966.

This book was done as part of series called Pioneer Books, "Biographies of the daring ones – the people with imagination and original ideas, who had the courage and determination to fulfill their purposes." It was written after Thomas did the Art of Animation, published in 1958, and before he did Walt's official biography in 1976. The style is a novelization written to young people in search of a vocation. It is more of a curiosity than an equal to Thomas' later work on Walt's life.

———. WALT DISNEY – AN AMERICAN ORIGINAL. Simon and Schuster, New York, 1976; Hyperion, New York, 1994.

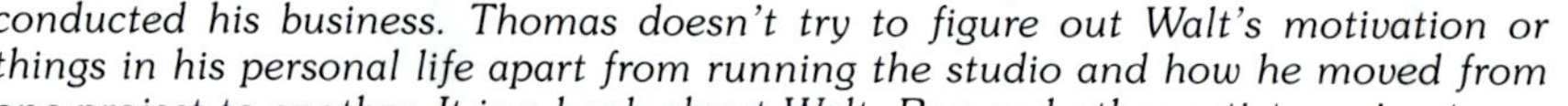

Bob Thomas was chosen to write this "official" biography based on previous work he had done for Walt Disney and the Disney Studio. It was done as a tribute and tackles a few of the more sticky issues in Walt's life. It is, however, completely based on facts, double-checked with the family and studio records. Many transcripts from Walt's memos and other writings are included to help communicate a sense of Walt Disney and how he conducted his business. Thomas doesn't try to figure out Walt's motivation or things in his personal life apart from running the studio and how he moved from one project to another. It is a book about Walt. Roy and other artists, animators, and production people are touched on as necessary, but Walt's role is stressed above all others. This is a key book to understanding the facts and achievements in Walt's life.

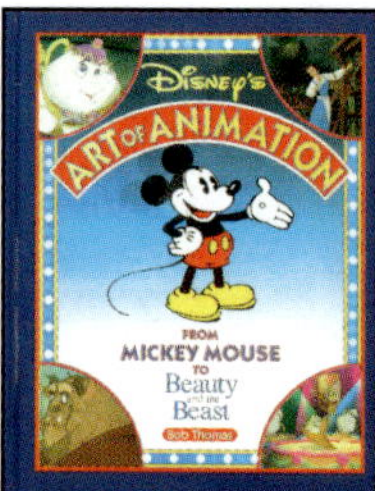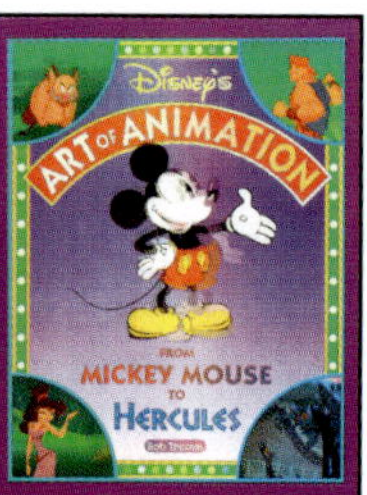

———. DISNEY'S ART OF ANIMATION. Hyperion, New York, 1991. Subsequent new editions released with new Disney animated features.

Thomas' modern update of both his 1958 work and that of Christopher Finch's 1973 book of similar title falls short of both, probably to meet the publisher's designated price point. Originally published with a lenticular casebound cover and updated with each new animated feature, the book was also available in paperback editions for most releases. The first eight chapters are the same in each variation of the title! A ninth chapter – A New Tradition – was added in later reincarnations. The remaining chapters deal with the making of and the story of the latest animated film featured on the cover. The chapters on the animation process found in Thomas' 1958 edition have all been eliminated, leaving only a brief history of Disney animated films. Much had changed since the '50s and a true update would have been welcome. The details that motivated Walt to have the first version published have largely been eliminated.

———. BUILDING A COMPANY – ROY O. DISNEY AND THE CREATION OF AN ENTERTAINMENT ENTERPRISE. Hyperion, New York, 1998.

Bob Thomas, the Associated Press Hollywood correspondent for over 50 years, knew and wrote the biographies of both Walt, and in this volume, Roy Disney. In each case he writes from the subject's point of view. This book brings an important balance to one of the greatest partnerships in American corporate history. It details how much Walt depended on his brother to run the financial side and make possible all the things Walt wanted to create. The financial community revered Roy as much as the public loved Walt. The story of Roy's successes aren't as dramatic as Walt's creative triumphs, but make for a good read and a better understanding of Walt. Roy protected Walt as much as he enabled his enterprises. He was the Disney family peacekeeper and ran legal, distribution, advertising, and merchandising in addition to all financial aspects of the corporation. These things never interested Walt, who only rarely attended board meetings or the annual stockholders' event. The

Thomas, Frank and Ollie Johnston. DISNEY ANIMATION – THE ILLUSION OF LIFE. Abbeville Press Publishers, New York, 1981 Deluxe and Regular Editions; Hyperion, New York, 1990 w/1981 copyright date. (Also see: Johnston, Ollie)

This 576-page book is the definitive text on the Disney style of animation, written by two men who helped create and refine the techniques of more realistic animated cartoons and features. Each step like squash and stretch, timing (the number of drawings between animator extremes), exaggeration, overlapping action, and many other principles are described and illustrated in great detail. This is a textbook on animation with background on the artists who collaborated to bring Walt's dreams to life at the Disney studio during the 1930s when the greatest strides in animation were made. Thousands of drawings and photos are used throughout the work. Vital reading for prospective animators or anyone seeking to understand the inner workings of the Disney Studio as it progressed from primitive cartoon shorts to feature-length animated films. The deluxe edition came slipcased with an actual 35mm film segment to use as a bookmark. Less expensive trade editions were also available. Fully indexed.

——. TOO FUNNY FOR WORDS. Abbeville Press Publishers, New York, 1987.

This book could be named Anatomy of a Sight Gag. Walt Disney preferred sight gags to dialogue or voice-over jokes in his cartoons. Thomas and Johnston attempt to explain the different type of sight gags and have masterfully categorized many approaches to this obvious humor. Highlights from Disney cartoons and animated features are used as examples. This reviewer found it difficult to focus on the text as the illustration kept distracting the intended concentration. The hundreds of gags rendered are just too funny for the words. One familiar with the films themselves will find the book more helpful, for while the key animation drawings are there, the timing and the context are not. Much of this is described. The pictures may be worth a thousand words, but the films develop subtle smiles to full belly laughs as only they can do.

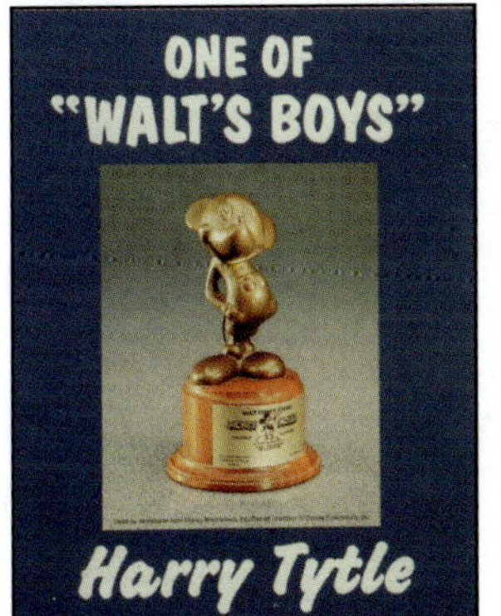

Tytle, Harry. ONE OF WALT'S BOYS. Privately Published, Royal Oak, Michigan/Mission Viejo, California, 1997. Limited Edition of 800 copies sold to the public.

The author met Walt and Roy in their polo-playing days and was hired as an inbetweener. He climbed the animation ladder, but direction and production proved to be stronger interests. He ran cartoon production and was named studio production manager in 1942. To arrange a meeting with Walt you had to go through Harry Tytle, who attended all meetings pertaining to production. He worked with Walt in an executive capacity for 30 years and kept a daily diary of his studio experience for 20 of those years, perhaps the most detailed account of Walt's studio life recorded. His book, documented with personal photos and drawings, is the most detailed one-source reference to the inner workings of the studio outside the Disney Archives. The author's personal commentary pulls no factual punches while perhaps avoiding some of the more colorful language found elsewhere. The book covers the years 1936 to 1976. It is rich in details about Walt's strengths and weaknesses, plus those of the revolving-door personnel that populated the studio from its golden age to the troubled times the studio began to suffer under committee management almost 10 years after Walt's death. Poor typography makes it difficult to read, but the added labor is worth the extra effort.

Walt Disney Productions. WALT DISNEY'S DISNEYLAND. Whitman, Racine, Wisconsin, 1964.

This hardbound Whitman Tell-A-Tale book contains large color photos of the Disneyland park and attractions as it approached its 10th anniversary. The tree and vegetation are well-established. Curiously, nearly all the photos selected for this book show attractions or areas since remodeled or replaced, so this short guide provides an interesting benchmark in the maturation of Walt's first theme park. He was still alive and no one considered the guiding light of the Disney empire would be extinguished a little over two years after this book was first printed.

———. MASTER PLANNING FOR WALT DISNEY WORLD. WED Imagineering, Glendale, California, 1969.

This 60-page book was released by the company as construction started on Florida swamps in 1969. Land preparation and canal excavation preceded construction on the Magic Kingdom, hotels, and other facilities. Black & white drawings, photos, maps, and charts support the text material dealing with subjects such as climate, expected attendance, economic impact on the state of Florida, EPCOT, and different timelines for the first five years of development. This benchmark plan underwent many changes. The monorail route was shortened and hotels were eliminated as a result. The plan calling for Eastern Airtimes to partner with Disney to build an airport on the property was also subsequently dropped. Many less-spectacular parts of the plan never happened and there is no mention of camping facilities that became a major factor by opening day. A great research document.

———. PREVIEW EDITION WALT DISNEY WORLD. Walt Disney Productions, 1970.

This 24-page booklet was distributed at the Lake Buena Vista Preview Center in the months leading up to the opening of Walt Disney World on October 1, 1971. Artist renderings and models displayed in the Preview Center were also reproduced in the booklet. It described the Florida Magic Kingdom, accenting some of the many differences from Disneyland in California. Then it detailed the hotel resorts planned, including the three master-plan hotels never built. The plan for the first five years provided details about the land use, major

attractions, and an outline for EPCOT. The most frequently asked questions about the future of the 43.5 square mile property were also addressed. The cover painting shows what the property would have looked like according to the plans in place when construction started in 1969 in contrast to the park as it opened in 1971.

———. TREASURES OF DISNEY ANIMATION ART. Abbeville Press, New York, 1982.

This oversized coffee table book was produced by publisher Robert E. Abrams with John Canemaker doing the introduction. It is a companion to Frank Thomas and Ollie Johnston's DISNEY

Walt Disney Studio. WALT DISNEY'S SNOW WHITE SKETCH BOOK. William Collins Sons & Co. LTD., London and Glasgow, 1938.

This book is more historical than a research tool to understanding the life of Walt Disney. It is a beautifully conceived presentation on the characters seen in the first Disney animated feature. There is a section for each one. The first is Snow White. There is a title page followed by a "how-to-draw" section. Brief text about the character faces a glassine title page through which a full color plate tipped onto a brown construction paper background is seen. The same format is used for each of the Seven Dwarfs, the Wicked Queen, the Witch, and the Prince. Supplemental studies of the animals, interiors, and the cottage exterior are also included. It was the first Disney art book published and remains very rare. It was reproduced in a limited edition by Applewood Book, but the reproduction didn't begin to compare to the original.

Williams, Pat with Jim Denney. HOW TO BE LIKE WALT. Heath Communications, Inc., Deerfield Beach, Florida, 2004.

This is a well researched Walt Disney biography and includes stories and quotes not found elsewhere. Others in the Disney organization are brought into the storyline, but the focus is on Walt. The book is part of a vocational guidance series, but offers a good read for Disney enthusiasts anxious for every detail of Walt's life. There is a religious undertone to parts of the book. It mentions some of Walt's more human frailties and the studio's animation strike in passing. Much of the book is the same biographical information found in other biographies and studio histories. It holds Walt up as an inspirational life example and presents him fairly with little mention of all the others who helped Walt's dreams come true.

Various Composers with Forward by Steven Spielberg. THE NEW ILLUSTRATED DISNEY SONGBOOK. Harry N. Abrams, Inc., New York/HA/Leonard Publishing Corporation, Milwaukee, 1986.

Walt Disney had an uncanny ear for picking songs for his pictures. There have been many books published on the songs from his cartoons and animated features in addition to individual sheet music for most songs. This book is one of the best to provide the piano/vocal music and remained in print for many years. One making a study of Disney music will want to exhaust all sources, but those interested in getting a feel for Walt Disney's master music selection talent can examine over two hundred pages of hit after hit that are still sung and recorded today. Pop hits range from "Minnie's Yoo Hoo," "The World Owes Me a Living," and "Who's Afraid of The Big Bad Wolf?," through all the animated classic hits, TV, and theme park melodies, to Mickey Mouse Disco, and "Love Come for Me," from Splash...73 in all. Color and black & white photos are used throughout.

Magazines and Periodicals

The Disney Public Relations operations have had tremendous success lining up and planning stories about studio activities. It was even easier when Walt was alive. He made great copy and proved to be a "go to" guy for top magazine and newspaper columnists when they needed a story. Thousands of articles were the result. The references cited provide a small sampling of the type of articles to be found. The important ones used for this book are included along with a selection of more typical stories. Often a routine article has one line or a quote worthy of the research time involved. Most of these stories are not available electronically. The very early ones provide benchmark information and it is fun to read the prediction of some pundits on the meaning or future of Disney's work and see how wrong they were. Also on DVD.

ALL ISSUES. The "E" Ticket. The "E" Ticket, P.O. Box 8597, Mission Hills, CA 91346.

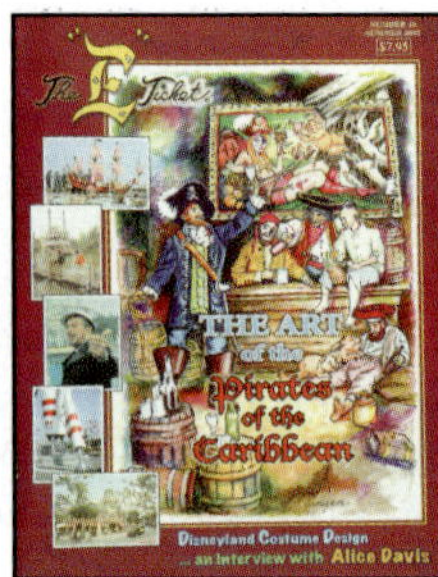

Each Issue of The "E" Ticket *includes in-depth articles about Disneyland and those who built it. It was the brainchild of Leon and Jack Janzen who grew up with the park. Their publication reflects the quality Walt Disney wanted in his park and the outstanding choices he made in picking the artists, engineers, architects, and craftmen who converted his dream of Disneyland into reality.*

THE AMAZING SECRET OF WALT DISNEY. The American Magazine, The Growell-Collier Publishing Company. Vol. CLX, No. 3, August, 1955.

This piece by Don Eddy, part of the publicity campaign for the opening of Disneyland, turned out to be one of the best magazine pieces written on Walt's private as well as corporate life. He agreed to have Eddy shadow him for several days at a time when he was very upbeat. It goes deeper than Walt's TV image, but retains respect for the "office" in a more polite '50s journalistic style. The author doesn't cover up the edginess of Walt's personality, but reports on it with more reserve than is found in treatments years later. It is probably the best reporting job done on Walt's life at the time, giving a nice cross-section of home versus studio activities while communicating a lot about the man. It's reprinted in Walt Disney Conversations. *(See Books)*

THE BIG BAD WOLF. Fortune, Time-Fortune Corporation, Vol. X, No. 5, November, 1934.

The success of The Three Little Pigs *caught the attention of this leading financial publication. The bulk of the story is a report on Walt and studio operations. It was one of the best of the era, but the treasure of the piece is a sidebar done on Roy titled "Mickey Mouse and the Bankers." It provides the dollar-and-cents information on how the studio operated in the early 1930's. Cost of production and the two-year return on investment are outlined as compared to the unusual financial success of* The Three Little Pigs. *The story reveals the Disneys were working on the bank's money and profits were being plowed back into the business to finance future production. Together with the 1940 Walt Disney Productions annual report, it is easy to see the Disneys were not getting rich as many employees and industry lenders believed.*

BRINGING FORTH THE MOUSE. American Heritage. American Heritage Publishing Co., Inc., New York, Vol. XIX, No. 3, April, 1968.

The article is a condensed version of Richard Schickel's book, The Disney Version. He was no Disney fan and it is curious why the publishers of American Heritage would employ him to write the story for this heavily promoted issue designed to appeal to a Disney audience. The Disney Studio did supply photos and drawings to help illustrate the story, but there is really nothing special about this coverage. It is included here because it is so often seen and is generally available to everyone doing research on Walt Disney.

DISNEY IN TV LAND. TV Guide, Triangle Publications, Philadelphia, Vol. 2, No. 43 October 23, 1954, 4-6.
    Reports on "Why Disney changed his mind about TV?" Walt states the Disneyland program will be 60% new programming – 40% films and cartoons from the Disney vault – some never seen before, like a scene cut from Snow White and the Seven Dwarfs. Walt is candid about the show being used to promote Disneyland and future theatrical releases. This article includes Herb Ryman's drawing of Disneyland and lists Disney's previous TV ventures.

EXTRAORDINARY MAN IN EXTRAORDINARY AGE. TV Guide, Triangle Publications, Philadelphia, Vol. 5, No. 50, December 14, 1957.
    This article promotes "Mars and Beyond" from the Man in Space series on the Disneyland anthology series. Walt reveals work has started on Donald in Mathmagic Land to be aired two years later and provides an interesting quote, "I'm really having fun with television. I haven't had so much fun since my early days in the business when I had the latitude to experiment. With TV it's like a cage has been opened – and I can fly again."

FANTASIA AND FANTASOUND. Theatre Arts, Inc., New York, Vol. XXV – No. 1, January, 1941.
    A review of Fantasia in its premiere showing at the New York Colony Theater November 12, 1940 provides an account of each section of the film as it was viewed at the time. There was never anything like Fantasia before and the reviewer was somewhat perplexed on what to review – a film, a concert, or an innovative form of animation. He treats all three possibilities, but focuses primarily on the concert aspects, noting the music editing of classical works to broaden their appeal. The most interesting part of this piece is the reviewer's take on Fantasound and his description of how it worked. No one had ever heard stereophonic sound up until the development of this system just 12 years after sound was first heard on film. It would take another 12 to 14 years before such systems became commonplace in movie theaters.

THE MAGIC WORLDS OF WALT DISNEY. National Geographic Magazine, Vol. 124 – No. 2, National Geographic Society, Washington, D.C., August, 1963.
    This 50+ page story is the most extensive ever done on Disney in any magazine. Coverage is divided into a Walt/Studio history, including an explanation on how animation works, and a walking tour of Disneyland. There is also some mention of preparations for the 1964-65 New York World's Fair. The background and history is mostly stock material from the studio PR department, but the walking tour of Disneyland is a unique approach starting with one of the best maps of Disneyland drawn by the magazine's cartographer. The walking tour is supported by a Disneyland portrait of on-stage and backstage activities captured in words and photos exclusive to this issue. The article freezes Walt Disney in his prime shortly before the opening of Mary Poppins, two years before he reveals his plans for Disney World, and three years before his death.

MICKEY MOUSE. Ladies Home Companion, Vol. LXI – No. 7, Crowell Publishing Company, Springfield, Ohio, 1934.
    The article leads with the degree of popularity Mickey Mouse enjoyed as the most recognized name of any person, real or fictional, in the world of 1934. Mickey was "more widely known than

Charlie Chaplin or Douglas Fairbanks, the leading male movie stars in western civilization. The Tribes of Kaffirs in Africa refused to accept any cakes of soap which did not bear the image of Mickey Mouse." It describes how Mickey was made an honorary citizen of France before his fifth birthday and how Hitler had denounced the characters because youths preferred emblems of the Mouse to wearing the swastika. Mickey's tremendous popularity in Sweden, India, Japan, and Russia where Stalin had to smuggle in prints are also chronicled. The article goes on to provide a typical biography of Walt and the studio's early years.

MICKEY MOUSE AND WHAT HE MEANS. Scribners, Charles Scribners Sons Publishers, New York and London, Vol. XCVI, No. 1, July, 1934.

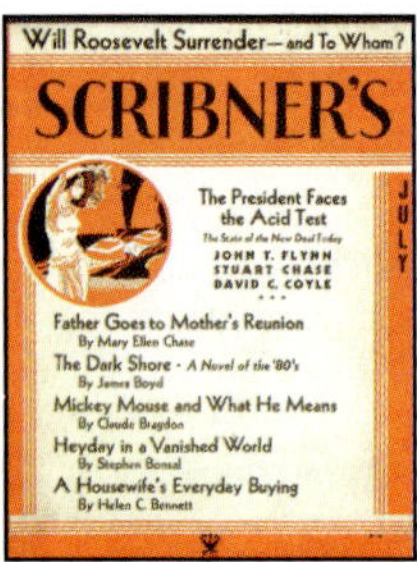

Author Claude Bragdon provides his views on how animation started with the Chat Noir *shadow plays seen in the Montmartre district of Paris in the 1890's. Then he linked to the animation of Winsor McCay before getting down to Disney for the final two-thirds of the article. After a 25¢ description of the animation process, Bragdon preaches how the use of color and more realism was taking animation in the wrong direction, away from the shadow plays he seemed to prefer. The criticism is silly in retrospect, but provides an early example of how the intelligentsia has rarely been in sync with the Disney audience.*

MICKEY MOUSE – ON NBC SUNDAY. Radio Guide, Regal Press, Inc. Chicago, Vol. 7, No. 12 for the week ending January 8, 1938.

Here is an example of where industry leaders said Mickey Mouse wouldn't work on radio and were right. Sunday evening at 5:30 p.m. Eastern and 2:30 p.m. Pacific on NBC wasn't the greatest time slot, but Pepsodent, the leading toothpaste at the time, signed a short-term contract to see if they could cash in on Mickey's popularity in an era of Snow White *and the raising fame of Donald Duck. The show didn't last long enough to make it into the most popular old-time radio history books.*

MICKEY MOUSE'S FATHER. McCall's, The McCall Company, New York, Vol. LIX, No. 11, August, 1932.

Standard early biography of Walt and his studio reports on the animation process by Pulitzer Prize-winning biographer Henry F. Pringle. One of the best examples of this type article. Cites merchandise sales in 1932 expected to be about $100,000 at retail. The author reports on a typical day and paints a detailed word picture of the Hyperion studio.

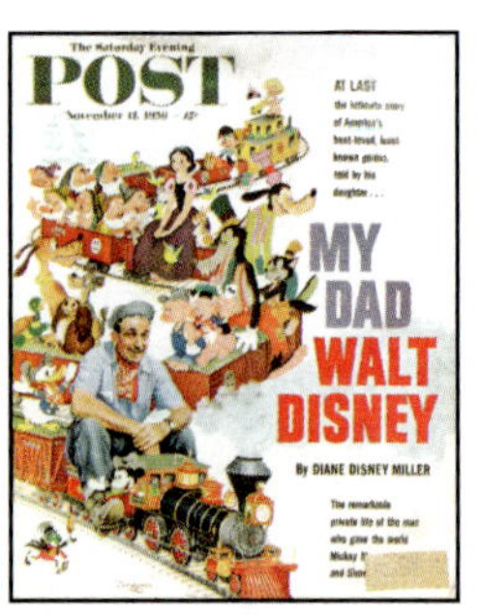

MY DAD WALT DISNEY. The Saturday Evening Post, The Curtis Publishing Company, Vol. 229, No. 20, November 17, 1956.

This article is Part One of the serialized book by Diane Disney Miller as told to Pete Martin. The magazine series has some photos exclusive to the Post and nice cover art by former Disney illustrator Gustaf Tenggren. The series of articles is an edited version from The Story of Walt Disney *published by Henry Holt & Company.*

RAILROADING WITH WALT DISNEY. Electric Trains, Fox - Shulman Enterprises, Inc., Philadelphia, Vol. 1, No. 3, December, 1951.

This story documents Walt Disney's half-mile Carolwood & Pacific Railroad built at his Holmby Hills home near Hollywood. This live-steam one-eighth scale line operated from 1951 to 1953 when an accident caused suspension of operation. Celebrity passengers like Edgar Bergen, comic Red Skelton, producer Walter Wanger, and artist Salvador Dali rode Walt's rails. Disney's interest in real and model railroads was recounted in this issue along with his wife Lilly's distaste for his hobby in her kingdom. When Walt decided to do something, he did it. The article is a neat departure from the normal Disney PR pieces,

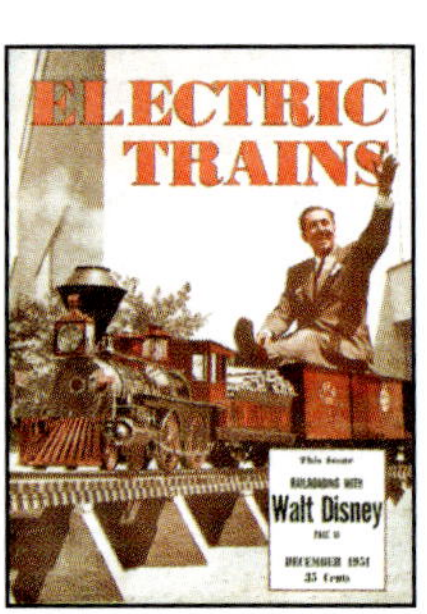

and also provides a brief studio history.

THE STORY BEHIND SNOW WHITE'S $10,000,000 SURPRISE PARTY. Liberty, MacFadden Publications, Vol. 15, No. 15, April 9, 1938.
The article is a love letter to Disney for having created the first animated feature, described as the most revolutionary event in motion picture history since the introduction of sound. The main value of the article is to get a sense of how the world, especially Hollywood, received "Disney's Folly" and the film we take for granted today.

WALT DISNEY. Wisdom. The Wisdom Society for the Advancement of Knowledge, Vol. 32, December, 1959.

This hardcover magazine provides a basic biography and studio history. There is a nice photo feature on Disney artists involved in various stages of the animation process and a section on his animated features. There is an extensive storyboard feature on 101 Dalmatians, then in production, and a description of the animation process bylined by Walt Disney. A section on live-action features spotlights Pollyanna before the section on Walt wraps up with a story on the creation of Disneyland and its just completed Tomorrowland expansion. The section ends with five pages of Disney quotes, many of which were exclusive to Wisdom.

WALT DISNEY: GREAT TEACHER. Fortune, Time Inc., New York, Vol. XXVI, No. 2, August, 1942.
This excellent report details training-film work the Disney Studio was doing for the U.S. military during World War II. The article begins with a story meeting on "Malaria & Mosquito." Storyboards from key sequences of noted films of the period are reproduced large enough to get a feel for the production. The films' storyboards in this fashion are: Emotion vs. Reason, Food Will Win the War, Education for Death, Donald Duck in Nutziland, Der Fuehaer's Face, and the non-war related, El Gaucho Goofy. This article is one of the few to cover this period of Disney Studio work.

Souvenir and Promotional Publications

There are numerous booklets sold at Disney theme parks published by Walt Disney Productions, The Walt Disney Company, or outside companies. Most of these titles were designed to be souvenirs of park visits. Other cast member instructional booklettes were written to explain specific Disney operations. The consumer books are normally highly illustrative type publications, while employees' handbooks tend to be full of helpful hints to make guests happy and provide background information on company traditions. This type of printed piece can be useful, particularly when different versions published over a period of time are compared.

Childs, Valerie. WALT DISNEY WORLD. Mayflower Books, 1979.
This grandiose color pictorial of the early years of Walt Disney World has limited text, but shows over 70 photographs of the park's first years. Included are photos of River Country, Treasure Island, 20,000 Leagues Under the Sea, and the Mickey Mouse Revue – all since closed or moved. A nice, concise history, plus basic facts and figures allow the reader to quickly size up the scope of the project area – twice the size of Manhattan Island. This book was sold around the world and at WDW, where it was a popular souvenir item.

France, Van. The Walt Disney Traditions at Disneyland. Walt Disney Productions, 1967.

Traditions is a training program handbook developed by Van France for the University of Disneyland as a cornerstone in new cast member training. This was one of the first editions printed after Walt's death. It includes a welcome by Roy O. Disney and Mickey Mouse. It provides some background on Walt, the Disney company, and Disneyland before covering the basic dos and don'ts of guest relations. The Disneyland "Look", teamwork, and safety are covered before the section on how every guest is to be given the VIP treatment by "accepting people for who they are", making them feel as if they "belong", the use of "smiling phrases", the use of "individual attention", and always having a "friendly smile." It's basic human relations stuff, but somehow made to work better in the magical atmosphere of Disneyland and its successor theme parks.

Walt Disney Productions. A Complete Edition About Walt Disney World. Walt Disney Public Relations, 1969.

This 28-page publication is similar to The Walt Disney World Master Plan prepared the same year construction began on the Florida Project. This version is more of a consumer publication, possibly prepared for the press and Disney employees. There are more pictures, eight pages in color. The cover illustration shows the planned route of the hotel monorail beam through the Contemporary Resort, along Bay Lake up to the Persian Resort, around and through Tomorrowland en route to the Polynesian Resort and the Transportation Center. The U.S. Steel design for the Polynesian Hotel, plus rare illustrations and models of the three never built hotels are shown in color. Construction photos, maps, and progress photos of new attractions support the text material, describing the first five-year plan. This type of document is always interesting in retrospect to compare what was planned to what was actually built. In this case the planning was fairly accurate.

——. Project Florida/ A Whole New Disney World. Walt Disney Productions, 1967.

This book was published about a year after Walt's death as prospectus and a sales piece while construction plans for Walt Disney World were being developed. It covers the new Florida Magic Kingdom and reveals many of Walt's concept drawings for his Experimental Prototype Community of Tomorrow (EPCOT). It talks about the impact WDW would have on Florida, and the role it would play in the continued growth of the state. The book acknowledges such a huge construction project was unprecedented. Time has shown Disney's power to attract other businesses and fuel growth in central Florida to be without equal and far exceeds what Disney could predict.

——. The Story of Walt Disney World. Walt Disney Productions, Orlando, 1971.

This souvenir/promotional booklet was sold at the Lake Buena Vista Preview Center and for the first few years Walt Disney World was

open. It provides a background on the Florida Project, complete with construction photos, drawings, and some of the earliest photos taken of the park. The text provides background on land acquisition, The Reedy Creek Improvement District, land development, differences between Disneyland and Walt Disney World, and the source of various components for the Florida Project.

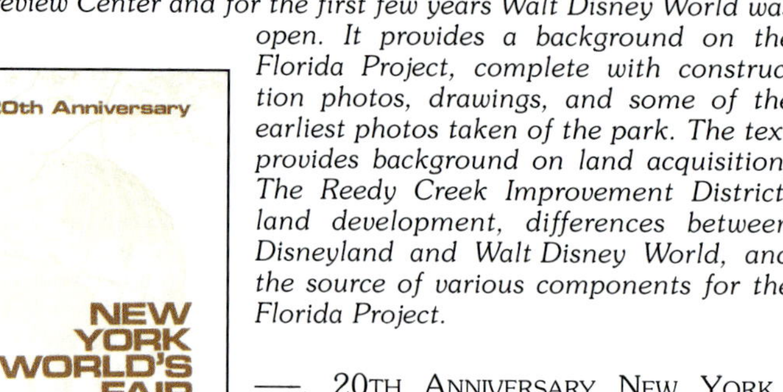

——. 20th Anniversary New York World's Fair – A Disney Retrospective. WED Imagineering, 1984.

This employee publication is only 12 pages, but it provides the history of each of the four exhibits the company prepared for the 1964-65

New York World's Fair. It provides a brief history of Walt's experiments with three-dimensional animation, dating back to 1951 when he was first planning Disneyland. It also reveals that five Disneyland attractions resulted from the company's work at the fair. Everyone knows the audio-animatronics from the Ford Magic Skyway were moved to a prehistoric diorama along the Disneyland Railroad. It is not well-known, however, that the WEDway PeopleMover was created beneath the 160 real Ford convertibles used to propel visitors throughout the largest exhibit on the grounds. The brochure is small, but it is loaded with facts, figures, photos, and information not easily found elsewhere.

Annual Reports

Reports for Walt Disney Productions were published for each year from 1940 to 1985 when the company was reorganized as The Walt Disney Company. Reports for the new entity have been published for each year thereafter. Both operated on a fiscal year beginning October first. These booklets feature letters to the shareholders describing corporate plans and activities, plus income, expense, and asset information. Early years break down licensing revenue and important data about theme park operations. As the company diversified it became more difficult to identify individual income amount without skilled inspection of the financial notes in the small print. The colorful "sell" sections of modern day reports still make for interesting reading.

Disney on Video/DVD

There was a time when you had to wait seven years between opportunities to see Disney animated features. Only short clips on 8mm film were available and most of those were silent. The coming of home video on tape and then DVD opened a whole new opportunity to enjoy not only the animated features, but all the Disney cartoons as well.

The Disney Family Foundation sponsored the production of *Disney – Man or Myth* which is excellent. The Leonard Maltin DVD Disney Treasures Edition series provides not only the Disney products, but valuable commentary, interviews, and production details as well. And it's all available for personal viewing in your own home.

The following is a list of the author's choice of the best information on Walt's life and work. Listing all the VHS or laser disc products would be a waste of space as these have all been replaced by better DVD products. There is one exception. *Snow White Live at Radio City* was an incredible stage production of this historic classic. It found a limited market because only a relatively few people were able to see one of the limited run sellout performances. Perhaps some day it will become part of a DVD package, but is not currently available except on a tape format. The Walt Disney Treasures DVD series with introductions by Leonard Maltin is a must.

WALT – THE MAN BEHIND THE MYTH. Disney DVD distributed by Buena Vista Home Entertainment, 2001. 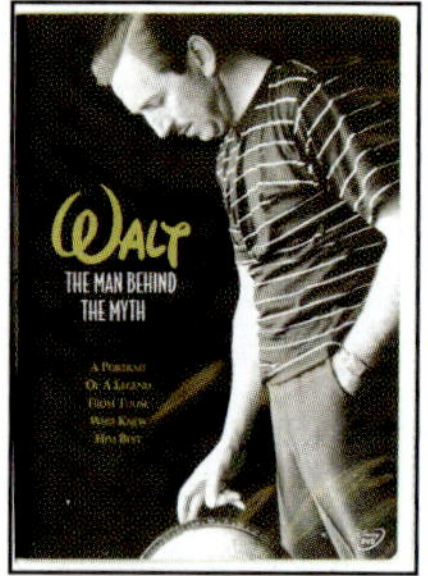

This is the official video biography of Walt produced for the Walt Disney Family Foundation. It runs 119 minutes and includes home movies and other rare color and black & white footage of Walt Disney's life. It includes material from the hours of Walt's filmed interviews retracing his career and presents an honest portrayal of Walt the man. His portrait is further brought to life in interviews with surviving family members, animators Marc Davis, Ward Kimball, Frank Thomas, and Ollie Johnston, plus Imagineering head Marty Sklar, Science fiction writer and friend Ray Bradbury, TV personality Art Linkletter, and several Mouseketeers. In addition, there are comments by Disney historians, Disney Archives founder Dave Smith, and many others. A great way to start for those new to Walt's life and a treasure for the committed Disney fan to hear from many who knew Walt well, several of whom have since passed on.

Treasure Editions with introduction, background, and interviews by Leonard Maltin.

Here is a list of all the Treasures Edition sets in this series available or announced before the printing deadline for this book.

–The Adventures of Spin & Marty (MMC)	–Mickey Mouse Club
–Behind the Scenes – Walt Disney Studio	–The MMC Featuring the Hardy Boys
–Chronological Donald Duck, Vol. One: 1934-1941	–Mickey Mouse in Black & White
–Chronological Donald Duck, Vol. Two: 1942-1946	–Mickey Mouse Black & White, Vol. Two
–Chronological Donald Duck, Vol. Three: 1947-1950	–Mickey Mouse in Living Color
–The Complete Davy Crockett Televised Series	–Mickey Mouse Living Color, Vol. Two
–The Complete Goofy	–More Silly Symphonies (1929-1938)
–The Complete Pluto, Vol. One	–On the Front Lines
–The Complete Pluto, Vol. Two	–Oswald the Lucky Rabbit
–Disney Rarities – Celebrated Shorts, '20s-'60s	–Silly Symphonies
–Disneyland: the Secrets, Stories, and Magic	–Tomorrowland: Disney Space & Beyond
–Disneyland USA	–Your Host, Walt Disney
–Elfego Baca/Swamp Fox – Legendary Heroes